GROWING UP
GREEN

LIVING, DYING, AND DYING AGAIN
AS A FAN OF
THE NEW YORK JETS

Andrew Goldstein

authorHOUSE®

AuthorHouse™ LLC
1663 Liberty Drive
Bloomington, IN 47403
www.authorhouse.com
Phone: 1-800-839-8640

Published by AuthorHouse 02/05/2014

ISBN: 978-1-4918-5979-7 (sc)
ISBN: 978-1-4918-5980-3 (hc)
ISBN: 978-1-4918-5933-9 (e)

Library of Congress Control Number: 2014902107

PROLOGUE

I ONLY HAD ONE TEAM

Ever since I first grasped the concept of professional sports leagues somewhere around age four or five, I've only ever loved one sport and one team. Sure, I watched baseball and was even a Yankee fan for a time, but I eventually lost a lot of interest in the game, to the point where I felt like calling myself a fan was a misnomer. (More on that later.) I follow the NBA, but I never really liked a particular team even though we had one in New Jersey for most of my childhood. And I would be extremely hard-pressed to name twenty active NHL players.

For me, the New York Jets were it for my entire childhood. Hell, they still are. They were the only team that ever made me think and act irrationally. They're the only team that has made me, a fairly level-headed person by most accounts, both run laps around my house with my arm raised and sit there on the couch ready to punch something, both within a week of each other and at ages where I should be long past such things. They've made me think the most, laugh the most, cry the most, and care the most. They have changed me for the better, worse, and everything in between to the point that I don't completely know what the heck they did to me over the years. Maybe that's what I'm trying to figure out by writing this book.

Your reaction to the last paragraph is probably a good indication of how much you're going to end up enjoying the rest of this story. It's probably even an indication of how much sense you're going to be able to make out of the rest of this story. It will classify you as a member of one of two very distinct groups on the topic of sports: sane, rational people and fans.

Fans will probably look at that second paragraph and nod. It might evoke memories of their beloved Showtime era Lakers or their long-suffering Red Sox winning it all in 2004 or even their very first Marlins game. (To the dozen people that might have significance for.) It might have been relatable or nostalgic or puzzling or—wow, I'm rambling already but you get the point. To a fan, those one hundred forty words meant *something.*

To a completely sane person, those one hundred forty words were clear signs of lunacy. A sane person might look at the second paragraph and think something along the lines of, "*What on Earth is wrong with this guy? He lets a group of fifty-some individuals who are completely unrelated to him dictate his happiness that much? He shuts down his life on Sundays to watch people play a game for seven hours? This is an obsession and he sounds like a complete head case.*"

Well, rational person, your measured and well-thought out logic is not welcome here. Fan is short for the word "fanatic" and, yes, you need to be at least a little bit crazy to support a team the way a proper fan should. There's something crazy about wearing a shirt with the name of a person you've never met, but know everything about, on the back of it. There's something crazy about camping out in the stadium parking lot five hours before the game in freezing cold temperatures because it's "tradition." Supporting teams that you know are going to fail, having lucky baseball caps, playing fantasy sports, there's something not normal about all of it. Every single convention of fandom can be reduced to nonsensicality by people who don't get what it means to be a fan. That's perfectly fine. In fact, they're probably the normal ones. However, if you're one of them, then you might not enjoy the rest of this book. But if you're one of those people who has that little bit of crazy inside them, or one of those people who don't, but want to find out what it's like to have it, then keep reading.

OK, you haven't closed the book, so we're off to a good start. Now we're going to take this a step further. All die-hard fans are a little bit abnormal, but some are on an entirely different plane altogether. I'm not talking about the fans that show up to Lambeau Field half-naked in November or dress up in ridiculous-yet-awesome costumes to go to games, although they're certainly worthy of recognition.

Maybe *insane* would be a better word to describe this special breed of fan than anything else. Most people have already heard that tired definition of insanity; to do the same thing over and over again and expect a different result every time. I've done just that for sixteen games per year plus a few fleeting playoff games—eleven of them, to be exact—over twelve years.

Over that time, the New York Jets have held one thing and one thing only constant. Losing. Sure, the players and the coaches and the particulars of the situation may change, but the ultimate result has not wavered in my lifetime or in the forty-five years since their 1969 victory in Super Bowl III. There have been close calls, not-so-close calls, heartache, false hope, false confidence, hopelessness, inconsistencies, smart decisions that somehow went bad, dumb decisions that always went bad, and about a million other things that I will try to scratch the surface of over the course of this book. Most of all, there has been the pervasive and overwhelming feeling over the twelve years I've supported the Jets that my favorite team is beyond salvation.

Yet both I and millions of others repeatedly subject ourselves to this sense of despair week after week, month after month, year after year. That little spark of craziness that you need to be a real fan becomes insufficient. To support the New York Jets, like I do, you have to be completely out of your damn mind. It's a following rooted in blind devotion to failure, a ridiculously high tolerance for disappointment, and, despite all evidence to the contrary, an unflinching belief that next year will be The Year.

Only a small fraction of sports fans in America truly know what this experience is like. Plenty of teams lose, but only a few have a died-in-the-wool tradition of losing in the most agonizing ways possible. Every fan suffers disappointment at some point in their life, but not every fan goes through dozens of them and still cares enough to remember every single one. And while errors in judgment occasionally plague every team, only several are plagued to the point where fans start to instinctually assume the worst for almost every possible situation before it even plays out.

That's really what this book is about; my personal trip through the insanity involved in being a Jet fan and how my relationship with the team has changed over the years. You'll see how certain people resonate with me after all this time and how they've shaped my opinion about sports to this day. You'll see every reason why I should have stopped caring years ago and every reason why I could never do that. Most of all, you'll see the uniqueness and, yes, the insanity of my experiences because nothing defines the act of being a fan more than those two things do.

Therein lies the toughest part about writing something like this; trying to resolve the direct contrast of insanity and uniqueness. Trying to show how doing the same thing over and over again and expecting a different result produces, you know, results that are actually different for each person. And if that's the case, is being a fan really even insane anymore?

The only way to reconcile these two is to try and tell a story that gets right to the heart of what makes us fans. If this book excluded the personal element and chronicled the misfortunes of the Jets in a purely factual manner, it would absolutely be insanity to still believe in them. Facts will say that fans have kept coming back in relatively large numbers to see the Jets ultimately fall short time and time again. These facts are an important part of the story, and it would be dishonest of me to pretend they're not just because I don't like them.

However, they're not the whole story. Fans are people, and the randomness of the fan experience comes from both the once in a lifetime mix of athletes on the field and how they are perceived differently through the eyes of everybody watching them. What you're about to read may or may not bear some resemblance to your experiences. You may or may not agree with or even like what I have to say about being a fan. That's OK, because your fanhood and how it has changed you is a story that is every bit as one in a million as mine is.

I cannot speak for every fan. All I can really do is tell my own story; the tale of how I've lived, died, and died some more with the fortunes of the New York Jets.

A LEGACY OF LOSING

For you to properly understand what the hell I got myself into when I decided to become a Jet fan, you need to know a little bit about their history. Not all of it, mind you, because God forbid that anybody should even *attempt* to write a book that lists every single screwed up thing that has happened to the Jets in their fifty-five year history. That thing would be the size of War and Peace; you don't have the time to read something like that, and I certainly don't have the time or masochistic tendencies to write it. But in order to fully comprehend the psyche of a Jets fan or the events that you're going to read about throughout this book, you need to hear a little bit of it.

The NFL has been around since 1920, almost forty years before the founding of its competitor for a whole decade, the AFL. To many, the NFL was considered to be the superior league and the AFL was their ragtag, upstart, and inferior little brother. Can you guess which one the Jets started in?

(Waiting)

(Waiting some more)

(Twiddling thumbs)

OK, time's up! If you guessed the NFL, then you and I are not off to a very good start. But if you guessed the AFL, you would be correct. The New York Titans (the team that would eventually become the Jets) were founded in 1959 as one of the AFL's original teams and were in direct competition with the Giants, who were founded in 1925 as part of the NFL. By the time the AFL launched, the Giants had won four NFL championships and twenty-two current Hall of Fame members had passed through their organization. So yes, the new Titans team had its work cut out for them. However, they would eventually rise to that challenge and capture the entire city's attention . . . . . by going bankrupt within five years of their creation. That would be a microcosm of everything that would unfold over the next forty-plus years.

Those first five years—1960 to 1964, were absolutely brutal. For four of those years, the Jets played in the Polo Grounds, a once-great baseball stadium that had been rendered an unmaintained dump since the New

York Giants baseball team (not to be confused with the Giants *football* team, which is still in New York) left for San Francisco in 1957. Sammy Baugh, the Titans' first head coach, signed a three year contract, was replaced two years into that contract, and the promised third year was reportedly never paid off. Baugh's .500 winning percentage stood for over thirty years as the highest winning percentage that any Titans/Jets head coach had ever achieved. Tickets to games were given away to people who purchased ten dollars' worth of groceries at Acme supermarkets. Players ran to the bank as soon as they got their pay in order to assure that their checks would not be bounced. Howard Glenn, the first player to die from injuries sustained on the professional football field, did so in 1960 while playing for the Titans. The threat of being shut down loomed over the fledgling football team after every single season.

So other than that, Mrs. Lincoln, how was the play?

But everything would soon change with the emergence of a young and charismatic quarterback at the University of Alabama. This QB went 29-4 over three seasons with the Crimson Tide and gained nationwide fame for his cannon arm and impeccable footwork. He even led the Tide to a national championship in 1964. Bidding wars between multiple NFL and AFL teams quickly escalated over the all-star QB's services for the 1965 season, even as a knee injury held him out of his final college game. The New York Titans ultimately won that bidding war, acquiring the QB for a then-record 427,000 dollar contract over three years plus signing bonuses, with a slick convertible thrown in for good measure. The luring of this particular quarterback to New York represented the AFL's first huge victory over the NFL and one of the many reasons for the 1970 merger. It proved that the AFL wasn't an inferior league; that it could attract big-name players and pay them the money to match. The future of football in New York, the hopes of a merger with the NFL, the AFL's future, and the ultimate destination of football all rested on the shoulders of this one quarterback. His name was Joe Namath.

The arrival of the QB that the press dubbed "Broadway Joe" and a 1963 name change ushered in a new age of New York football. Not the brand of football played by the boring, old, "three yards and a cloud of dust" Giants. Their name suggested a mammoth, lumbering dinosaur of a team straight out of the game's pre-historic age; the old, antique guard.

Modern times, however, were sleeker and more exciting. No longer would football be played one boring run at a time. Instead, the brand-new era would be defined by an aerial assault, spearheaded by the game's first superstar and franchise QB. With the arrival of their superstar QB, the Titans saw the opportunity to change their name to something that reflected this brave new world. And thus was born unto the world the team that lends its name to the title of this book—the New York Jets.

Along with the name change came the era of Namath. It's impossible to overstate how desperately football needed an injection of personality like Broadway Joe. Remember, this was the 60s. The winningest team in the NFL at the time, Vince Lombardi's Packers, were led by head coach Lombardi and quarterback Bart Starr, two people who could not have given less of a crap about promoting the game. Their job, as they saw it, boiled down to winning and executing their game plan, not a single bit more. Great team? Absolutely. Sexy story that would turn people's attention away from Mickey Mantle? Not a chance. Nothing was coming close to bumping baseball off the front page in any city that had a team. Baseball players were the athletes who did movies, who appeared in commercials, who were treated like living deities. It's not just that Babe Ruth and Joe DiMaggio were great baseball players; they were great salesmen, promoters, and celebrities. That's what Joe Namath brought to football and to the Jets that had never been seen before. Sure, both the NFL and the AFL had great players, but they never had a *star*, a guy who could transcend his sport and place himself in the epicenter of popular culture in America. Not until Joe, anyways.

The Jets were mediocre from 1965-1967 as Namath learned how to play in the pros. After the 1967 season, Weeb Ewbank, an initial investor in the New York Titans, bought out the other members of his ownership group and assumed full control of the Jets' day-to-day operations. He moved the team to the newly built Shea Stadium and set about the task of essentially building a football team from absolute scratch. His timing was fortuitous, as the Jets were about to have the greatest season in their brief existence, a season that hasn't been matched to this day.

Broadway Joe and the Jets lit up the NFL in 1968, going 10-3 and making the playoffs, where they faced off against the Oakland Raiders in the AFL Championship game. This was a revenge game for the Jets after losing the demoralizing and infamous "Heidi Game" to Oakland earlier in the season. *Time Out: The "Heidi Game" was so named because the Jets took a three-point lead with just over a minute left, prompting NBC to assume that a Jet win was inevitable and switch their programming from said game to the movie "Heidi", thus preventing the TV audience from seeing the two touchdowns that the Raiders would score in those remaining sixty-eight seconds. To this day, I have an unnatural hatred for "Heidi", even though I've never seen it and wasn't alive at the time. It's a fan thing. OK, time back in.* The Jets did indeed end up getting sweet revenge after a 27-23 victory over the despised Raiders. This set up what many people, including me for reasons that will become obvious, believe to be the greatest game in the history of the league. The game? Super Bowl III. New York Jets vs Baltimore Colts at the old Orange Bowl Stadium in Miami, Florida.

First of all, let me preface this by reminding you of the relationship between the AFL and the NFL. The eventual merger that would join the two leagues together had been announced, but would not go through for another year and a half still. The logistics of the merger had already been worked out, but people were just beginning to discern how the AFL-NFL balance of power was oriented. The consensus opinion among football types, by a fairly large majority, was that the NFL had proved itself to be the far superior league. They had been around at least four decades longer, depending on when you want to date the true "start" of the NFL. They fielded more talent, would go on to have more teams survive the merger, and had justified their position as the superior conglomeration by having their signature team (the Packers) kick the asses of the AFL's best in the first two Super Bowls. The eventual merger, it was said, would be less of a marriage between equals and more of a giant expansion draft for the NFL. That attitude would be reflected in the gambling line for the Jets-Colts matchup. At game time, Baltimore was favored by *seventeen points*. When you consider that 64% of *all* games played between 2002-2012 ended with a margin of victory less than fourteen points, it says a lot when the best team is widely believed to be that much better than the second-best team.

Of course, that led to the most famous moment in Jet history and one of the most well-known incidents in NFL lore; The Guarantee. Broadway Joe Namath, the fearless Jet quarterback/celebrity appeared three nights before the Super Bowl at a hotel banquet hall to accept the Touchdown Club of Miami's Most Outstanding Player Award. Namath, whose partying habits and enviable bachelor life were both well documented, was intoxicated and then some. A Colts fan began to heckle him from the crowd, saying that his team would easily defeat the underdog Jets. Namath, in his drunken stupor, immediately responded with the eight most famous words in NFL history. "We're gonna win on Sunday. I guarantee it."

Boom. *The Guarantee.* The newspaper headline wrote itself, as did the story. This was something never seen before in the NFL; a player actually saying something. NFL players were usually cut from the mold of Lombardi's Packers or Don Shula's Colts. They were workmanlike people who didn't say much, largely kept most of their truly meaningful moments behind closed doors, and who largely treated the public eye as a distraction. Namath had already begun to change that paradigm with his product shills and flamboyantly extravagant lifestyle. (There are actual photos of him wearing a mink coat on the sideline when he was sitting out due to injury.) But this was just too much. The quarterback of a seventeen-point underdog publicly declaring that his team would win? Suddenly, everybody's attention shifted to this cocky kid from Beaver Falls, Pennsylvania and his boisterous prediction.

Nowadays, something like this wouldn't be that big of a deal because we're used to it from athletes. As the era of Buzzfeed, the Twitter, and whatever else the kids are using nowadays slowly dawns, trash-talking has become too easy. Any old athlete can pick up his/her smartphone and make a guarantee, and it's just as easy for anybody (athlete or otherwise) to fire back at them. There's no artistry to trash-talk anymore, no opportunities for apocryphal "yo, you are not going to BELIEVE what Joe Namath said last night" stories because everything is so public now. Every "feud" and every piece of "bulletin board material" feels like a pro wrestler desperately trying to promote his new persona. That's the beauty of The Guarantee: it wasn't contrived in the least. No marketing advisors thought of the gimmick and talk shows weren't on the air to brutally strip away the moment's grandeur with endless replays. All it came down to was the banquet room of a hotel thick with cigar smoke, an inebriated backcountry upstart who had it out for the football establishment, and a momentous declaration. For the pure spontaneity of the occasion, we'll never see another moment that quite matches it.

Of course, Joe Namath's guarantee would have meant nothing if not properly vindicated on the field, which it was in a 16-7 Jets win. The Jets switched up their offensive style to counteract the tenacious Baltimore pass rush, running the ball down the Colts' throat with bruising halfback Matt Snell, who finished the game with 121 yards rushing and a touchdown. Colts' QB Earl Morrall threw three first-half interceptions against a staunch Jets' D, which caused Shula to actually *bench him in the middle of the Super Bowl* for an injured Johnny Unitas, who didn't fare much better. The defense of the seventeen-point underdogs dominated to the degree that it actually caused the opposing team's best player to be benched in the season's ultimate game. Call me the next time you see that happen anywhere else.

So the clock ticked down to three zeroes and the AFL's underdog Jets had won their first and only Super Bowl. Fans rushed the field as the two teams exchanged postgame pleasantries. A gaggle of onlookers, both media and otherwise, surrounded the golden boy Namath as he ran towards the Jets' tunnel, his Guarantee having proven true. As he ran, his arm shot up. The quarterback's index finger pointed toward the sky, rising above the mob on the field, emphatically signaling that the Jets were indeed number one. Roll credits.

Now, you may be sitting here and saying, "But Andrew, you said that the Jets sucked. Look, you even named the chapter *A Legacy of Losing*. This sounds an awful lot like you're over-exaggerating things. In fact, everything with The Guarantee and the Super Bowl upset sounds pretty awesome."

Well, after losing in the playoffs the next year, the Jets went on to post a losing record in *eleven straight seasons*. Eleven years, the entire length of the seventies, was spent toiling away in the now-AFC's cellar, nowhere near the playoffs. Namath, unfortunately, was both blessed with extraordinary physical gifts and blighted with knees that couldn't utilize those gifts. Years of low hits had taken their toll on the wunderkind, rendering him unable to move around in the pocket. Things got so bad that the New York Post dubbed him the "million dollar statue" and called for his immediate release. When he eventually got off the bench and into games, his reckless tendencies and diminished arm strength tended to lead to more interceptions than they did touchdowns. He was unceremoniously cut from the roster after the 1976 season and retired soon after. Other members of the Jets' 1968-1969 championship team, such as general manager Weeb Ewbank and running back Matt Snell, also retired from the game over the coming years, leaving the Jets totally foundation-less. Meanwhile, AFC rivals such as the Steelers, Raiders, and Dolphins all won multiple Super Bowls over the course of the 70s, an era that ended up defining professional football and carving out an identity for the game. The Jets were a twelve-year old relic of a time gone by, struggling to mediocrity at best and languishing in complete helplessness at worst.

The Jets did little to help themselves improve over the course of their existence by repeatedly and flagrantly screwing up in the NFL Draft. The draft is the NFL's primary improvement mechanism for crappy teams. Every year, the worst team in the league is rewarded with the first pick in the next year's draft of all college football players that are eligible to move up to the NFL. Essentially, they are rewarded for being bad by getting priority choice of the league's future talent pool. Since significant trades almost never happen in the NFL and using free agency to sign existing good players tends to get really expensive, the draft is essential. You get a number of NFL-ready guys on your team, some of whom will have an impact either immediately or in the not-too-distant future, and you get their services for peanuts compared to what you'd usually have to pay in a bidding war on the free agent market. That's why it is absolutely *critical* that teams not misfire with their draft choices. And boy, do the Jets ever have a history of misfiring.

You can actually Google "Jets draft mistakes" and you will instantly be redirected to pages and pages of material containing every single grievous oversight that has ever been committed in Jets' history. Allow me to share just a few with you.

- With the ninth selection of the 1995 draft, the Jets passed up a chance to sign consensus top-five pick and future Hall of Famer Warren Sapp, a mountain of a defensive tackle that would go on to be the best player at his position while playing for the Tampa Bay Bucs. Instead, the Jets took a tight end named Kyle Brady. He was released from the team after four years.

- After a disappointing 7-9 finish in the 1983 season, the Jets set out to improve their decrepit offense. Specifically, they were in desperate need of change at the quarterback position, The Jets opted for Ken O'Brien from Cal-Davis University, a highly regarded college quarterback that never really won anything significant with the Jets. The player picked three spots later by the Miami Dolphins? Dan Marino, only one of the five greatest QBs to ever play the game. Marino would go on to break pretty much every significant career passing record in the book en route to a 147-93 career record with the Dolphins. O'Brien went 50-55-1 at the helm of the Jets' offense.

- Two years after screwing up their quarterback pick, the Jets naturally recognized that it was time to screw up on a wide receiver selection as well. To wit, the Jets took Al Toon out of the University of Wisconsin. To his credit, Toon had a fine career for the Jets and was even selected to the Pro Bowl three separate times before retiring early at the age of 29 due to suffering eight or nine concussions over his playing career. (And those are the ones that we know about.) Unfortunately for Toon, those solid statistics would be overshadowed by Jerry Rice, the wide receiver taken by the San Francisco 49ers a mere six picks later. Much like Marino, Rice went on to completely rewrite the record books and redefine the standards of excellence for his position, all while winning no less than three Super Bowls.

- The 2003 NFL Draft featured thirty-seven defensive players that were taken within the first two rounds. Of those thirty-seven, eleven of them went on to be selected to the Pro Bowl at some point in their career. The Jets used both of their picks on a defensive player, which means that they had a 57.5% chance of at least one of those players making a Pro Bowl. (If I butchered the calculations there, I would like to sincerely apologize to Ms. Gunther, my 12th grade stat teacher. Sorry 'bout that.) But because these are the Jets we're talking about, neither Dewayne

Robertson nor Victor Hobson (the two players chosen), ended up making a single Pro Bowl. In fact, both players were cut from the Jets within six years and out of the NFL within eight.

• After another disappointing season in 1990, the Jets took running back Blair Thomas with the second pick in the draft. Thomas held out for much of training camp and demanded to be paid more than what the Jets were offering him. When he finally did get paid, he proved to be the latest in a long line of draft busts by eclipsing the hundred-yard mark for a single game only twice in his career and rushing for just over 2,000 yards total during his six-year stint in the NFL. (For a point of reference, 1,000 yards is usually considered to be the benchmark that constitutes a pretty good *season* for a running back.)

I'm gonna go ahead and stop listing all of these inexcusable draft-day miscues before I actually pull the hair off of my head one strand at a time, but I think you get the point. The Jets, throughout their history, have been a woefully un-savvy franchise, and their failure to accumulate talent through the draft is just one example of that. Adding to the mystique of the annual bungled draft is the location of the whole boondoggle: Radio City Music Hall in the heart of Manhattan. There are plenty of Giants fans in the hall and every team is usually represented by at least a few die-hards, but the leaders of the rowdiness and general hooliganism in the crowd have been, and will probably always be, Jet fans. Every Jet selection is met with either raucous cheers or hearty boos, the overt hopes of a new franchise player and the covert dread of another draft day frittered away behind each one of them. Meanwhile, the fans of most other teams snicker behind the Jets' fans back, waiting to see how they'll make a mess of things again.

Despite repeated instances of draft-day foibles, the Jets managed to make a few gains over the next twenty years. Granted, some of those gains were drastically overridden by the sheer number of losses, but still. To their credit, they did make the AFC Conference Championship, the penultimate round of the playoffs, twice over the next twenty years. Of course, since these are the Jets we're talking about, they lost in both games. The first one came in 1982 after a strike-shortened nine game season, when the Miami Dolphins defeated the Jets 14-0 in a mud-infested affront to football entertainment. Miami linebacker A.J. Duhe intercepted three of New York quarterback Richard Todd's passes, the last of which was returned for a touchdown in the fourth quarter to seal the Dolphins' victory, in what would forever be known as the A.J. Duhe game. The Jets would not go that deep into the playoffs for another fifteen years.

After that game, the Jets went on to some mild success in the mid-80s (a first-round playoff exit in '85 and a divisional round exit in '86) before falling back into up-and-down mediocrity. Wait a second, did I say "up-and-down?" My bad, I really meant to say "consistently down." From 1987 to 1996, the Jets recorded exactly one playoff appearance and one season with a winning record. The Namath era and The Guarantee might as well have happened centuries ago, and even the suggestion that the Jets were New York City's dominant team would be immediately met with guffaws and a few "Hey, that's a good one!" type reactions, even from Jet fans. Things reached rock-bottom in the pitiful era of head coach Rick Kotite, which somehow lasted both two years total *and* two years too long. Under Kotite, the Jets ended up with a sterling 4-28 record over the course of the 1995 and 1996 seasons, which I believe currently ranks as the third worst two-year stretch in NFL history, winning percentage-wise. Somehow, even in a league that is specifically designed to avoid such a thing, the Jets managed to finish with the worst record in consecutive years, partially because of the Kyle Brady over Warren Sapp draft miscue. Throughout both seasons, Jet fans carried on the informal-yet-dreaded tradition that is bestowed upon the fans of the clear-cut worst team every year; wearing brown paper bags over your head at the stadium. (The implication being that you're too embarrassed/sad/disgusted to actually watch your team.) Signs reading "Fire Kotite!" were commonplace at Giants Stadium, and they stopped only when rumors began to circulate that Kotite was indeed set to be fired at the end of the year. Of course, they were immediately replaced by signs that read "The End Of An Error" and even more paper bags, but they were replaced nevertheless. To add the final bit of insult to the two-year injury—because, by God, the Jets apparently hadn't had enough of either yet—a highly touted quarterback prospect from the University of Tennessee chose to remain in school for his senior year instead of declaring his eligibility for the 1996 NFL Draft. The next year, the Indianapolis Colts had the first pick of the draft and took this particular quarterback, whereas the Jets would have been able to take him if he had declared in the year where they held the number one pick. This quarterback's name? Peyton Manning. Only one of the best players in NFL history and someone who will absolutely be inducted into the Hall of Fame on the first ballot. So, fourteen years apart, the Jets had opportunities to pick two of the best players to ever play the game, both of which played a position that the Jets sorely needed to improve in the years that they were available. They ended up getting neither of them. Typical, classic Jets.

But something happened in the Summer of 1996, something that would change the course of football history forever. None of the experts ever could have predicted it, but it happened against all odds. In the morass of a Jets' season marred by complete ineptitude, a hero would rise. Yes, on August 21st, 1996, only weeks before the Jets would embark on their doomed 1-15 campaign, I was born.

Oh yeah, and the Jets hired the greatest coach of all time approximately a year after that. In terms of importance, the two events were about even, I'd say.

Yes, the Jets landed the man known as the Tuna, legendary head coach and eccentric taskmaster Bill Parcells. Even sweeter was the fact that both he and eventual Hall of Fame running back Curtis Martin (who was signed by the Jets only a year later), were wrested from the grasp of the New England Patriots, in what would soon be considered the first shots fired in their bitter rivalry. (Trust me, there will be much, much, much, much more on this rivalry a little bit later on in this book.) After a bitter dispute over Parcells' contract with the Pats, the Tuna was allowed to depart for the Jets. Parcells had already served as the head coach of the crosstown Giants teams that won the 1986 and 1990 Super Bowls and his pedigree was well-known throughout the league.

His impressive resume, though, was the secondary reason that the Jets were attracted to him. Parcells had this distinctive, "I'm doing things *my way*, damnit" attitude that had a knack for cleaning up malcontents within football teams. His average press conference was an incredible tour de force, an unparalleled mixture of two parts utter disdain and one part acerbic sarcasm. He had a legendary temper, a wise-ass persona that seemed to have a counter for anything that anybody could possibly say, and an uncanny way of knowing the right buttons to push on players and teams that would get the most out of them. He'd dispense soft-spoken and fatherly advice to the quiet running back Martin, but he'd just as soon start lobbing insults and barbs at number one receiver Keyshawn Johnson, knowing that his enormous sense of pride would drive him to work even harder so he could shut his own coach up. He controlled every aspect of the Jets, so much so that he even assumed the role of general manager in addition to being the coach, something that was becoming almost extinct in the modern NFL. Even at his Hall of Fame induction ceremony in 2013, he insisted that his shrine be placed next to that of Giants' linebacker Lawrence Taylor, a man with which Parcells had some legendary shouting matches, so he can "keep an eye on that sucker." That's essentially Bill Parcells in a nutshell.

The results were immediate. In the 1997 season, the Jets surged to a 9-7 record and came only a three-point loss to Detroit away from making the playoffs. Keep in mind that this was *one year* after they finished 1-15. Their eight win improvement from 96 to 97 was the largest bump in wins from one year to the next in league history.

After the season was over, Neil O'Donnell, the quarterback that the Jets took before Marino, was cut from the team and replaced with a free agent acquisition named Vinny Testaverde. Behind Testaverde and Parcells, the Jets would go 12-4 en route to their second AFC Conference Championship appearance, which pitted them against the Denver Broncos. Denver QB John Elway, a first-ballot Hall of Famer, was on the verge of retirement and playing in his final home game. If he had any doubts about whether or not he would retire, the Jets helped to resolve some of those misgivings by beating him up for the first half's entirety. Gang Green took a 3-0 lead into the locker room at halftime and scored early on in the third quarter to make it 10-0 . . . . .only to promptly gave up twenty-three unanswered points in the second half and lose 23-10. Classic Jets. The next season, Testaverde tore his achilles tendon in the season opener against New England and the Jets stumbled to an 8-8 record without him.

And then Parcells walked away. He gathered all of the Jets in the locker room, told them that he wouldn't be coming back for the next season, and walked out as his players stood there speechless. In his ensuing press conference, he cited a creeping lack of motivation for the job as his reason for stepping down. Something like this almost never happens; a coach at a high point in his career walking away from a team that could win a championship is almost unheard-of. Parcells' departure and its inevitable fallout would be enough to fill a whole offseason's worth of newspapers with all on its lonesome. But all of this was *before* things got really weird.

The Jets' acting defensive coordinator and Parcells' right-hand man, Bill Belichick, was promoted to the position of head coach in order to replace the Tuna. Then, something really weird happened. Bill Belichick quit. Yep, he did. The coach that is now known as one of the greatest of all time coached the Jets for exactly one day. In fact, the press conference that was planned to announce his hiring turned into an announcement of resignation from Belichick. He scrawled a quick resignation note that simply said, "I resign as HC of the NYJ" just minutes before taking the podium and embarking upon a half-hour long rambling session that outlined, in no uncertain terms, why he was leaving. Wait a second, did I say "no uncertain terms?" My bad, I actually meant "very uncertain terms." As a matter of fact, the uncertain status of the team's ownership, which was in the process of changing hands from Leon Hess to Woody Johnson, was the only reason he gave for his unexpected resignation. If you're a football fan, you know the rest. Belichick eventually accepted the position of head coach for the New England Patriots and went on to lead them to three Super Bowls, not to mention a thirteen-year stretch that saw New England atop the AFC East eleven times. (That stretch, as of this book's publication, is still counting.) If Belichick doesn't win those Super Bowls, if quarterback Tom Brady goes to some other team, if Belichick turns out to be just another run-of-the-mill coach, then everybody would remember him for leaving the Jets alone at the altar. Now, though? Nobody ever brings it up. It's old news, an insignificant part of the greatest coach of the past decade's still-growing legacy. For the Jets, though, it was another franchise-altering opportunity that came and went. So, just to review, they had the chance to employ the greatest quarterback of the 90s, one of the best defensive tackles in history, the greatest coach of the 2000s, AND one of the two best quarterbacks of the 2000s. None of them ended up playing for the Jets.

So the Jets slid into mediocrity in 2000 with new head coach Al Groh, finishing 9-7 and missing the playoffs. At the end of the year, Groh resigned to take the head coaching job at the University of Virginia. Herm Edwards took over a decent Jets team and made the playoffs during the 2001 season, but they were ousted by a far-superior Oakland Raiders squad in the first round.

Now, everything that you just read in this chapter sets the stage for everything that's going to happen in the rest of the book. I mean, how would *you* feel if you were a supporter of a team like this? Angry? Frustrated? Sad? Hopeful? Excited for the day they turn it all around? All/some/none of the above? Well, I've felt all of those things and more while cheering on this perpetually sorry franchise. Every Jets season carries with it their history, this legacy of losing that underscores everything they do. And every season that falls short, every sixteen games plus playoffs that doesn't end with a Super Bowl, adds another chapter to the legacy. When the newly united NFL was in its infancy, the Jets had it all. Star power, a quarterback, one of the best head coaches in the league, toughness, a coolness that attracted fans from New York and everywhere else. They had all of this, and a Lombardi Trophy. And it all went away in the blink of an eye. For the past forty years and counting, they've been trying to get it back. Every season has brought bits and pieces of that miraculous 1968-1969 journey to the table, but very few have ever gotten close to bringing the full package back. Jets fans follow a perplexing and disappointing team, waiting for the day when they turn the universe on its side.

Yes, that's the day that would make the missed field goals, intercepted passes, bad draft choices, and all of the other things that have malaised the Jets worth it. The day when they win the Super Bowl. That's the day that Jets fans have been waiting for since the sixties. Sometimes, it seems too distant to even dream about. Other times, it seems agonizingly close, a prize just waiting—nay—*asking* to be taken. No matter how close that day seems, though, one thing remains the same. It never actually arrives.

So Jets fans, like fans of most franchises, continue to wait. To wait, and to hope against hope that this year's team will be the one. *That's* the life of a Jets fan, as far as football is concerned.

Soon, I would live that life too.

BELIEVING IN NEXT YEAR

My grandparents' family room is much like any other family room. Wall-to-wall beige carpeting lines the floor, interrupted by two striped couches and a black leather chair, both of which are placed on the left side of the room and face the now-flat screen TV. (It seems so inconceivable to me that there were times in my life where I actually watched a non-flat screen TV.) Above the TV hung a clock that bore the insignia of the United States Marine Corps, one object of many in the room that reflected Grandpa's service record. Almost all of the others were on a shelf located across the room and next to the door that lead to the garage. Pictures of their kids and grandchildren; my mom, Uncle Ray, Uncle Jamer, cousin Victoria, and me, either rested on various tabletops or adorned the wall. On small wooden tables next to the couches, the most recent newspapers and magazines were often strewn about, waiting to either be read or thrown in the garbage. Three solid, heavy doors on the right side of the room lead to a closet, the bathroom, and the back patio, respectively. The room has a slight opening in the middle that leads to a stairwell which is enclosed on both sides and has transported many an appetizer from the kitchen to the living room during family gatherings at Thanksgiving, Easter, and birthdays. The door directly to the left of the stairwell leads to the newly-refinished basement.

OK, I'm done with the tedious imagery for now. Maybe some people like those long-winded descriptions of exactly what a place looks like, but I don't like reading them and I've put down a ton of books because they contain exactly that. (I'm looking at you, *Jane Eyre*.) And if I don't like reading them, then I sure as hell don't like writing them. However, I felt like this particular description was important because I want the reader to know exactly where I first discovered the game of football and, by extension, planted the seeds for two books, a future career, and basically my entire life.

I read everything as a kid. Absolutely everything. Books, magazines, the scrolling ticker at the bottom of the screen during the news, instruction manuals, tourism guides for places that I'd never heard of, you name it. So, as luck would have it, I was staying over at my grandparents' house on August 15th, 2002, just six days before my sixth birthday. After taking a nap on the couch, I began to look around for something to do for an hour or so dinner time. So, naturally, I immediately discovered that day's paper resting on the table and began reading the top page of the pile. Luckily for me, that page was the sports section. After flipping through it for awhile, a column entitled, "New York Jets Kick Off Their Preseason Tonight vs Baltimore" appeared. Of course, all of the relevant information, analysis, and stats went right over my head because I was five years old. Two names, though, did not. For whatever reason, I remembered Wayne Chrebet and Vinny Testaverde.

I didn't know the first thing about football at that point, but I remembered those two names. There was something about the way they sounded. *Wayne Chre-bet. Vinny Test-uh-ver-day.* I kept saying these names over and over during the course of the few hours leading up to the game, a timespan which I later identified as the unofficial beginning of my announcing career.

Then, the game started. My grandparents were both sitting on the couch with me and watching the game. As I watched the game, I began to do the thing that must have driven both my parents and my grandparents out of their mind when I was a kid. I started asking questions.

Now, my parents encouraged curiosity. They always kept tons of books around the house and were talking to me about topics ranging from fish to politics by the time I was five years old. However, they neglected to realize that they had created a monster. A monster that would soon bring every single conceivable football question to bear on his poor grandparents.

Grandpa, why is there a yellow line on the field? Grandma, how come that guy isn't wearing the uniform of either team? And why did he just throw a flag on to the field? Where is this game being played? How did all of those fans get there? Wait, the team is called "New York" but they play in New Jersey? Why are they tackling him like that? What positions do Wayne Chrebet and Vinnee Tes-teh-vur-day play? Do they not like each other? Who's that guy on the sideline with the funny hat? Why are there so many commercials? What is Miller Lite?

The answers, if you've never watched a game of football before, are as follows:

The yellow line is the first down line, the guy that's not wearing the uniform of either team is the ref and he just threw a flag to call a penalty on a team for a rules infraction, the game was being played in Baltimore, most of the fans drove to the game, I'm just as confused as you are about the New York/New Jersey thing, they're tackling him like that because they're paid to, Chrebet is a wide receiver, Testaverde is the quarterback, I don't know whether football players generally like each other, the guy on the sideline with the headset (which I mistook for a hat) is the coach, there are so many commercials because CBS would like to remain in business, and Miller Lite is beer.

You think reading that entire last paragraph was exhausted, long-winded, and confusing? Imagine being my grandparents and having to answer all of those questions and tons more while the game was being played in front of them. And they, bless their hearts, answered every single one of them. After that night, I knew that I liked the game of football. I wasn't sure which team I liked or what the hell was going on for most of the game or why I even liked football. I just knew that I liked it.

Of course, both my grandma and my grandpa saw this as an opportunity to sway me towards the Jets. My favorite sportswriter, Bill Simmons, actually wrote about this very topic; parents and other family members swaying kids to support their team. He asserted that kids below the age of six will believe absolutely *everything* that their parents tell them. As he puts it, you have precious little time between when a child grasps the basics of competition and when he/she decides to make their own decisions about which team to root for. You have two years, tops, to commence brainwashing your kid into loving your team. Neither my Mom nor my Dad ever liked or watched football that much, so it was up to my grandparents to take over their parental duties and do the sports brainwashing for them. Grandpa had stronger allegiances to *people* within football than he ever did to any team, so the first thing that I learned were the names of every single person on his unofficial Favorite People in Football list. *Bill Parcells. Phil Simms. Curtis Martin. Joe Klecko. Lawrence Taylor. Vinny Tessaverdey.* (I hadn't quite obtained the ability to properly pronounce his name at the tender age of five.)

Then, a few weeks later, we were at a family brunch and my grandpa handed me the sports section from a newspaper and pointed me towards the Jets game. No sales pitch, no phony stories about how the Jets were superheroes or anything, none of that little kid stuff. He just circled the game on the list and highlighted the time and TV channel. Just like his favorite coach of all time, the aforementioned Bill Parcells, Grandpa always knew exactly which buttons to push in order to get somebody to do something. See, I wasn't a typical kid. I didn't watch cartoons, couldn't name three Disney movies, didn't like ice cream or pizza, never liked Spongebob, and wanted to be a game show host when I grew up. (Yes, all of my friends still wonder why I chose to lead this awful, bizarre, profoundly botched childhood. I honestly don't know the answer to that question.) If the grown-ups were doing it, I wanted to do it. Every single opportunity I had to be different than other people my age, I took. So anything that was different than what the other kids were doing was right up my alley, which naturally led me to football. So my Grandpa knew that if he just pointed me in the Jets' direction, then my curiosity would take it from there. Very clever guy, my Grandpa.

So, after brunch, I sit down to "watch" my first Jet game. Of course, I put the word "watch" in quotation marks because the way I went about taking in a football game back then was so radically different from the way that I currently do things. If you have kids or can remember absolutely anything before the age of seven, you know that the K-2 age group has the shortest attention spans on Earth. You couldn't get me to focus for three straight hours if Richard Dawson came over for dinner, so forget about a football game. (Note to anybody living in the 21st century: Richard Dawson was the host of *Family Feud* from 1976 to 1985 and, by my five year-old estimation, the coolest person to ever live. I was born about twenty years behind my time.) When the Jets were on the goal line, I was trying to determine whether the leather chair in our living room would make a good trampoline. On crucial third downs, I was running all over the family room like a maniac until my Mom commanded that I settle down.

But when I did watch, I ended up doing what I always did when my favorite shows were on. Slowly, I got up close to the TV, maybe a foot or two away, and paced in front of it. The game was far too exciting for me to even consider sitting down, so I decided that I needed to stand. This is something that I continue to do to this day, especially when there's a good game happening. From the very start of the game, I'll get within eighteen inches of the TV and walk back and forth across the floor with my arms folded, while also pointing at the screen and making comments to myself. If I had a play card and a headset, I'd look like I was trying to call the plays from my family room. Yes, I know it's weird. But it's routine, and it was a routine that was established during that first game against Buffalo, which the Jets won 37-31 in overtime.

After that game, I became totally engrossed in football and the Jets. I started asking for Jets books, Jets jerseys, really, just anything with a Jets logo on it. There was nothing I ever wanted more than to get football everything for Christmas: video games, actual footballs, more memorabilia, autographs, cards, and anything else that had the slightest thing to do with football. My free time became increasingly occupied by committing to memory everything I could about both the Jets and football. I could name ten players on any team in the league. I knew the year (1969), score (16-7), and opponent (Baltimore Colts) of the Jets' first and only Super Bowl win. By the middle of the year, I had memorized the score and opponent of every Jets game (in order) for both 2001 AND 2002. The two people who asked me for that information at the time couldn't have been more impressed.

This was also the period of time where I somehow got the impression that I could be a football player. I went out to the backyard almost every single day and ran around with a football, imagining myself as the next great running back (a la Curtis Martin) or the greatest receiver to ever play the game. (Jerry Rice had nothing on Wayne Chrebet according to six-year old me.) When I wasn't doing that, I was neglecting what little responsibility I had in order to play *NFL 2K3*. Of course, I had absolutely no idea what to do or how to control the players, but I didn't care. I was just happy that somewhere, somehow, there was a football game being played on a screen.

You know, that whole season was probably the most fun I ever had around football. It didn't feel so serious to me. If the Jets won, I was happy. If not, I was a little bit bummed out for five minutes, and then I got over it almost immediately. Back then, there was never this impulse, this visceral calling that commanded me to care deeply about every game. No worrying about what the Jets' playoff chances were, no constantly updating Twitter, no writing deadlines to meet, nothing at all. Just the game and me. Football was just a game, and I found it just as fun as I did my handheld mini-pinball gizmo. I'd watch it every chance I could, but it ultimately didn't matter who won. It's really the irony of ironies when it comes to this book, a self-reflective narrative about how sports assumed its proper place in life over time, that sports had been in its proper place from the beginning.

Those were the days of innocence, the times where I could get all of the enjoyment out of the game with a fraction of the emotional investment. Two games outside the division lead? The Patriots have the tiebreaker advantage? Vinny Test-uh-vertay was benched and we have a new starting quarterback? Who cares!? It's football, and it was fun.

You know, I've often wondered why it is that I strayed from this stance on the sport I love, and why it took me almost my whole childhood to push myself back in that direction. My Grandpa was always a little upset after the Jets lost, so maybe I started caring too much because I didn't want *him* to be sad. Maybe as my friends started to watch football and pick their favorite teams, I felt the need for my team to be better than the ones they chose. Maybe it's nobody's fault at all and losing this idyllic attitude towards sports was inevitable. Or perhaps the answer is all of the above, a combination of some of the above, or none of the above. Who the hell really knows the answer? Everything changes so much over time that it becomes impossible to discern why football transforms from a part of life to life itself.

All I really know is that I wish I could go back and re-live one of those football Sundays. Just one, maybe for a couple hours. Just so I could remember what it feels like to truly enjoy football, pure and simple. You know those super-cheesy "falling in love again" style rom-coms? You know, where the girl gets amnesia or the guy goes back in time to when he first met his wife? Yeah, I hate those movies, but at the same time, I wish I could do something like that with football. That sense of childish wonder and excitement blended with inquisitiveness, it's something which can never truly be re-captured. In the words of Bruce Springsteen: they'll pass you by, those glory days.

The season drew near its end with the Jets at 8-7 and in a position to win the AFC East, an accomplishment that they had not achieved for the past couple of years before that season. Leading up to their Week 17 showdown with Green Bay, the final regular season game, I was depressed. The season was over after that game. So what would happen after that? Would football fall off the face of the Earth? My six-year old cranium was getting extremely worried about this, to the point where I couldn't focus in Mrs. Kane's class for the whole week. (Sorry about that, Mrs. Kane.) It got to the point where, once again, I started asking questions. And since sports was the one topic on which my super-genius Dad, who knew every answer to everything ever, was not fluent, there was only one source that could respond to my queries about whether or not the NFL would spontaneously disband after the season ended. Grandpa. After arriving home from school on Friday, I dialed his number in a panic.

"Hello?" said a deep, commanding voice.

"Grandpa, it's me", I said. "After this week, is there no more football?"

It is at that moment that my dear Grandpa probably realized the full extent of how in to football I was. I ran home from school and arrived at my house five minutes early for the sole purpose of calling him and asking him that question. A brief silence ensued on his end, which in retrospect, I can only assume was Grandpa rubbing his temple and sighing. And once again, to his credit, he took the time to patiently explain to me that no, football would be back next September. Whew. But then, I asked, how would they know which team is the best from this season? They had to have had a reason for playing those games, right?

Grandpa said, "Well, of course they do. After this week, the twelve best teams go to the playoffs. They last for a whole month. If you lose in the playoffs, you don't play again until September. If you win, you keep playing football. At the end, there's this game called the Super Bowl. The best team is the one that wins the Super Bowl."

Whoa! Another month of football after this week!? A Super Bowl? You could have knocked me over with a pencil. This was all too awesome for me to even handle at the time. A whole 'nother month of football and something called a Super Bowl. Wow.

Wait a second, I thought. *Are the Jets going to go away after this week? Are they good enough to be in the Super Bowl?* Naturally, I had to pose these questions to grandpa as well.

"That all depends", he answered. "If the Patriots lose this week and the Jets win, they'll play next week in the playoffs. Maybe, if they keep winning in the playoffs, they can make the Super Bowl."

"But what if they don't, Grandpa? What if the Packers beat them this week?"

After another brief silence, he replied, "There's always next year."

Beautiful. There's always next year. That was quite possibly the best thing anybody had ever said to me during the entire first five years of my life. Within days, it became my go-to statement for everything. Jets didn't win the Super Bowl? There's always next year. I forgot to brush my teeth? Hey, there's always next year. I need a blanket statement to explain why I didn't do my homework on time? Always next year, am I right?

What grandpa taught me with those four words was that no matter what the outcome, life goes on. If the Jets didn't make the playoffs, the sun will still rise in the morning and time will continue to march forward. It's a lesson that I wouldn't remember until years later, and it's something that I'll undoubtedly tell my children someday. Life goes on. There's always next year.

Fortunately, I didn't have to wait until next year, which was fantastic because if there's one trait that the 0-10 demographic lacks any semblance of, it's patience. That would prove to be a non-issue, however, as New England lost to Miami on a last-second field goal. More importantly, the Jets ran roughshod over the Green Bay Packers. Sure, Green Bay had already secured a playoff spot and thus decided to rest all of its starters, but I'd rather not taint a glorious childhood memory with facts, reality, and all that other boring stuff. Once again, I ran around my living room, fists wildly punching the air, overcome with jubilance that my Jets were going to be able to compete for a Super Bowl, whatever that was.

After a first-round 41-0 demolishing of the Indianapolis Colts, the Jets had to travel to a place known as the Black Hole, more formally referred to as Network Associates Coliseum in Oakland, and do battle with the Oakland Raiders. Back then, the Raiders were *good*. In fact, I think they might have been the first team I ever really hated. Not just because of how good they were, but because of how *mean* they were. The Oakland Raiders have a reputation for having the most violent, unruly, and generally terrifying fans in the NFL. Everything that these guys can do to potentially psych the opposing team out, they do. These denizens of the Black Hole wear Darth Vader masks, bleeding skull helmets, and innumerable other kinds of apparel, solely for the purpose of intimidation. They were owned by a larger-than-life man by the name of Al Davis, a cunning and combative team owner that coined the phrase, "Just win, baby" and acted accordingly. He made a point of feuding with former NFL commissioner Pete Rozelle over every little thing. One time, he even posed as a reporter and asked the head coach of the next week's opponent to draw up the play that he used to win a recent game. That very week, the Raiders used that play to score a touchdown. And even though the Raiders and football in general have gotten far tamer since the 1970s (believe me, *much* tamer), Oakland was still the villain for me. They had a scary logo of a pirate with an eye-patch. Their fans would sometimes riot in the streets, regardless of whether the team won or lost. And, even though I didn't know this at the time, the Raiders were the very team that eliminated the Jets from the playoffs the year before. Everything that I ever heard about them on the news or from my grandpa continually reinforced the notion that Raiders=Lucifer. By game time, I was convinced that this divisional playoff contest between professional football teams was akin to a battle of Right vs Wrong, Good vs Evil, and Simba vs Mufasa.

Well, hate to break it to you, but Mufasa kicked Simba's ass. By a lot. I was completely taken aback, in a way that I never thought I'd be. See, everything that you ever watch, read, or listen to as an average five-year old kid has the good guys winning. Pick quite literally any Disney movie that you can think of: good guy wins. If you're a parent, peruse every single book you've given to your kid: good guy wins. Even in life, as far as they know, the good guy always wins. After all, around that age is when you really learn right from wrong, so there's a very obvious reason why we as a society don't expose Kindergartners to things like *Goodfellas*. (Well, that and the scenes of Joe Pesci repeatedly stabbing a guy in the trunk of his car within the first two minutes. That's a pretty decent case against showing *Goodfellas* to little Joey in of itself. But I digress.) To little kids, it's the same script every time. Here are the good guys. Good guys have conflict with bad guys. Conflict gets resolved in a peaceful way. A lesson is taught. Good guys win.

The thought of the Raiders winning never once crossed my mind, which is why it surprised me that they obliterated the Jets 30-10. I'd never considered that the villains can have a significantly better pass rush and a more effective running game than do the good guys. The minute details of the game escape me at the moment, considering that it happened when I was in kindergarten, but I remember being more confused than anything else. I thought that the football season would play out much the same way that *Like Mike* did and Wayne Chrebet would get magic Nikes just in time to win the big game. But on that day, reality interceded and taught me my second important lesson; the world is unfair sometimes and the good guys don't always win. Essentially, that game served as my first dose of reality. The silver-and-black clad Raiders moved on to the AFC Conference Championship, and the Jets went home.

I think that's the part that really bummed me out, actually. Winning and losing didn't totally concern me at that point in my life; it would be another two years before I was even truly upset over a Jet loss. (Wow, I approached these games so much more level-headedly at age five than I did at age fifteen.) I just didn't want the Jets to go away for nine whole months. It was kind of like how you'd feel if the season finale of a TV show you liked was just OK. You're a little bit disappointed because you're not seeing it again for almost a full year and your last memory of it wasn't fantastic, but it's not like you're actually upset over it. A little bit peeved, maybe, but not actually upset. That was me. Sports were just another thing in my life. And, perhaps most importantly, there was always next year.

Meanwhile, I'd begun to take more and more of an interest in the game. I remember that when naptime arrived in first grade, I would discreetly sneak in a copy of the Pro Football Almanac for that year and read it over and over again. Every single one of my sloppily handwritten essays and completely indecipherable drawings were related to football. All of my spelling tests, addition practice worksheets, and book reports were signed "Go Jets!" It got to the point where my first grade teacher probably would have loved to trade me for just about any other kid on the face of the Earth. Since most kids in the early years of elementary school follow a distinct monkey see/monkey do pattern, people were starting to become enthralled with this strange and totally foreign activity called *football*. I took a little bit of pride in being the first one on the bandwagon, and was happy to go around dispensing my wealth of football knowledge to anybody who would listen.

But a weird thing suddenly started happening. Of everybody that had suddenly started following football, almost none of them were Jet fans. There were Giants fans, Eagles fans, Steelers fans, and miscellaneous other fans, but Jet supporters were just about nowhere to be found. What I found over the years (but especially at that age) is that fandom runs in the family. Kids will support the teams that their parents like because, before a certain age, your parents are the coolest people alive. They're the ones that can always scare away the monsters under the bed and get the straw into the Hi-C juice box on the first try. Sports become a way— perhaps one of the best ways—to bond with your parents (usually your Dad), so kids tend to root for the same team as their parents root for. And when these people's parents were kids, football was just starting to become popular, which means that many of them were pretty much on their own for choosing their favorite team. For most of that time period, the Jets absolutely sucked, which meant that these parents gravitated away from them, largely to the much more respectable Giants. Then, they passed their favorite team on to the kids.

Even without the parental influence, kids can identify a loser surprisingly well. If there's one thing that little kids love the most in the world, it's winning at things, and if there's one thing they hate most in the world, it's losing at things. That's why there are so many Yankee fans in California, and that's also why half the crowd at Tropicana Field in

Tampa Bay will be rooting for the Red Sox when they come to town. People just don't like losing. The Jets, as the previous chapter has made you privy to, have not had a particularly success-laden history, and they weren't a particularly good team at the time either. So all of my classmates, under the influence of family and tempted by success, chose other teams. It didn't make any difference to me, though. Besides, who wants to watch football when you can play it?

Yes, the idea that all forty-some Caucasian pounds of me would somehow end up blowing away scouts at the NFL Combine and playing running back every Sunday had not yet been purged from my head. I'd be just like Curtis Martin, the Jets' running back at the time, except I would score a touchdown on every play. At least that's what would happen in my local flag football league, where I ran for at least four touchdowns a game, which isn't necessarily hard to do when you're the only one out of twelve that is focused on winning and not having fun. Every single play where someone else scored a touchdown, I would throw a fit until I got the ball again. Then, at the end of the season, the coach handed out fliers for the next step of that Pop Warner League; the first year of *tackle* football. The kind where people can actually get big boo-boos and even break stuff. I took one look at the diagram on the front, illustrating how to wrap and tackle properly, then quickly abandoned all hopes that I could ever play football professionally. Playing the game wasn't worth getting torn to pieces by bigger kids. (Little did I know that this decision would foreshadow the precarious future of the game, when hundreds of kids with actual athletic ability would make this choice for themselves as concussions became more and more of a problem.) I'd like to think that a higher power was looking out for me by ensuring my lack of athletic prowess, thus preventing my slow and painful metamorphosis into a Terrell Owens clone.

So, with my lifelong dream of about a year and a half thrown into the Grand Canyon and shattered, I began to look for a new career path at the age of six. One November Sunday, I sat down to watch the Jets, who were in the throes of a disappointing season and making all of my classmates that chose different teams look downright erudite.

You may be asking yourself, "Wait a second, did you take the time to type "smart" into an online thesaurus for the sole purpose of coming up with a highly interesting yet totally unnecessary adjective?" Well, you're damn right I did! And it rhymed! Let nobody tell you that Andrew Goldstein doesn't pull out all the stops for his readers. Also, let the record show that Andrew Goldstein has now become infatuated with the obnoxious habit of referring to himself in the third person . . . . Wait a second, what was I talking about? Oh yeah, how bad the Jets were. Tangent over.

Anyways, I was watching the suddenly-mediocre Jets lose yet another game when I suddenly put two and two together on a brilliant plan. See, for my whole life, I've been repeatedly told that I talk far, far too much. Parents, family members, friends, teachers, everybody. And if I wasn't being told that I talked too much, I was being reprimanded for talking too loudly. Most other people would take that advice to heart and talk less, but I instead looked around and concluded, "I must be pretty darn good at talking." So, as play-by-play man Jim Nantz and color commentator Phil Simms announced another Jets' loss, it hit me. *Why can't I do that?* My hand reached for the mute button, and within seconds I was stumbling my way through mock commentary of the Jets' game. This was the greatest thing ever. My job description would be to talk about the Jets and to get as close as possible to the game of football, all without the bodily harm. And thus, my dreams of broadcaster were off and running. That's another great thing about sports, by the way, it encourages talking and thinking from its fans. Not everybody knows the game like a broadcaster and obviously not everybody can be up in the booth, but just about everybody can know enough to talk about the game with another fan just by watching it. Sports are a social experience, and that was more than enough to satisfy me, the ultimate in social first-graders at the time.

My broadcasting career was just about the only positive thing that came out of the 2003 football season, as the Jets stumbled to a 6-10 record, good for last place in the AFC East. To be perfectly honest, I don't remember much of anything worthwhile from that season. It was kind of an awkward year anyways, one where the novelty of loving football had worn off and so did my dreams of playing the game. The Jets never recovered from a preseason injury to starting quarterback Chad Pennington, who had replaced Vinny Testaverde (finally got his name right sometime over the Summer) a little ways into the previous season.

He fractured his wrist after taking a hit in the final preseason game and had to sit out for the season's first six weeks, a time in which the Jets sputtered to a 1-4 start. (They had one of those early weeks off.)

One of the few things that I *do* remember about that season is NFL insider Adam Schefter going on Sportscenter the day before Pennington's return to the field and expressing concern that Pennington may not be fully healed yet. I was entirely taken aback at the fact that NFL players had to play with injuries that they hadn't recovered from. That is, until my grandfather told me about a guy named Jack Youngblood who played in a Super Bowl with a broken leg and described him like he had fought through a routine common cold. That story had two pronounced effects on me. Firstly, it reinforced my personal inconvenient truth: namely, that I was not *nearly* tough enough to play actual football. No way, no how would I ever consider playing the game again. The second thing that the story drove home was the fact that football players were apparently more Supermen then they were humans. All fans, and especially little kids like me, have this tendency to look at these incredible footballing machines in heavy pads and think that they're something greater than human. They run faster, they jump higher, they're taller than your parents are, and it seems like they hit the gene pool lottery to the point where they are somehow detached from the rest of us Earthlings. It took until my second year of football to realize how much sacrifice and pain was required to develop the skills that go hand-in-hand with that raw physical ability.

Unfortunately for Pennington, my newfound belief that football players could just slap a band-aid on injuries and return to action immediately turned out to be unfounded. He was never quite the same after that injury. Most other people didn't notice because, well, most other people didn't have enough time on their hands to ponder questions like, "Does Chad Pennington seem a little bit different to you?" But as I watched the Jets game, I sensed that something wasn't right. He stopped throwing the ball deep and seemed a little bit more pensive under pressure than he was before. As it turned out, Schefter's fears about Pennington's rushed rehab were right on the money. His wrist hadn't healed correctly and would forever be screwed up to some degree, at least as far as his football skills were concerned. For the rest of his career, his absolute absence of anything resembling arm strength, due to his inability to flick his wrist like he used to, would be something of a joke among Jet fans and critics alike. It was one of those times as a fan when you're initially in denial. *But . . . . but I saw him just last year and he didn't have these problems! Maybe he'll be better by next week! I swear, the old Pennington is going to come back soon!* But eventually, you accept the new normal; that he isn't going to be the same. Obviously, Pennington wasn't anything like a Hall of Fame caliber athlete even before the injury, but he had showed a good deal of promise. And while he did go on to have a fairly productive career as a league-average QB, there's no denying that the wrist injury left a lot of his talents on the table.

And if Pennington wasn't a superhuman, if *he* could get hurt, then *I* could as well. So no, I would not be playing football again.

For the 2004 season, Pennington was back after a full four months of rehab and so were the Jets. They raced out to a 5-0 start and had the entire fan base thinking Super Bowl. In truth, they benefited from a fairly easy schedule early on, but little kids who just turned seven don't necessarily factor strength of opponents into their thought process. I was all in on that year's Jets team. That was the first year when I went to Giants Stadium. (More on that in the next chapter.) It was the first time that I watched all sixteen Jet games, which was something that I took way more pride in than I probably should have. I even dressed up like Wayne Chrebet for Halloween and wholeheartedly ignored my parents' eye-rolling. The Jets were going to win the Super Bowl that year, and I wanted to make sure I enjoyed the hell out of it.

The Jets cooled off slightly over the course of the year and finished with a still-respectable 10-6 record; not enough to oust the 14-2 Patriots from their perch atop the AFC East, but enough to grab a Wild Card spot and a trip to San Diego for the first round of the playoffs. Gang Green survived that game against the San Diego Chargers by a 20-17 score in overtime to move on to the next round. (Apologies for the lack of details about this one: for some reason, I really don't remember much from it and Googling the details so I can pretend that I recall everything seems a tad dishonest. Maybe I blacked out once the game went into overtime.)

The AFC Divisional Round pitted the Jets against the Pittsburgh Steelers, who went 15-1 in the regular season behind rookie QB Ben

Roethlisberger, in the freezing confines of Heinz Field. For the first time, I felt a little bit of fear during the week building up to the game. I liked how the Jets season had turned out so far, and I guess that I subconsciously didn't want to mar it with an inevitable loss to Pittsburgh. Still, that didn't prevent me from talking about the game to every single person I knew, to the point where they were probably sick of me after Wednesday. Eventually, my Dad came up with a brilliant idea; a father-son bonding day. We'd go to the New Jersey Sportsman's Show in the afternoon, come home and grill up some baby-back ribs, and watch the game. Even though Dad didn't watch football in the least, he'd make the effort for me, which is just another reason why he's the greatest.

Well, things didn't necessarily turn out as planned. The sportsman's show was just something to kill a couple of hours before the game, so my mind was otherwise occupied for the entire time. This effect was greatly compounded by the fact that I was—and still am—about as far away from an outdoor person as you could get. As Dad tried to draw the slightest bit of interest from me in tractors, fishing equipment, mountain bikes, and camping trips, I gave obligatory mhms, uh-huhs, and head nods while thinking about the upcoming game. It could not have distracted me any less from what was going to unfold in about six hours. For some reason, I *felt* something about this game that I'd never quite felt before but would feel all too often in the years to come. I didn't just want the Jets to win, I *needed* the Jets to win. That's what was going through my head while my Dad tried to point out different types of RVs to me. If he'd taken me to that show on any other day, I'd chalk it up as two and a half hours of my life that I would never get back and forget about it. But when you're a fan, you tend to remember certain events in life, both of significance and not of significance, in terms of sports. And for whatever reason, I remember where I was and what I saw, almost verbatim, before that game against the Steelers.

Fast forward six hours to game time. The Jets and Steelers were locked in a heated battle, trading punch for counterpunch throughout a closer-than-expected game. This would already be excruciating enough if my dad weren't sitting on the sofa opposite me. Now, in every fan's life, there's usually one or two people that you try to *avoid* watching games with. More often than not, it's your super-young kid, spouse, mom, or non-fan friends. Sometimes, it's somebody who's a fan of the other team. It's nothing personal, but fans need to be around like-minded fans in times like these. It's just how our brains work. We need somebody who can understand when to cheer, somebody that has the fan sixth sense to know things like, "I'd better not say anything at this particular moment", somebody who truly gets it. My dad, incidentally, falls about as far away from that "gets it" category as humanly possible. If it's a key third down and the game is tied, you can always count on Dad to suddenly jump in and ask, "Now what is that blue line thingy across the screen?" Game-winning field goal attempt about to go up? Dad will be there with his favorite football query, "Now, what is a play-action pass?" (I've explained that to him—and I tell you this without exaggeration—exactly thirty-four times over the course of eight years. Seriously. I've kept count over the years) And that's not all. He shouts "WHOA!!" and "Oh! OH!" at five yard runs on first down, changes his allegiance depending on who's winning, occasionally falls asleep for an entire quarter, and asks you for a complete game recap when he wakes up. I usually put up with it because he's my dad and ~~he pays the mortgage on the house~~ I love him so much. But the one exception to that rule is when the Jets are on. In fact, I make a concerted effort to *not* watch the Jets game with anybody else, a tendency that might stem from this particular matchup.

All throughout the game, Dad hit me with a barrage of questions that made me finally understand the utter torment that I must have put my grandparents through two years prior. At least, though, I did it during a meaningless preseason game and not a do-or-die fight to the death. He shouted "GO STEELERS!!" whenever they made a good play. Every fifteen minutes passed with at least one question, some of which included "What's the score?", "Which team does Derek Jeter play on?", and "So which one is the running back, again?" Dad was in his fifties. I was seven. And this all happened while the Jets tried to save their season on the TV in front of us.

This game, despite most experts' predictions, was neck and neck right down to the end. The score was tied at 17-17 for much of the fourth quarter. Pittsburgh was starting to look tired. Most of the Steelers, through their body language and overall demeanor, seemed to say, "Damn, these guys are little bit more than we bargained for." In fact, the Jets embarked on a potential game-winning drive with just under five minutes left in the fourth quarter. They managed to march their way all the way down to the Pittsburgh thirty yard line when the drive stalled with two minutes and three seconds left on the clock, which left a forty-seven yard field goal between the Jets and the AFC Conference Championship; the last game before the Super Bowl. This could only mean one thing. Enter. Doug. Brien.

I've found that all fans have an athlete at some time in their lives, in whatever sport, that make them immediately expect the worst whenever they enter the game. Sometimes the feeling is justified, sometimes it isn't, but whether or not it's explainable never alters the overwhelming sensation of dread that comes along with the words, "And here comes (insert player here)!" It sounds mean to say and it felt downright rude as I was typing the words, but it happens to be true. There are just some athletes that you don't trust in big situations, and for me at the time, Doug Brien was one of those guys. He was the Jets' often-shaky field goal kicker—as if there's any other kind of Jets field goal kicker—that had already missed five kicks during the regular season, one extra point (something that no kicker should ever miss unless he's being kneed in the groin as he's swinging his leg), and one crucial field goal the week before in San Diego. And now he was about to trot out for a forty-seven yard kick to save the season in a stadium that is notorious for screwing with kickers. (Heinz Field's open end, which overlooks the Allegheny River, is despised by kickers the world over for its maddeningly unpredictable and ever-changing wind directions/speeds.) So no, I wasn't exactly bursting with confidence.

I was in the process of chewing the last of my fingernails when Brien lined up to take the kick. My Dad, finally sensing the gravity of the moment, reclined on his easy chair and said nothing. The room seemed to spin as Brien glanced towards the uprights and then back down towards his holder. Dad probably would have been wise to grab the phone and dial 911 in the more-than-likely event that I passed out from sheer nerves. If this is what *I* felt, I can only imagine how Brien must have felt. After what seemed like a lifetime, the ball finally spiraled back towards the holder. Brien took a mighty stride towards it and kicked the thing for all it was worth. As the ball spun through the air, it looked like it had enough distance. The only question was whether it would make it throu-

DOINK!

The ball smacked into the upright and tumbled away from the goalposts. Two referees that stood right where the ball would have landed began to walk onto the field, waving their arms in a horizontal motion to signal that the kick was no good. My Dad groaned. I fought back tears and held my hands over my forehead. *That's it*, I figured. *We just blew it.*

But wouldn't you know it, the Jets got another chance. Pittsburgh quarterback Ben Roethlisberger took the ball from there and immediately threw it right into the arms of Jets' linebacker David Barrett. The first play from the rookie QB Roethlisberger after the biggest break of his football life was an interception. Go figure. New York managed to move the ball up to the Steelers' twenty-five yard line before the clock ticked down to only a couple of seconds left. Doug Brien would have a chance for redemption. He went through the same routine—glance at the uprights, hold his arm outwards towards the center of the goalposts, look back down at the holder—and then kicked the ball again. This one wasn't even close. I mean, his kick hooked so far to the left that it might as well have gone directly into Lake Erie. The Jets just had two chances to send the Steelers home and overcome their tortured past, only to miss both of those chances.

In all fairness to Brien, these were fairly difficult kicks. I probably made them sound a lot easier and more routine than they actually were at the time. But to a seven-year old kid like me, the distance and wind direction on a field goal attempt were non-factors. "Doug Brien misses two difficult field goals late in the game" was instead reduced to "Doug Brien sucks and I'll always hate him because he was paid off to miss those kicks and he's the worst so he should just retire right now and go play for someone else because he's a doodyface." At least I think I said something along those lines. When you're bawling your eyes out because a field goal kicker broke your first-grader heart, things you say don't always make a ton of sense.

Since the game was tied, an overtime period was played immediately following the missed kicks. Realistically, though, the Jets had about a million different forks sticking out of them after the Brien field goals. I knew that they didn't have a chance in hell of coming back to win after what just happened, but I still watched and held out hope, just in case. Long story short, they didn't come back. Pittsburgh kicker Jeff Reed booted a significantly easier thirty-three yard field goal through the uprights to end the game and send the Jets to their couches until next season. Game over.

I think I felt physically sick watching the ending of that game. On Monday, I'd have to go into school and walk by the classroom of my first grade teacher Mrs. Kane, a rabid Steelers fan, who would undoubtedly want to talk to me about the game. Ray, my best friend for about a year, loved the Eagles, who had won their divisional round game. So now I have to hear it from him too. It was the first time that I really felt a connection with a team, and that team didn't win. I just sat there, totally shell-shocked, tears beginning to well in my eyes. My Dad tried to say something to cheer me up, but I couldn't hear him and I'm not sure I wanted to. Eventually, after about fifteen minutes of me not responding to any of his attempts to make me feel better, he asked me, point blank, "If the Jets make you this unhappy, why not just stop watching football?" He then walked out of the family room and up to bed.

I kept saying it to myself in my head over and over. (Or it might have been out loud; I didn't totally care at that moment in time.) *Football made me unhappy, so why continue watching it? Why not just swear off the game of football?* It made so much sense to me, so that's what I pledged to do. Fuming, I swore to myself to never watch another football game ever because, hey, that's the kind of thing that kids do when they get angry. Satisfied that I had fully and successfully cut off my nose to spite my face, I turned to go up to bed too.

But something didn't feel right that night. I kept tossing and turning in my bed, turning over the pillows constantly in hopes that they'd somehow become more conducive to sleep, and ultimately finding out that they weren't. After staring a hole in my dresser for roughly thirty minutes, I decided I'd wander back downstairs. I was too depressed to care if my parents caught me watching TV past my bedtime. So I flicked on the TV and there it was. Another football game. The Jets-Steelers matchup was the early game that evening and the Atlanta Falcons vs St. Louis Rams game happened to be the nightcap. Remembering my earlier promise, I immediately moved to change the channel.

Then, I saw Atlanta convert a nice pass for a first down. My thumb hung over the buttons, but did not press them. Next play, a long Atlanta run. By the time the Falcons marched into the endzone, I'd dropped the remote and allowed a smile to creep back on to my face for the first time since the day began. Yes, even though the Jets let me down, I still couldn't help but love football. It had become a part of me, and it was far too late to consider leaving it behind.

And as for the Jets, well, there's always next year.

MEADOWLANDS

I was really confused. I was excited, don't get me wrong, but I was confused more than anything. There were a lot of concepts that I didn't quite grasp at the tender age of seven, and the idea that I was going to go to a real, actual Jets game was one of them.

My seventh birthday came about two or three weeks before the 2004 season and my Uncle Jim (hereby affectionately referred to as Jamer) surprised me with tickets to the Jets' Week 5 game against the Buffalo Bills. Four tickets, one for Grandpa, one for Jamer, one for Dad, and one for me. We were gonna show up for a four o'clock game at approximately noontime and do something called "tailgating", whatever that was. And then, we were going to watch the Jets (hopefully) destroy the Bills.

For me, the thought of it was a little bit intimidating. When you're a little kid, everything seems big and beyond your ability to fully comprehend. As the shortest kid in my class at a time where being tall made you cool, even my tallest *classmates* seemed so big that they were beyond my ability to comprehend. So imagine how I thought of a gigantic stadium with a huge parking lot filled with thousands and thousands of people. To me, Giants Stadium (which was shared by the Giants and Jets but, naturally, had solely the Giants' name on it) was terra incognita. I'd seen pictures of it, heard about it, and saw it on TV, but I never actually thought that I could go there. Yet, I was about to do just that in two months.

Every single sports fan has some memory of their first game. Either you remember your first game or, if you were too young to do so, whoever took you certainly does. It's a hallmark life experience, no different than the first day of Kindergarten or your first birthday. Your first game is when you first meet your *other* family, the one that you chose for yourself. It's when your passion for your team expands beyond the living room and you first realize that there are thousands of people who think just like you do.

It's a system shock because you *think* you have the whole picture when you watch on TV, but you don't. The advantages of attending a game lie in the nuances. They lie in the things that you'd never think were important and that you can't possibly appreciate unless you've seen them and felt them. TV doesn't show the wispy smoke billowing up from the grills in the parking lot. TV can't possibly express to you how loud the crowd actually is. When you go to a game, the turf is pure green. When you go back home and watch it on TV, the color of the turf seems like a manufactured shade of green that's drawn straight from a Sherwin-Williams paint canister. *Everybody* should have the opportunity to go to a pro game or a highly anticipated college game at least once in their life, just to get a chance to experience everything that I've described and everything that I'm about to describe.

So the Jets win their first four games of the season, which means that I'm about to see the *undefeated* New York Jets in my first game ever. In fact, that's what I told everybody over and over again in the week leading up to the game. I'm sure my second grade teacher was counting the hours until 3:00 on Friday after hearing about my trip to see the *undefeated* New York Jets beat Buffalo for the hundredth time.

The first thing that I remember from the game was the tailgate, which I quickly found out was the greatest thing invented by anybody, ever. (At the time, I said that without a hint of hyperbole, but now I realize that claiming it was the "best thing ever" might have been a bit overblown. It's a close second, nestled comfortably in between NFL Sunday Ticket and Buffalo Wings.) Our car rolls past the gate to the parking lot and instantly, I see nothing but green. Rows and rows of fans are camped out next to their vehicles, almost all of them wearing Jets gear. (The Buffalo fanbase, if you can believe this, is not particularly well-represented in opposing stadiums. I saw, maybe, ten people in Bills gear throughout the whole day.) And when I say "rows and rows" of fans, I'm talking about a whole parking lot that has a radius of at least a half a mile with almost every space occupied by somebody, almost all of them with a full array of tailgate supplies. To this day, I have no earthly idea how anybody successfully navigates their vehicle into a spot without running over six fans (at least one of which is in a throwback jersey), ten bags of chips, and at least one portable George Foreman grill. The place is just packed with people, some of whom showed up the previous evening and slept in their cars. Fans don't screw around with tailgating.

To wit, let me describe the "tailgate supplies" that almost every single group of fans had with them. We start with the most basic supply in the tailgate arsenal: the grill. Everybody was grilling something; burgers, hot dogs, brats, you name it. The second most important piece of the tailgate ensemble; a healthy beer supply on ice in the cooler. Wait, you think that ten o'clock A.M. is too early for a Heineken and a bratwurst? What rock have you been trapped under for all these years?

The third thing that's absolutely essential for your tailgate is a football. The more it looks like it has been to hell and back, the better. Preferably, you'd bring along the same football that your dad has been bringing to tailgates since the mid-70s. If the leather is starting to peel off the ball or the laces are starting to unravel, you know that it's properly broken in. After all, you need to burn off the bratwurst calories somehow.

These are the three things that I saw just about every single group of fans have in their possession. I also saw satellite dishes being mounted on telephone poles, TVs mounted to the back of vehicles, giant tents, flags, every kind of retro and alternate jersey imaginable, face painting setups, beer pong tables, chips, noisemakers, signs, Fireman Ed hats, lawnchairs, and even more beer. You know, just to name a few.

So now, imagine bringing a seven year old kid into this environment. It was . . . . a bit overwhelming if you can believe that. We unloaded our tailgating gear in a cramped parking space, just like everybody else did. I had only recently discovered the glorious slice of heaven that is a New York Strip steak, so when I heard that burgers were essentially steaks that were shaped a little bit differently, I was sold.

And then we started tossing the football around. It was at that first tailgate that Jamer taught me the route tree. He told me what a Go route was. And a curl route. And a slant, screen, post, hitch, dig, out, in, and flea flicker. Before that toss, I had always thought that both teams entered each play with little to no planning and that huddles were just so the players could catch their breath. Those passing plays with Uncle Jim in the lot of the old Meadowlands first introduced me to where the wins and losses and heroes and goats are really determined; on playcharts, in film rooms, and within the players' minds. I may have been a football fan, but I couldn't actually speak a word of football until that day. And if I never start learning that language until later in my life, then there's a good chance that both of my books are never written. These are the things that you learn when you're a seven-year old and a rabid football family takes you to your first game.

The brats and the alcohol and the football tosses aside, tailgates are all about sharing an experience with your dysfunctional yet lovable sports family. All of the things that you do at home that some people will just *never* understand (the chants, the lucky jerseys, the pre-game traditions) are things that you get to do at tailgates. You step out of your car, take one breath just to see it rise into the cold October air, look around, and think, *"Alright, all of these guys are in this with me."* There's so much individual expression that's tolerated and celebrated within a tailgate, yet almost everybody's part of the same group. You feel a sense of brotherhood that comes from an event which can't be replicated anywhere else. It's not like the crowd before a concert or even the gathering that precedes New Year's in Times Square. When you're at a tailgate, you're surrounded by thousands of people who, for better or for worse, attached their lives to a team just like you did. Tradition, kinship, laughs, memories, and an experience that you'll remember for the rest of your life, all before you even make your way into the stadium.

About an hour before the game, the migration inside the concrete coliseum begins. Fans drop their spatulas and get up from their lawn chairs to start making their way towards the monstrous construction. Hordes of ticket-holders, many of whom are drunk, almost drunk, or plan on being drunk before the second quarter, make their way past the long line of ticket-rippers and push their way through the gleaming metal turnstiles. Suddenly, there it is. Giants Stadium.

The outside of the stadium looked fairly normal, with about three or four escalators on either side lifting the fans up to the various interior floors. At each corner of the stadium, two humongous circular spires, referred to as "gates", twisted up into the bright blue *New Jersey* (no, not New York) sky. These spires served as additional walkways for fans to enter the stadium and, in the case of the now-infamous Gate D, a space for inebriated idiots to fulfill their quota of sexual harassment for the month. (Just Google "Gate D Jets" and read away unless you're under eleven or twelve years old. If you are, then trust me when I say that it would just be better to wait until you're older. It's not one of the prouder moments in Jets history) Once inside the rotunda of the stadium, people selling food, beer, t-shirts, face paintings, and other assorted objects line the walls, packed in storefront to storefront. This constant row of vendors paused only when the wall opened and a set of stairs led down to the interior of the stadium. From that gap, you could get an unobstructed glimpse of the seats and that beautiful field.

For today's fan, watching football on TV lets you see the big picture. That's just a fact. With the advent of the Red Zone, laptops, high definition televisions, NFL Sunday Ticket, Fantasy Alerts, Wi-Fi, and everything else that makes tracking football from your home effortless, you actually *miss* more action when you go to the game than if you just stayed home. But when you stay home, you don't get to experience the atmosphere.

When I walked into the stadium for the first time, my seven-year old senses were on overload. The music blaring inside the stadium was louder than my stereo could play it, which I didn't think was possible. (Remember when boomboxes and stereos were some of the coolest things that a kid could possibly have? We've come a long way since 2004.) The jumbotron was three times bigger than any TV I had ever seen. I had seen the size of the crowd on my television at home, but it never hit me how gigantic the mass of people congregating inside the stadium really was until I got to be a part of it. The seats were filled with a rollicking sea of dark green and white, with only brief interruptions for the brave souls that chose to wear Bills' jerseys into what quickly became their personal version of Hell. The game was at 4:15, so every person of legal drinking age had at least a few in them by that point in the evening, and people were generally acting the part. (Hey, I'm not condoning it. I'm just saying that it happens and it's part of the ambience.) Everybody was screaming, cheering, chanting, cursing, and clapping, all before the intros even started. Players for both teams were out on the field running some pre-game drills. The kickers were booting field goals, the quarterbacks and wide receivers were tossing the ball around, and everybody else was stretching.

All throughout this process, a giant clock next to the jumbotron ticked down the time until the game started. When the numbers on that timer slipped below ten, both teams made their way into tunnels on the opposite side of the field from each other. I could see people moving some devices near the entrance of the tunnels, but I wasn't sure what they were. One of them seemed to be some sort of cannon, and another was a vertically-oriented, perfectly straight apparatus with an open top that said "Jets" on it. The crowd grew progressively quieter as the clock continued to tick away. After a few minutes, I heard the public address announcer boom, "Welcome to the Meadowlands for today's matchup between the Buffalo Bills (BOOOOO!!!!!!) and your NEW YOOOOOORK JEEEEEETS!!!"

A large cheer erupted from the crowd, louder than anything I had heard in the pre-game warmups. Then, the players began to crowd into the mouth of the tunnels and prepared to jog out onto the field. First, the Bills. They were introduced in a dull, monotone voice as "the visiting Buffalo Bills." They all made their way over to the sideline among plenty of boos and expletives from the fans. Then, the Jets made their way out of their own tunnel, to many cheers from the crowd. However, I noticed that some of them still remained obscured from view in the depths of the tunnel. Even stranger to my seven-year old brain was the fact that the Jets who were already on the field did not go over to the sideline like the Bills did. Instead, they lined up across from each other in two rows, starting from the edges of the tunnel and extending outwards onto the field. The PA Announcer started calling the names of each player remaining in the tunnel. *SHAUN ELLIS!* A burst of smoke came from the cannons set up beside the tunnels. *DEWAAAYYNE ROOOOBERTSON!* The crowd went nuts as fire shot out of the vertically-oriented device next to the line of players and into the early evening air. *CUUURRRTIIIIS MAAAARTIN!* One by one, the players charged down the open space between the two rows of their teammates, arms extended and palms open, high-fiving each one as they passed. *CHAAAAAD PENNINGTON!* Everybody saved their loudest applause for the quarterback, the last guy to make his way out of the tunnel and on to the field. In retrospect, it felt a little bit weird that everybody was losing their minds over Chad Pennington, but we were 4-0 for the first time in forever, so what did we care? (I don't mean to insult Chad Pennington. He's one of my favorite Jets and I still own and wear his jersey. But with the way that crowd was carrying on, you would have thought that it was a 60s Beatles concert or something.)

After the introductions, the national anthem, and the coin toss, the teams lined up for the kickoffs. Once again, a hush fell over the crowd. A man in a Jets' jersey and a green fireman's hat, hoisted up on another fan's shoulders, appeared on the Jumbotron. He motioned for the crowd to quiet down by waving his arms dramatically in a downward motion. Any Jet fan who didn't know to quiet down the first time (example: Me) was either silenced by the fan on the Jumbotron or implored by their neighbors to be quiet. In my case, grandpa and Jamer were the ones to tell my dad and I to pipe down. I had no idea what was going on, but my instincts told me to be as silent as everybody else was. (Thus making it one of the very few times when my gut told me *not* to talk.) The Bills' kicker raised his hand to signal that he was ready to kick the ball off and begin the game. As he did that, the man in the fireman's hat raised *his* arms over his head. Just as the Bills' kicker swung his leg to strike the ball, the earsplitting chant came.

J-E-T-S! JETS! JETS! JETS!

Yep, that was the first time I noticed Fireman Ed, a member of the Hall of Fans and the Jets' de facto mascot. See, the Jets aren't famous for their cheerleaders like the Dallas Cowboys are. They don't have a recognizable mascot, like the Phillie Phanatic for the MLB's Philadelphia Phillies. Nor do they have a famous cheering section, like the Dawg Pound in Cleveland. We have Ed Anzalone, a New York City firefighter that spearheads the J-E-T-S chant at kickoff and after the Jets score. I don't remember too much about what happened during the game besides the fact that the Jets won (some Googling revealed the final score; 16-14), but I'm never going to forget Fireman Ed and the J-E-T-S chant. These traditions are something that fans fiercely protect, and with good reason. Much like a football team needs to have an identity, their fanbase needs to have an identity. That identity is built through traditions like the chant. It's built through people like Fireman Ed who keep the faith and take an active role in making sure everyone else does too. And part of that tradition, part of taking a young fan and making him one for life, are moments like the one that happened after the game.

So after the game, we make our way from our suddenly freezing seats on to the concourse, along with a throng of happy, drunk, and happily drunk Jets fans. Even though the game ended and the vendors began to close the metal gates over their store windows, the din of the crowd did not subside. After all, the New York Jets—yes, the freaking New York Jets—were 5-0. Random J-E-T-S chants could be heard all the way from the parking lot and across all levels of the concourse as the masses began to file out of the stadium. As we stepped on to the escalator that would deliver us to the parking lot, I (barely) peered over the sides of the escalator to take in the scene in the parking lot.

WE'RE 5-0 BABY, YEEEAAAAHHHH!!!!!
SUPER BOWL!!!!!!!
LET'S HEAR IT FOR PENNINGTON!!!!!

Everybody was whooping and hollering all the way down the escalator. People were hugging, chest-bumping, high-fiving, pounding fists, raising their arms above their heads in victory, and greeting complete strangers like friends just because they had a Santana Moss jersey on. It felt like the crowd was dying for somebody, *anybody*, to initiate a J-E-T-S chant, because they responded every single time someone started it. I probably could have started it, but seven-year old me had a long day and was too exhausted to speak, let alone incite even more pandemonium. As we walked through the parking lot, I could see more white smoke escaping from among the cars into the darkness. Some intrepid fans, instead of waiting in the gridlock of traffic that was sure to ensue, chose to restart their grills and begin the tailgating process anew. More beers were opened, more brats were cooked, and it wasn't until the wee hours of the night that the last tailgaters exited the lot.

I finally dragged myself into the back seat, buckled up my seatbelt, and began to fall asleep as I tucked the football that Jamer and I played catch with to my chest. Before I went down for good, Jamer looked over at me and asked, "Was it worth it to come here?"

Using my last bit of strength, I managed to mutter, "Yeah, it was."

"Would you come back next year?"

I didn't answer. My eyelids had checked out for the day. I distinctly remember having to be carried back into my house when we got home because my dad couldn't wake me up. But the smile etched across my face as I drifted off to sleep told Jamer all he needed to know. Oh yeah, we were coming back.

Everything that I just described wasn't particularly unique. In fact, most fans who have attended games in person can probably attest to experiencing something similar. But the feeling that I got when I stood on that escalator, the little voice inside my head telling me to remember everything that I saw, that's something that tied me to the team forever. It's those little things, those little slices of life, that make you stay with the same group of guys time and time again.

So we've gone back every year. Each season, for one game, Jamer gets tickets for himself, my Dad, my Grandpa, and me. Each season, my Dad and I get up early and make the forty-five minute drive to my Grandpa's house in Cranford. Each season, we drive from there to the same Marriott parking lot and wait for Jamer to meet us there. Each season, we go from there to the tailgate and do the same things that I did the first time I went. And each season, I walk away from it happy.

Over the years, I've seen some characters both among the tailgating masses and among the crowd inside the stadium. I've seen people with wacky tattoos, people wearing giant panda masks, people wearing actual airplane headpieces, people who were drunk beyond belief (which probably describes all of the above), and everything in between. However, none of them are more memorable to me than "HERE WE GO!!!" guy. This story is a nice litmus test for whether or not you're a fan. If you are, then you'll probably nod at this story, chuckle a little bit, and say something along the lines of, "Yep, I know exactly what he's talking about." People who aren't fans will probably just shake their heads and wonder why I found this so enjoyable. Allow me to explain.

It was Week 3 of the 2009 season and the 2-0 Jets were the toast of New York after beating the Patriots. They entered this matchup with the Tennessee Titans looking to go 3-0 for the first time since 2006 and rookie quarterback Mark Sanchez was the early favorite in the rookie of the year race. Actually, I don't know why I'm telling you this stuff because the context of this particular event is really not that important. Like so many other times when you're attending a game, the story isn't so much about what happened during the game as much as what happened in the stands.

A couple of minutes after we found our seats, a group of five or six fans walked down our aisle and sat down in the row in front of us. The person who happened to sit in front of me was a heavyset red-head with bad facial hair and a Jets cap. I said to myself, "Please, just don't let him be one of those obnoxious drunks." See, I had heard horror stories of people sitting near people who were wasted and the guy eventually (inhale) cursed excessively, tried to punch someone, threw up on people, threatened another fan with bodily harm, stood up in front of other people trying to watch the game, passed out, or was generally an annoyance to everyone in his vicinity. (Exhale.) These people are really fun to watch and add some innocent enjoyment to the game *so long as they're in another section*. When you're eyeing the throw-up threat across the aisle or enjoying the two belligerent drunks who are about to throw down in the section in front of you, it's part of the gameday atmosphere. (Once again, I'm not condoning it, but it is a part of life at football stadiums.) However, when they end up in your section, that's when things get dicey. And if the overweight red-head who sat down in front of me weren't an obnoxious drunk, then I wouldn't be telling this story. But alas, he was and I am.

First thing's first, the guy starts dropping random f-bombs loud enough for the entire section to hear it. The weird thing is that this was thirty minutes before the game, so maybe he was cursing and carrying on just for the hell of it. Or maybe he was too drunk to even begin to notice how loud he was yelling. (Probably the second one.) I leaned over to Dad and whispered, "I wonder what his parents would say if they were here." (I'm gonna take a second to climb down from my high horse after that one.)

Grandpa, who heard me say that, tapped me on the shoulder and pointed to the people on either side of drunk redhead. Yep, two of the people that this schmo came in with were his parents. They were just carrying on as if their son weren't serenading the whole section with profanities. I think Drunk Redhead nearly spilled his beer all over them as they were calmly discussing what to do for dinner after the game. On a semi-related note, I was able to spot the one Titans fan in our section as the walking trainwreck in front of me wouldn't stop his obscenity-laced dialogue. After a little bit of thought, I resolved that Drunk Guy was definitely crazy enough to try and throw the Titans fan off the second deck by the third quarter. But I digress. The point is that I knew that Drunk Redhead was out of his mind even before he turned around, looked at me, and delightfully screamed, "Hey, you're a redhead! Us gingers need to stick together!" (Note to reader: I am not a redhead. But at that precise moment, I was just happy that I was the one person in the world that he apparently didn't despise.)

When the game started, this guy would just stand up at random moments in the game—*entirely* random moments—and scream at the top of his lungs, "HERE WE GO!!!!!" It seemed like every five minutes, this guy felt the need to belt out another "HERE WE GO!!!!!!" for the whole stadium to hear. What's weird is that he'd never do it when something exciting was happening. I kept waiting for it every time the Jets were down near the goal line or a big third down was coming up. Nope. Instead, the Titans would be punting on 4th and 13. As the ball gracefully tumbled through the ai—HERE WE GO!!!! Jets just ran for a three yard gain on first and ten? HERE WE GO!!!! TV Timeout? HERE WE GO!!!!!!! At halftime when the high school kids were play— HEEEEEEERE WE GOOOOOOO!!!!!!! This guy was probably the greatest walking, talking billboard that Bud Lite has ever had.

The four of us (dad, grandpa, Jamer, and I) started developing somewhat mixed opinions about this guy. Dad and Grandpa, the morally sound ones in our group, thought that this guy was a disgrace. Grandpa, at one point, even told him to shut up and implored the people sitting next to him to assist in that effort. Surprisingly, the guy said sorry and promised to tone it down a little bit. Why? Because, he said, he didn't want to upset the little kid in back of him; AKA Me. He then reaffirmed his declaration that "us gingers need to stick together." (Once again, I was neither a little kid nor a ginger.) Of course, he invented about half a dozen new ways to utilize the f-word in the next ten minutes and eventually both Grandpa and Dad just resigned themselves to dealing with him.

On the other hand, Jamer and I were loving this. Every single time he let out another "HEEEERE WE GOOOOOO!!!", Jamer nearly keeled over with laughter. I didn't want to laugh and risk losing the protection that my red-headedness gave me (or didn't give me), so I decided to keep it to a muted chuckle. Still, I was leaning over to Jamer throughout the day and trying to come up with prop bets like "how many f-bombs will he drop?" and "next HERE WE GO; under or over three minutes." (In case you were wondering, I lost the first prop and won the second to break even for the day.)

So that's how it went throughout the day, with HEEEERE WE GOOOOO!!! guy whooping and hollering and cussing the whole time. Eventually, we all just looked at each other and laughed about it. And as the Jets stopped the Titans on fourth down one last time to preserve a 24-17 victory, he looked to the sky and let out an earsplitting roar. As we exited the stadium, conversation immediately turned to this guy. We all agreed that it was something we would never forget and I immediately became profoundly sad that I didn't capture one of his screaming episodes for my cellphone ringtone. Just as we were approaching our car, we saw the guy and his family getting into their Honda Civic with one of the sober members of their group behind the wheel. He recognized me, pointed in my direction, and let out one last deafening "HEEEEEERE WE GOOOOOO!!!!!!" for good measure. Then, the Civic's engine revved and they were gone. I chuckled one more time and then climbed into the backseat of dad's Mercury. What else could you do? He was just part of the dysfunctional family.

Admittedly, it's a really weird story and now you can probably see what I mean when I said that people who aren't fans would find it difficult to grasp why this was so memorable. Maybe it was one of those "you had to be there" moments, but I think that every fan will have one of these stories if they go to the game in person a few times. Because that's what happens when you go to games. You meet some of the strangest, saddest, happiest, best, worst, and most memorable people that you're ever going to meet in your life. You always come back with an anecdote or two about seeing an unbelievable moment in person or about the guy who sat in front of you that wouldn't shut up. But either way, you come back with some kind of connection that you didn't have before, and you come back with a story. *That's* the kind of thing that you can't get from sitting in a luxury box, and you can seldom get it from watching TV. To make those connections and to have those experiences, you need to get an average seat. You need to get up early and make that drive to the stadium. You need to walk into the stadium thirty minutes early, before it gets too crowded, to really appreciate what's going on down on the field. You need to *be there.*

A football game, or really any kind of sporting event, is life condensed into a radius of only a few miles. Within that radius, you meet people that you're going to keep in touch with for the rest of your life. You're going to hear, smell, touch, taste, and see things that will resonate with you. You will be a part of a community of fans, something that is far greater than the sum of its parts. Sometimes, you and that community will suffer losses together and look toward better days in the future. Sometimes, you'll celebrate the wins together and try to hold on to that all-too-brief moment of victory for as long as possible. And ultimately, you'll find out that it won't matter as long as you have people to share it with.

I'll always remember looking at that parking lot on that October day in 2004, my mouth agape. I'll laugh when I think about the HEEEERE WE GO!!!! guy and chalk it up to him being just another crazy fan. I'll remember exiting Giants Stadium on that escalator and absorbing everything around me.

I'll never forget meeting the world for the first time in the Meadowlands. Never.

MANGENIUS, IMMORTALITY, AND BROADWAY BRETT

The Pittsburgh loss that I described at the end of chapter two set off a distinct downward spiral for the Jets. After a 4-12 showing in the ensuing 2005 season, Gang Green decided that they had seen enough of head coach Herm Edwards, who they promptly dismissed. His replacement would be Eric Mangini, a thirty-five year old product of New England coach Bill Belichick's extensive coaching tree. He had spent the previous eight years working as the New England coach's subordinate; three years as a defensive assistant when Belichick was with the Jets, four years as a defensive backs coach in New England, and one as a defensive coordinator.

Looking back on the circumstances that surrounded his hiring, it's easy to see the rationale behind bringing him in as the head coach. The Jets had been seriously unstable in the years leading up to the 2006 season, going from making the playoffs to missing the playoffs the following season three separate times in the eight years before Mangini's arrival. Maybe the Jets' management thought that Mangini had discovered a winning formula while working with Belichick that he could bring to New York. Maybe they thought that hiring away Belichick's newly anointed defensive coordinator would be a good way to stick it to both Belichick and the Patriots. Maybe I'm overthinking this and the Jets genuinely thought that he was the best man for the job. I guess we might never know.

Even when I was in fourth grade and didn't grasp the game nearly as tightly as I do today, I still felt somewhat leery about bringing in Belichick's assistant to be the head coach. Wasn't the whole point to try and beat the Patriots, not become them? I wanted to have a unique Jets team that defined its own identity and beat New England on their own terms. It just *felt* wrong to have somebody who was part of the Patriots' brass running my team.

However, all of my apprehensions quickly went out the window after Mangini's first season. The Jets finished the season with a 10-6 record and made the playoffs a single year after going 4-12. Quarterback Chad Pennington's return from yet another injury was the only major roster difference between that year and the dismal previous season, and he couldn't possibly be worth six wins, right? So who or what else could it have been? The logical answer would be that Mangini was responsible for turning the Jets around.

If you start digging a little bit deeper, though, giving Mangini all the credit starts to look a little bit less logical. The 2006 Jets went 4-4 in their eight games before the bye and went 3-3 in games decided by one possession. After the break, the Jets played only two of their remaining eight games against teams that finished .500 or better. They split those games and went 2-0 in games decided by one possession. Under the right scenario, one more loss could have dropped the Jets to 9-7 and knocked them out of the playoffs. One missed field goal (they won three games by a margin of three points each) or one other misstep could have very easily ended the Jets' season.

Apparently, the New York tabloids didn't care to dig a little bit deeper. They needed something exciting to put on the cover of their sports section and it certainly wasn't going to be resident scapegoat/ Giants' QB Eli Manning, who had just lost six of eight games to end the season *and* lost to the Eagles in the postseason to top it all off. The Yankees weren't doing anything at the moment, Isaiah Thomas was in the process of tossing the Knicks' salary cap into the Hudson River, and apparently whatever was going on with the Rangers and Islanders didn't warrant that front page. That left the playoff-bound little brother of New York City football, the New York Jets, as the sexiest story to put in bold typeface across the top of the sports section. And the logical posterboy of the reborn Jets was their new head coach, Eric Mangini. Actually, scratch that. He was now referred to in New York as *Mangenius.*

Suddenly, everybody wanted to jump on the Mangenius bandwagon. ESPN stories about the Jets now had almost twice as many comments as did stories about other teams. Sportscenter showed pictures of the New York Post in the days leading up to the Jets' Wild Card playoff game with New England. Eventually, I started correcting anybody who called him Mangini. His name was Mangenius, he was the next Bill Belichick, and that was that. Even after the Patriots casually dispatched the Jets by a score of 37-16 in their playoff game, I was convinced that we had finally found a head coach that would become a fixture in the Jets' organization. As it turned out, that 10-6 regular season was the peak of the Mangini era. He proceeded to go 13-19 over the next two seasons before he was fired at the end of 2008.

I'm not saying that what Mangini accomplished that season was insignificant, because it wasn't. What I am saying is that the Jets could have very easily missed the playoffs that year no matter how competent Mangini was. In professional sports, public opinion is drastically swayed by victories and defeats, even when the line between the two becomes so thin that it can no longer be seen. I'm not talking about the classic "down by one, two outs, bottom of the ninth, bases loaded, Game 7 of the World Series" scenario that every kid who has ever loved baseball plays out in his backyard. No, I'm talking about more subtle things like a fumble taking a bounce out of bounds instead of to a player or a field goal bouncing off the front of the crossbar and missing instead of hitting the middle of the crossbar and deflecting through. Games of unspoken inches like these are played out time after time in every game on the NFL schedule. This unseen battle weaves itself through the fabric of football and sports in general, affecting public perception and changing legacies in ways that we can't possibly acknowledge. Enough of those unseen battles broke the Jets' way in 2006 to catapult them into the Playoffs, against all conceivable odds.

And I guess what I'm trying to say through my annoyingly flowery verbiage is that the Jets actually weren't that great and Eric Mangini was no more nor less a genius than (insert any previous Jet coach except for Bill Parcells here) was, a fact that was laid rather bare in just nine months' time when the 2007 season rolled around.

Have you ever supported a team that went to the playoffs, and then totally reversed course a year later? Very few things in sports are more painful, right? The thrill of supporting a team that actually has the chance to win a championship is one of the best feelings in sports, and to have reality yank it away from you is one of the worst. It comes back to that time-tested debate of, "Would you rather have had something and lost it, or never had it at all?" I can't attest to what it feels like when my team never has success at all because I'm not a Cleveland Browns fan.

(Sorry for the low blow, Cleveland. I'm rooting for the Browns to get to the top one of these years. The joke was just too easy to make and I'm not that witty, so I made it. You understand, right?) But to have it and then lose it is infuriating. You just stare at the TV set after your team has lost another game and wonder, "Wait a second, what the hell happened to these guys? Weren't they just in the playoffs eight months ago?" You keep waiting for the players, the coach, *someone* to light a fire under the team, only to give up after watching them set *themselves* on fire instead, week after sordid week. On top of all that, you have to endure the inevitable "What's wrong with the (insert team here) and how worried should the fans be?" conversations from every single columnist and TV analyst, which of course just makes you even more angry and more worried than you already were. Stretch that feeling out over four-plus months, add more abject sadness into the fanbase and ineptness into the team, and you now know what the 2007 Jets season was like.

People knew that it was not going to be a particularly auspicious year for New York's AFC representative from the outset when the New England Patriots and their seemingly unstoppable offense rolled into Giants Stadium and delivered a 38-14 curb-stomping of the Jets. I watched that game and couldn't even bring myself to be upset about it, because I realized immediately the extent to which our biggest rivals outclassed us. See, I find that I only really get upset about the Jets when I know that they *should* be winning. If they offer me hope—really, any hope whatsoever—I'm sucked back in. But this? There was no hope to be found here. The Jets might as well have not even run out of the tunnel. The Pats marched up and down the field on our sorry defense, especially when Brady threw to a guy by the name of Randy Moss, a name that I would become very familiar with over the next four years.

Randy Moss was one of the greatest receivers that the game will ever see. He owns a bunch of franchise and NFL receiving records, and he's at least in the top ten for every relevant receiving record that he doesn't own. The guy had absolutely everything that you would ever want from a wide receiver; size, speed, athleticism, the ability to catch balls in traffic, great route-running, fantastic acceleration, the strength to fight through just about every cornerback jam, everything. He started his career with the Minnesota Vikings, where he spent seven years tormenting defensive coordinators and catching everything that was thrown his way. After getting released by Minnesota for some behavioral incidents and spending two years toiling away as a member of the Oakland Raiders (otherwise known, from 2002 onwards, as the Team Where NFL Careers Went to Die), Moss somehow found his way onto the Patriots' roster for the price of a fourth-round pick. The Raiders were convinced that Moss was damaged goods and wanted to flip him to anybody for anything they could possibly get. If the Pats did a little bit more negotiating, they probably would have gotten the guy for a barrel of footballs and maybe some tackling dummies. But the bargain didn't really matter to Moss' critics, who claimed that his skills had atrophied so much in Oakland that he would be of little use to most teams. Besides, they said, who wants to deal with his attitude and effort issues? And to top it all off, he was slapped with the kiss of death; the authoritative proclamation that he was a "distraction." That's how New England ended up getting one of the greatest receivers that the game will ever see for the price of a single fourth-round pick

Everybody has a team that they particularly don't like as fans, but most of those teams also have one particular player that just *kills* you. Every single time you play (insert team here), you're worried that (insert player here) will totally take over the game. For the Yankees, it was David Ortiz. For the 80s Pistons, it was Larry Bird. And for the New York Jets, it was Tom Brady and Randy Moss. They absolutely murdered the Jets on a few different occasions, and it all started on that Sunday. It was rookie cornerback Darrelle Revis' first game as a member of the Jets, and he was matched up one-on-one with Moss for most of the day, which was only slightly more humane than putting him in a zebra costume and throwing him into the lion's den at the Bronx Zoo. Needless to say, Moss torched him. Nine catches for 181 yards and a long touchdown catch later, the Jets were totally beaten. Every single time it looked like we were going to force a stop and finally get off the field, Moss would wrap his massive hands around another Tom Brady throw and keep the drive alive.

It wasn't just Moss, though; it was *everybody*. No Pats' receiver had less than two or three yards of separation on just about every single play. Whenever the Jets tried to disguise their formations on defense, Brady seemed to know exactly what to do. Every throw was delivered on a rope; right where it needed to be. Wes Welker, a new addition to the Pats' receiving corps from Miami, moved right into the space created by defenders who vacated their usual posts to go cover Moss and caught passes all day as a consequence. On the rare occasions that both halves of the deadly Moss-Welker duo were covered, somebody else was open. As the Pats matriculated their way up and down the field, the wheels of the greatest offensive machine in pro football history began to rotate ever more rapidly. Poor Chad Pennington and his fully human Jet teammates had no chance whatsoever of matching the Pats on this day. New England ended the day with a 1-0 record and the Jets with a 0-1 record, but they might as well have called the division for the Pats after that game. Honestly, it felt like I was being beaten up, yet I was so impressed that I didn't totally care. I knew that I was witnessing the beginning of something historic.

That's another thing about fans; they recognize and appreciate greatness. I've always believed that true fans have to love the sport first and the team second. And while there have been numerous times where I have strayed from that belief, I always come back around to it at the end of the day. If I'm too upset after a Jets' loss to even watch the highlight show afterwards (doesn't really happen now, but happened all the time in middle school), then I would force myself to step away for a little while and remind myself why I loved football. The point is that being a fan means appreciating greatness, especially if it's something that you'll never see again and even if it's against your own team. If even part of you thinks that someday, somewhere down the road, you'll regret not being able to say to your kids that you watched something happen or saw somebody play, then you have an obligation as a fan to watch. Even if it involves your team's collective ass being kicked.

The 2007 season will forever be remembered by the records of 16-0 and 18-1. The former is the Patriots' unblemished regular season record, the first of its kind. (The '72 Dolphins went 14-0 in the regular season.) The 18-1 refers to their total record for the season, playoffs included. We'll get to the significance of the "1" a little bit later, but just know that this season belonged to the Patriots from the outset. The Jets ended up going 4-12 that year and benched Chad Pennington, so that's why they're not going to matter so much for the next couple of pages or so. New

England, the Jets' hated rival, is what mattered that season, both because of the records at the beginning of this paragraph and, on a personal level, they helped me make one of the best friends that I'm ever going to make in my life. So, in a way, the Pats beating the tar out of the Jets over and over again led to a new friend, a newfound appreciation for the game, and some of the (hopefully) best parts of this book. But I'm digressing, so let me start from the beginning.

Shortly after the Pats rolled through the Jets, word started to trickle out about some kind of suspicious activity surrounding the game. Specifically, the reports indicated that major news was about to break regarding the Patriots. My eleven-year old, Jet-crazy mind immediately started overflowing with conspiracy theories. Is it possible that the Pats took the same performance-enhancing drugs that all the baseball players were taking? Did the Jets have a deal with shady mobsters to throw the game, 1919 Black Sox style? Perhaps someone committed a crime of some kind during the game. Or maybe my suspicious about Bill Belichick being a football cyborg had been confirmed and he would be banned from the game for life. As it turned out, *all four of those theories were true.*

(I know it sounds crazy, but I'll explain. Just take a second to digest that.)

(Just one more second.)

. . . . Yeah, none of those things were actually true. (Be honest, part of you wanted to believe that all of them were true. Don't deny it.) But the truth was almost as good as any one of those. When you watch the NFL for a little while and listen to coaches give interviews or discuss strategy, it becomes obvious that trade secrets do not exist. Players that move on from one team to another happily divulge whatever relevant information they have about the previous team's playbook. Coaches regularly come up with inventive and brilliant new schemes that allow them to have enormous success, and then freely give tips to coaches from other teams about how to implement those same strategies. The Jets hired Eric Mangini away from Belichick and the Patriots in hopes that he would bring with him some of his mentor's vast bank of football knowledge. In this particular case, that includes knowledge about the video camera.

Apparently, Belichick ordered various Patriots' staff members to plant visual recording devices in on-field locations. These devices were aimed at Jets' coaching personnel, specifically defensive coaches. The idea was that the recordings would be viewed by a member of the Pats' coaching staff, who would try to interpret what the hand signals being made by the videotaped coaches meant. Once he found a correlation between a particular hand signal and a certain tendency, he would communicate with Belichick via headset and tell him what each signal corresponded to. In doing so, the Patriots would slowly decipher the Jets' defensive schemes and gain a competitive advantage. Smart? Absolutely. Cunning? Sure. Completely and totally against league rules? You bet.

Apparently, the league had heard rumors about teams trying to steal each other's signals even before this incident and wanted to put a stop to it. To that end, in the Fall of 2006, the league issued a memorandum specifically detailing where recording devices could not be used. Some of these places included the sideline, the coaches' booth, the locker room, or any part of the stadium that can be accessed by staff members of either team. Belichick would later allege that he thought videotaping was OK, so long as the video was not viewed while the game was being played. As Belichick would later learn from NFL commissioner Roger Goodell, this was decidedly not OK.

But how did he get caught? Well, he had used this tactic fairly frequently over the course of his last seven or eight years with the Patriots, at least often enough for Eric Mangini to know that he did it. After the beatdown the Jets suffered in Week 1 at the hands of New England, Mangini decided to throw the rulebook at his old boss. He alerted NFL security that the Pats were videotaping from the sidelines and other locations on the field, which was confirmed when the officers confiscated a camera from Pats' video manager Matt Estrella. They then did a sweep of the entire stadium, and their search eventually arrived at a narrow crevice in a wall near the Jets' end zone. Tucked into the confines of that gap was—you guessed it—another camera.

Busted.

The Pats were fined 250,000 dollars for the incident and Belichick was personally fined 500,000 dollars, the largest financial penalty ever levied against a coach in the history of football. New England was also denied their first-round selection in the following year's draft and forced to hand over every single scrap of paper/second of tape that was even remotely related to the incident. Unnamed sources were starting to come forward and levy complaints that New England had used video cameras rather creatively in other games as well, including in some of their significant playoff victories. And to think that this all happened because the Pats decided to try and put one over on a team that they were going to beat by at least two touchdowns anyway.

Was this really that big of a deal? No. Did the Pats really gain that much of an advantage from this anyways? Probably not. Did the media, Jets' fans, Patriots' haters, and sports conspiracy theorists eat this thing up like a bowlful of chili? You betcha. They even came up with a snazzy name for the scandal that was splashed across the cover of just about every single New York newspaper. The snafu would be forever known as Spygate. (Or by its unofficial longform name; Spygate: A Tabloid Copy Editor's Dream Come True)

This is when I fully embraced my utter disdain for the Patriots. Sports fans are already irrational people, so imagine how overboard an eleven-year old sports fan would go with the "New England was cheating!" narrative. I went from being kinda neutral about the Patriots to finding them totally irredeemable and revolting in the span of a few days. Still respected the hell out of them, but I hated their guts nevertheless. You, the reader, are probably sitting there wondering, "Wait a second, what does all of this have to do with meeting one of your best friends?" Even if you weren't wondering that, you're probably nodding your head yes to that question in an attempt to humor your humble narrator, right? You're too kind. But I am once again digressing, so let me get back to the story.

A few days after SpyGate, I noticed a kid wearing a number 83 Patriots jersey. (83 was Wes Welker's number, if you're interested.) It was the day we got a new seating chart in math class, and I happened to be seated next to him. I had never talked to this guy before in my life. However, he was wearing a Patriots jersey, which means that I had to needle him about SpyGate for a little while. As soon as the teacher turned her back, I leaned over and whispered, "Hey, what's your name?"

"Matt", the kid said, not turning his head to look at me.

He probably wanted to be left alone and was perfectly content minding his own business. I, however, was never one to take much of a hint. Keeping a keen eye on the teacher to make sure that her back was still turned, I leaned over again and whispered, "The Jets would have won that game if the Patriots didn't cheat!"

His ensuing facial expression indicated to me that I had hit a nerve. Without missing a beat, he turned to me and whispered back, "Yeah? Well, the Jets suck!" And with that, the seeds for a beautiful friendship were planted.

By the way, when I said that I had to poke fun at him for SpyGate "for a little while", I really meant every single day for at least a month. The same brief conversation that I just described was probably repeated a good three or four dozen times over the course of the next thirty days or so. We had some of the least intelligent football debates I can ever imagine anyone having; the kind usually reserved for internet message boards. We used every single insult, curse word, totally inaccurate statement, and ridiculous hypothetical that our sixth-grade intellect could muster against the other person. Eventually, I no longer needed to seek Matt out in the hallways or in the cafeteria. He started looking for and approaching *me*, all for the pleasure of telling me that the Pats were undefeated and that the Jets were 1-6 or 1-7 or whatever the hell their pitiful record was at the time. After some more time passed, we started talking about things other than football. Video games, music, things that were going on at school, and all the things that you usually talk about with friends happened because of football.

This is another reason why being a fan is more than just rooting for a team. It brings people together. Nothing gets a conversation going or ties people more firmly together than do sports. Religion, politics, grades in school, and things of that ilk are all too dicey to bring up with someone you've just met. No socially competent person would ever start off a first conversation with, "Hey, I'm a Republican/Democrat! How about you?" The classic movies/music/food/etc small-talk staples are OK, but they're transient. Almost nobody remembers epic debates with their friends over what the worst 80s song was, or when Al Pacino reached his peak as an actor. (Except for me, apparently, because I've had both conversations with Matt, Ray, and a few other friends in the last week.) By in large, people just aren't as passionate about those things as they are about sports. (Once again, I'm speaking in generalities.)

But sports fans are already unofficially part of a family, whether they realize it or not. It takes a certain type of person to love a sport or a team, to develop this passion over years, to know which moments mattered. Because of this unique mindset, finding another fan is like finding a very distantly related member of your family. A several-million strong, happily dysfunctional clan of all shapes and sizes, but family nevertheless. I've become friends with people that I had never spoken to simply by being in a fantasy football league with them. Matt and I became friends by going back and forth about the Jets-Patriots rivalry. Every single time (and I do mean *every single time*) that I've ever seen someone consistently wear team memorabilia, especially NFL teams, I will engage that person and end up talking to them for at least a couple of minutes. I've found that nobody can really help complaining about the new free agent signing or talking about what happened in the last game. The same is true for when someone talks to me while I'm wearing a Jet t-shirt, especially my semi-retro Chad Pennington jersey. If there's time, I'll strike up a conversation with whoever stopped me. All of this happens because sports fanhood is, like I said, an inherently social experience. Being a fan is all about talking to the person next to you, giving your buddies grief if their team lost, having dumb arguments that you'll laugh about someday, and doing all the other things that friends do with each other. A conversation between two sports fans lays the groundwork for friendship. And that's something that I learned throughout the 2007 season, even as the Jets slid down the ranks of the NFL and Matt's Patriots continued their scorched Earth campaign against the entire league.

Long story short, the Pats completed the regular season undefeated and ripped through their division and conference round opponents in the playoffs. All that stood in the way of immortality was the scrappy New York Giants. (In case you're not familiar with sports doubletalk, "scrappy" is a euphemism for a team or player that sucks on paper, but is somehow doing well.) For me, it was the Super Bowl From Hell. The spying, cheating, stereotypical-villain-in-a-sports-movie Patriots were going against the "Big Brother of New York" Giants in the biggest game on Earth for NFL immortality. Essentially, whoever won, I lost.

Of course, seeing as how the Patriots went 16-0 and broke almost every relevant offense-related single season record, nobody gave the Giants a chance at all. Over the two weeks that led up to the big game, Matt spent every single day bragging about how the Patriots were going to finish the season undefeated and steamroll the Giants by thirty points. He had good reason to think that they would do so; Vegas favored the Patriots by two touchdowns. But the more that Matt kept talking, the more I got the sneaking suspicion that he was about to get his heart broken. I dared not vocalize that opinion for fear of being called an idiot, or a butthead, or whatever the chic insult was in sixth grade. However, I just couldn't shake this feeling that something bad was going to happen to the Pats. What ended up happening that Sunday is everything that's great about being a fan and everything that sucks about it, all wrapped up into one mind-blowing two minute drive. Even though the Jets had nothing to do with the game, I still feel like I need to include it in this book because I learned more about the highs and lows of being a fan in those two minutes than I did in almost any other time throughout my decade of watching sports.

All game long, the teams had played each other to a standstill. The Patriots were hanging on to a slim 14-10 lead. Eli Manning and the Giants faced second down with five yards to go on their own forty-four yard line. I'm standing in front of the TV and hyperventilating, even though I have absolutely no rooting interest. I wanted the Patriots to lose, just so I could toss it in Matt's face. My hopes were very nearly crushed when Manning took the ensuing snap and proceeded to throw the ball over the head of wide receiver David Tyree on the right sideline. Pats' cornerback Asante Samuel leaped for the ball as it continued to sail closer to the sideline. I decided that I couldn't watch. After a second or two, I lifted my head to see what was probably a joyous Patriots' sideline celebrating a Super Bowl-clinching interception. Instead, I saw the ball bouncing along the sideline. Samuel had dropped it. This was the break the Giants needed.

On the next play, Manning took the snap and was immediately harried by two or three different New England pass rushers. One of them reached around the offensive tackle and grabbed a fistful of Manning's jersey, but the Giants' signal-caller managed to break free, spinning out of the pocket as he did so. After scrambling around for a few moments, he stepped up to his left and launched the ball downfield toward David Tyree, the lone white jersey amid four New England Patriot defenders. Tyree leaped into the air and trapped the ball between his fingertips as safety Rodney Harrison desperately tried to knock it away from him. As he went down to the ground, he secured the football against his helmet to complete an impossibly difficult miracle catch. First down, Giants. The Giants would score a touchdown three plays later to give themselves a 17-14 advantage with thirty-five seconds left on the clock. After New England's failed Hail Mary attempts, the New York Giants had officially done the impossible and won the Super Bowl.

This was probably the most traumatic experience of poor Matt's life, right up there with the time he first saw the "Dancing in the Streets" music video. He came in to school the next day in a borderline catatonic state, not speaking to much of anyone or showing any signs of responsiveness. Obviously, in these especially depressing circumstances, any truly caring friend or morally decent person would keep his mouth shut. The first thing I did when I saw Matt? I zipped open my backpack, whipped a football out, and held it to my head with one hand, recreating Tyree's catch. It's a real credit to him that he didn't just haul off and punch me right there. Did I stop at that? Nope. I said the words "18-1!" and "Hey, who won the Super Bowl?" so much that he had every right to never speak to me again. Actually, he didn't really talk to me over the next few weeks, only offering a few "shut up" remarks to try and disarm my relentless barrage of assholery. After about a month or so, we eventually repaired our relationship and continued with our bickering. Did I finally learn my lesson after nearly losing a pretty good friend? Of course not. My Uncle Ray, a huge Giants' fan, gave me a book called *"A Team to Believe In: Our Journey to the Super Bowl Championship."* It was Giants' coach Tom Coughlin's account of the season and it had a few pictures in the middle. I remember that he put a bookmark right on the page with the picture of the Tyree catch. As a Jet fan, that stung a little bit. (Fine, it actually stung a lot.) But I had already resigned myself to the fact that my team sucked, so why not torture Matt some more with it? When we walked into math class, I approached him and said, "Hey, I have something to show you. Could you possibly close your eyes for a second?" Matt did. When he opened them, he saw the picture of the Tyree catch staring back at him. He just sadly shook his head and resumed getting ready for class. The lesson here, for all the young fans out there, is that when your friend's team suffers a crushing loss, *don't rub it in*. Seriously, don't do it. Let them get through their grief in whatever way they want to. Throwing salt on the wound is probably the surest sports-related way to lose a friend that I can think of.

Anyways, back to the Jets. After a miserable 4-12 season in which they were forced to stick Chad Pennington on the bench, the roster clearly needed something of an overhaul, especially at the quarterback position. However, the 2008 draft class was relatively light on quarterbacks, so the Jets added another chapter to their history of screwing up draft day by taking Ohio State defensive end Vernon Gholston with the sixth pick. Gholston played three seasons with the Jets, never broke into the starting lineup, and recorded zero sacks before being mercifully released. Meanwhile, there was still no answer at the quarterback position, a statement that could aptly describe the Jets in most seasons since Namath left. Awesome.

That brings us to the man that would immediately be dubbed Broadway Brett upon his arrival with the Jets. Brett Favre spent the last sixteen seasons with the Green Bay Packers and was one of the five best quarterbacks in the league for most of that stretch. He gained a deserved reputation as a fearless gunslinger that could throw the ball harder, farther, and into tighter windows than anyone else could. The only problem was that, like every other athlete, he couldn't beat Father Time. During the last two or three years of his time in Green Bay, he was in his upper thirties and thinking about retirement. After the 2007 season, he actually did retire, only to change his mind and decide that he wanted to come back to the Packers. The only problem was that he announced his un-retirement in late July, well after Green Bay management had moved on from him and found a replacement. (The replacement, by the way, was Aaron Rodgers, one of the best QBs in the league at the time of this book's release. Some teams just get all the breaks.) So Favre handled the situation like any tactful person would, by publicly declaring his frustration at the Packers' front office and implying that they should be willing to undo their entire contingency plan just for him. Then, Favre actually flew to Wisconsin to attend Packers' training camp after publicly feuding with them all offseason, as if they were going to hand him back his starting job like nothing ever happened. Maybe he wouldn't *beat* Father Time, but he was determined to go down swinging. GM Ted Thompson and head coach Mike McCarthy ended these pipe dreams by telling Favre that they were no longer interested in his services. So that left poor Favre out to dry, totally committed to football but not to a team. And there are the poor Jets, second-class citizens in their own city, the Patriots' biannual punching bag, one of the dregs of the NFL. Suddenly, both sides looked at each other and said, "Hey, wait a second!"

So it came to pass that the Jets signed Favre, thus carrying on their storied front office tradition of addressing organ failures with band-aids and chicken soup. His contract would pay him twelve million dollars for that one year.

I get why Brett Favre had to be signed. He was available for relatively cheap, the Jets needed somebody who they could put on the front of their program (not to mention a human being who was capable of playing starting quarterback), and the Giants' Super Bowl victory reinforced the whole "We need to win NOW" mentality among the fanbase. Regardless of why it happened, I wasn't totally sold on the move. I mean, really? We're willing to spend all that money on a thirty-some year old quarterback who wasn't sure that he wanted to play football just four months ago? OK, so we bring Favre in, he improves the team enough to the point where we get a two or three win bump, and that would leave the Jets' record at . . . . 6-10 or 7-9. Best case scenario would be 9-7. The natural cycle of how contenders are built in sports goes from really bad to moderately bad to good to contender and then right back around to really bad. Obviously, there are a lot of different ways to build a championship-caliber team and many teams buck this trend, but that's generally the most common path taken. You'll notice that nowhere on that cycle is an "average" option. That's what the Jets would be with Favre. Average, kind of directionless, miles away from beating the Patriots, up against the salary cap, and a good four or five losses away from attaining one of the top draft picks. I had no idea what to expect from the Jets except for unabashed mediocrity.

Let the record show that, for the first eleven games, the Jets far surpassed my expectations and shocked the football world. An 8-3 record (including a victory over New England and undefeated Tennessee) put the Jets in a most unfamiliar place; at the top of the AFC East. When your team keeps piling up win after unexpected win like this, you get totally sucked in to everything that's happening. You keep hearing about how these miraculous championship runs and lucky breaks happen to other teams, but you never really expect them to happen for yours, even though you hope they do. So when it happens, the fan sixth sense kicks in and says, "Hold on a second, maybe something's really happening here." I'm convinced that being a fan loses its innocence when you stop having those moments every season, when you become cynical enough to not trust your team. You arrive at that moment, that place, by your team punching you in the face so much that it becomes second nature to see the next right cross coming and reflexively duck out of the way. I had not reached that point yet. I thought that I had, but I was just as gullible as ever. Which meant that it was time to be punched in the face again.

The next week, the Jets lost 34-17 on their home turf to Denver. I spent so much time clenching my hands into fists over the course of the game that there were some shooting pains in my fingers for a day or two afterwards. This, of course, was the better than the alternative; throwing things and being a mess for the whole night. It hadn't happened in roughly two or three years, but I could feel that it was about to happen if I didn't show some amount of self-restraint. So, I did. My parents, of course, knew that the best course of action for when the Jets were losing was to not talk to me for a little while. After about half an hour, I'd be (somewhat) normal again and resume rational thought, but not before talking to myself, squeezing the hell out of a stress ball, sitting there and sulking, or doing whatever I did to get over believing in something that let me down again. There would be plenty more of that to come in the next couple of weeks, as the Jets followed up their whale-turd of a performance against Denver with another no-show against lowly San Francisco on the road, dropping their record to 8-5. In two weeks, they went from being a surefire first-round bye team in the playoffs to possibly not even making the playoffs. I'm telling you, this team will give you panic attacks every single game if you let yourself take the game too seriously. Unfortunately, I took the game *far* too seriously and paid the emotional price for it. I think I might have cried for at least five minutes after the Niners' loss, which just shows how much I let football influence me.

After a close win over the lowly Buffalo Bills, the Jets proceeded to drop their next two games against Seattle and Miami respectively. They finished 9-7 and out of the playoffs once again. I couldn't even muster up enough energy to be mad for those last two games. By that point, the writing on the wall was visible from space. Gang Green could not have been more done than they were going into those last two weeks.

The reasons for their collapse were many. Favre had been woefully inconsistent and far too trigger-happy. The Jets would put these drives together and then Favre would uncork these beautiful spirals . . . right into triple coverage. It was like he thought that everything would work itself out if he just threw the ball hard enough, which was a philosophy that, in his defense, was able to sustain itself throughout much of his career. However, while that mentality worked perfectly when he was in his mid-twenties, post-unretirement Favre couldn't pull that off anymore. So, he often ended up throwing it right to the defense. As a fan, there are certain plays that just make you scratch your head and say, "wait a second, what the hell?" That was me after most Favre interceptions. I was less angry and more just confused. *Hold on, what did Favre just do? Did he really just try to throw it thirty yards downfield while two defenders were dragging him to the turf? Why would he ever feel the need to do that?* After seeing this kind of thing happen over and over again, some fans were semi-seriously wondering if Favre had some debilitating injury that the rest of us didn't know about. Well, funny they should ask, because he actually had a torn biceps tendon that the Jets failed to report to the league for the last month of the season. That tends to put a bit of a damper on one's ability to throw a football with accuracy.

Of course, it wasn't just Favre and his unreported injury that contributed to the Jet collapse. The defense was a total mess: teams essentially did whatever they wanted with total impunity from an offensive standpoint. Darrelle Revis was starting to come into his own, but everybody else in the Jets' secondary became easy prey for opposing quarterbacks. No pass rush, no push at the line of scrimmage, poor tackling, just everything you could ever hate about a unit of eleven people whose job is to stop the other team from scoring. That plus an injury-riddled quarterback, an offense which simply *insisted* that the opponents take the ball back from them either on downs or by turnovers, a teamwide penchant for drawing penalties, and a shaky coach-fanbase relationship led to the downfall. So . . . . good times! And by that, I mean really depressing times. In fact, I don't think I even watched most of the last Jets' game. To this day, I can't decide whether I quit on my team or if it was the right thing to take a break from them. And the fact that I still think about this crap today should give you some idea about how far from normal I am. But hey, it's sports and it's worth every moment. At least that's what I continually say to convince myself that writing this book is a good idea. Once again, I'm digressing.

A day after the Jets' season went down the tubes in Miami, I woke up and went downstairs to get some breakfast. As I rounded the corner into the kitchen, Mom walked in from the garage. She had just gotten home from the gym and looked generally pleased, like she had some good news to tell me. "How did your workout go?", I asked, walking to the fridge for some orange juice.

"Great! Hey, guess what?", said Mom, a huge grin on her face. "I was on the treadmill and I saw ESPN on the TV next to mine! Can you believe that Manginano guy got fired?"

I had to do a double-take. "Wait, what?"

"Yeah, he was fired! Aren't you proud of me for knowing that!?", she exclaimed, a satisfied grin etched across her face. The coach just got fired and she reacted like she'd just found a hundred dollars on the ground because she knew before I did. I couldn't help but laugh a little bit and nod my head. Sometimes, you need someone who doesn't watch sports regularly to intervene and keep things in perspective. Thanks, Mom. (It bears mentioning that my Dad currently can't name an active player on the Jets, much less the coach. He once asked me, in all seriousness, if Babe Ruth played for the Jets.)

As for Mangini, he never had much of a chance after the season fell apart. He was an average coach that had the fortune of getting dealt a good hand in '06 and the misfortune of having to deal with a bad one in 07. The 2008 season was the last chance for Mangini, and things just didn't break his way. He was out. With that move, the Jets had finished knocking down most of what they had spent the better part of the 2000s building. It was time to start over.

THE OTHER TEAM

I have to confess that I wasn't being entirely honest when I said that I never had another team besides the Jets. It wasn't in the same sport, mind you; that would be complete blasphemy. I would not be able to live with myself if I was one of those gutless "hedge my bet" type of fans who pulled the old "Well, the Jets aren't very good right now and I really liked Baltimore when I went there on vacation last year . . . . so I'm going to switch my allegiance to the Ravens just in time for the Super Bowl!" routine. (Dad, I hope you're reading this.)

No, I liked a team in a different sport. I watched all their games, memorized all their players, purchased memorabilia, played as them in video games, and did just about everything with them that I would do with the Jets. I realize that I'm making it sound like I cheated on the Jets with another team or something, but that's kind of what it felt like. For about four or five years, I loved the New York Yankees almost as much as I loved Gang Green.

And why wouldn't I? They had everything that the Jets didn't and achieved things on a yearly basis that the Jets could never match. Year after year, the Yankees made the playoffs. In fact, it was an oddity when the Yankees *didn't* make the playoffs, like somehow the natural order of things was thrown out of whack. Sports Illustrated and the writers on espn.com always anointed them the World Series favorites in their postseason predictions columns. The Yankees won at least ninety games every single year and always led the league in either home runs or team batting average or some stat that validated their place at the head of the MLB table.

That's why it was so shocking when the Red Sox came back from a 3-0 series deficit in 2004 to eliminate the Yankees and eventually break their eighty-six year World Series drought. It's not just the improbable comeback or the unbelievable moments or even the history between the two teams. It was about reversing everything we thought we knew about baseball. The Yankees were supposed to win and the Red Sox were supposed to lose. That's all there was to it. That was the way things were and that's the way things would presumably always be. My seven year old brain couldn't even *conceive* of the Red Sox winning anything. It was like waking up and finding out that the laws of gravity no longer applied. I was more amazed than upset, as if I was somehow aware that I'd be telling my kids about the time when the Earth stood still, water ran upstream, and the Yankees lost to the Red Sox.

Their success when I was watching them was only bested by the success of previous generations. Over their century-long existence, they've employed people by the names of Babe Ruth, Lou Gehrig, Mickey Mantle, Mel Allen, Casey Stengel, and Joe DiMaggio. Twenty players currently have plaques in the hall of fame inscribed with their insignia, soon to be twenty-two when Derek Jeter and Mariano Rivera are inducted. They've won twenty-seven championships, which is over a quarter of the total World Series played since their inception. Over the course of Yankee history, they've fielded some of the most talented teams in any professional sport, let alone baseball. The Yankees' past has been marked by everything that Jets' history lacks; consistent winning, domination of other teams, transcendent talents, and a consistent impact on their sport and the way it's played.

Of course, pinstripe pride and tradition doesn't pay the bills, so that's when it helps to have a little bit of money to throw around. The Yankees are the third most wealthy sports team in the world and are worth an estimated 1.7 billion dollars according to Forbes magazine, a figure that is only bested by Manchester United (an English Premier League Soccer Team) and the NFL's Dallas Cowboys. Because of Major League Baseball's lack of any real salary cap, the Yankees are free to use as much of that 1.7 billion dollars as they can muster to sign players. That's how the Yankees have led the league in opening day payroll for fifteen straight seasons. I mean, I can't remember a player that the Yankees really wanted ever turning them down because of money. Not once. Alex Rodriguez, Mike Mussina, Gary Sheffield, Mark Teixeira, Reggie Jackson, Babe Ruth's historic $100,000 contract, it was all table stakes to the Yankees. If you were a marquee free agent, the Yankees were going to show you the money. If they wanted you to re-sign with them after your contract expired, they made sure to give you the incentives to do it. Bottom line: if the Yankees wanted you, they found a way to get you more often than not. Money was never an object.

There is no more polarizing team in all of sports. *Everybody* has an opinion about the Yankees, even and especially those who know very little about them. I've seen well-written and detailed analyses of how well suited the Yankees' business plan is to the current times, and I've also seen tens of thousands of fans yelling "YANKEES SUCK!" whenever they play on the road. I've even heard of the crowd chanting "Yankees Suck!" at a random Red Sox-Rays game in May. Wake me up the next time that happens for any other team. Everybody I know that likes sports either loves or hates the New York Yankees. It's practically un-American to be indifferent towards them. They've been called the Bronx Bombers, the Bronx Zoo, the Pinstripers, the Evil Empire, everything that's right with baseball, everything that's wrong with America, and a million other things. The best way to explain it is through one of my experiences at Sports Broadcasting Camps in Boston. One day, I got up to speak in front of the camp and made the mistake of wearing a Yankees hat. Immediately, about a fifth of the crowd erupted in cheers (the Yankees fans) and the other four-fifths savagely booed me. Obviously, the camp was predominantly Sox fans, but I saw people wearing memorabilia related to no less than fifteen different major league teams in the crowd, all booing my Yankees cap. The next year, I wore a Jets hat when I got up to speak, and nobody said a word.

Everything that I wrote in this chapter indicates an organization that is well-run and produces positive results almost without fail, to the point where everybody else resents them for producing those results. They're the sports version of U.S. Steel, a titan of industry whose assets and sphere of influence are surpassed only by the sheer brand power of its name. Pick the Yankees and you're almost guaranteed a front office who will make most of the right moves, a team that will be perennial contenders for a World Series title, and a legacy of winning that stretches back to before World War I.

Do you have any idea how *boring* all of that gets?

I know that after spending the majority of this book complaining about the Jets, saying that I couldn't find it in myself to really get behind the Yankees because they won all the time makes me sound like equal parts hypocrite and ingrate. There are probably more than a few reasons why I'm not writing this book about the Yankees, but their predictability is probably reason number one. It sounds like a dumb argument to make, but just bear with me while I try to make it.

The Jets make you run the gamut of emotions. They take you from high to low to the middle and then back to the low, and that was just in the last ten minutes. After watching them for over a decade, I still can't totally predict what they're going to do. I feel like I've seen everything, and yet I'm still totally prepared for something I've never seen before. Isn't that what makes sports so great?

The Yankees, on the other hand, pretty much stopped surprising me after about year number three of watching their games. Big free agent out there? The Yankees are going after him. New MLB season about to get underway? It'll end with the Yankees in the playoffs. What's the fun in rooting for somebody if you can already guess how it's going to end? Eventually, all of the Yankees' games started to blend together to the point where I couldn't pick out which moments and players were really meaningful to me and if you can't even do that, then what's the point of supporting them?

If you're like me and have ever heard the phrase "Wait 'till next year" after your team gets sent home for the season, you know how painful it is. To think that you just went through a whole year's worth of games believing and waiting for something to happen only to find out that it was all for naught is one of the worst feelings of any fan's life. You feel like asking for a refund of the dozens or hundreds of hours that you spent in front of the TV, sweating out every last play.

But at least with the Yankees, I could always definitively say that there would *be* a next year. That's why I wasn't really even that upset after the Red Sox series in 04; because I knew that they'd be back there again next year, or the year after that. I'd wait four months or so, then baseball would be back and the Yankees would start kicking ass again. Because of that mentality, I never felt that much sorrow after they lost or extracted much satisfaction from their wins. Like I said, they never really took me through the emotional peaks and valleys like the Jets did, and I realized that. I began watching them less because they made me feel less. They made me feel like a regular, sane person who just happened to be watching a baseball game, and I didn't like it. Eventually, I knew that I had to stop calling myself a Yankees fan when I kept cavalierly saying,

"Oh well, life goes on" immediately after the game whether they lost or won. A real fan shouldn't feel that way.

In football, next year is almost literally next year; between seven and eight months to be exact. But next year was never a guarantee when it came to the Jets. In fact, a big reason why the Jets carried more weight for me was the possibility, no, the fairly substantial probability *that there would be no next year*. I remember every single high point in my life as a Jets fan because behind every one of them was this unspoken feeling that this was it, that I'd never get to feel any better about my team than the way I did in that exact moment. If "there's always next year" hurts, imagine getting sent home from the playoffs after a promising season and thinking, "wait another five years." The Jets showed me what the Yankees couldn't; that success is transient and that if you don't take the time to fully experience what's happening *now*, you may not get the chance to do it again. When I was pre-writing for this book, I was able to assemble a page and a half-long list of every person, moment, and experience related to the New York Jets that really mattered to me, all in about twenty minutes. I couldn't possibly do the same for the Yankees.

Really, though, that's just part of why I ended up sticking with the Jets over the Yankees. Maybe it had something to do with the fact that I was watching football games on a relatively consistent basis for about a year and a half before I even really knew what baseball was. By the time I was watching Yankee games on a consistent basis, I was almost seven and had a solid year or so of exposure to football under my belt. When you're young, and I mean around five years old, things that you really connect with tend to resonate more strongly with you than things you experience when you're older. That year before baseball was full of football games (both college and professional), all the NFL 2K3 I could bear to play, Jets memorabilia, and running around like a maniac in my backyard while pretending to be Curtis Martin and Wayne Chrebet. I'd connected with football on a level that I knew I never could with baseball, much in the same way as you connect with your first pet in a way that you can't quite replicate with future pets. I wasn't changing the Jets pennant hanging above my desk for a Yankees one, and I would have tried to fight anybody who tried to change the channel from the Jets to the Yankees.

There was also my tenure of actually playing football, which lasted from the tender age of five all the way up until I was almost seven. Still, I actually believed that I could be in the NFL for those two years and absolutely nothing else would do for a career. When I realized that my goldfish had about the same level of athleticism that I did, I soon abandoned my NFL ambitions for the passion that I have now: getting paid to talk about sports on television. Any delusions that I may have had about becoming Derek Jeter were broken by about my third game of kid-pitch baseball. Actually running around with a football tucked into my arms (while holding it high and tight with all five fingers on the ball, of course) tied me to the game in ways that I could never be tied to baseball.

For me, every single football game, Jets or otherwise, was an event. College football Saturdays happen twelve or thirteen times per year and NFL Sundays happen seventeen times every year, playoffs not included. Some people count down the days until the end of school or their next vacation, but I always counted down the days until football. *C'mon, you can get through today. Just four more days until Jets-Dolphins. Three more days until USC-Notre Dame. Hang in there a little while longer.* Because of that week-long wait, you have more time to digest what's happening, talk about it, think about it, really *feel* it. I gained a greater sense of appreciation for everything that took place on the field because it only happened once every week. Every victory, every defeat, every moment is magnified due to how short the schedule is and how much space is in between each game. The end result is that Sundays from September to February become appointment television for fans, a miniature holiday all unto itself, the kind of thing that you constantly think about when you're planning your schedule and prepare for hours ahead of time. It's kind of like if your favorite TV show has only ten episodes per season. You make sure to really take in what's happening in all ten of those episodes because you know that it's going off the air for the year in just a few weeks.

Baseball, though, is on every single day for months on end, which kind of deflates the significance behind any given day of baseball. A win in football is infinitely more valuable than is a win in baseball simply because it represents a greater portion of the total number of games; one out of sixteen is a bigger fraction than is one out of one hundred sixty-two. Because the average game doesn't carry as much meaning in baseball, I never really found the same urgency in it as I did in football. If the Yankees lost a game, I handled it rationally because there would be one hundred sixty-one more opportunities to make up for that loss. There would be another game tomorrow, and the next day, and the day after that. If we're going to carry on the TV show analogy, then baseball would be a little bit like *Law and Order* or *CSI* in the respect that there are so many episodes/games that the significance of each one becomes a little bit dulled. Great show? Yes. Enjoyable to watch? Absolutely. If you're channel surfing late at night and are just in the mood to watch TV, would you be satisfied with stopping at baseball/*Law and Order*? In most cases, yes. But is it commanding your attention like *Breaking Bad* would? Probably not. Which one are you going to watch while sitting upright on your couch and which one are you going to use as background while you're doing something else? More and more, I found myself watching intently for football and kind of half-watching Yankee games.

Another disadvantage to baseball's schedule is the tendency towards consistent results. Fans watch sports to try and see things that we've never seen before. We want to see teams go from worst to first and vice versa every season. We want to see breakout players that we've never heard of and once in a lifetime performances from the game's best. Much of what I just described could be categorized as a collection of outliers: things that fall outside what usually happens on a day-to-day basis. Outliers tend to correct themselves over baseball's one hundred sixty-two games. Teams that go from worst to first in June often go back to being the worst by the first of September. Unknown players that break out at the beginning of the year often fall back towards the pack after a month or two. In baseball, the best teams often end up with the best records and the best players often end up with the league lead in the various statistical categories. This is because things tend to regress towards the mean with a bigger sample size. Obviously, this isn't necessarily a bad thing, nor is it true in all cases. In fact, a baseball fan could probably point to hundreds, if not thousands, of instances that prove me wrong. But for some reason or another, baseball just didn't resonate with me anymore.

In fact, I probably could have saved myself a few thousand words and two or three hours of trying to come up with a logical explanation by just writing that last sentence. *It just didn't resonate with me.* Everybody has their own quirks, and one of mine is that I *cannot* be a casual fan of anything. I either have to engross myself in it or leave it alone. I tried to love baseball. I really did. But when I *know* that so many special moments happen on a baseball diamond every day and I find myself not appreciating them as much as I appreciate the ones in football, then I can't really call myself a Yankees fan or a baseball fan. When I found myself doing things like playing video games instead of watching Jeter step up to the plate and forgetting Robinson Cano's number, I knew that I would never have the proper enthusiasm needed to really appreciate the game. Being a fan is all about personal expression. What you do, what team you choose to support, who your favorite player is, and the reasons you do all of these things speak to who you really are. And baseball, as great a game as it is, just never really formed the connection with me that I thought it should have. So, I eventually stopped following it.

But amid all of this talk about why baseball never quite worked for me, I should take some time to mention what it *did* do. Namely, it made my childhood a hell of a lot more fun. I mean, who *hasn't* played in their local little league for at least one season? What kid hasn't at least tossed a baseball or tennis ball up and tried to hit it with a metal bat? I spent hundreds of hours either watching the Yankees or trying to take expansion franchises to the World Series in All Star Baseball 2003. I carried around the same beaten-up copy of the SI MLB season preview issue for months after it came out. Baseball taught me to appreciate not just the game-winning home run and the big strikeout, but the little things. I began to notice how Derek Jeter would fight to drag an at-bat to ten pitches before he found just the right pitch. I looked forward to seeing Tim Wakefield pitch, for no other reason than to revel in the baffling twists and turns of his knuckleball. The way Ichiro would hit the cutoff man every time, the sheer range that Jim Edmonds would cover in centerfield, the power that one flick of Manny Ramirez's wrists could generate, these are all the "little things" that I grew to love, even if I stopped loving them as much after awhile. So even though baseball wasn't for me, I'm glad it was in my life.

However, I feel like the real reason I started falling more and more in love with football (and more out of love with baseball) has everything to do with the teams involved. Like I said, it just became no fun to root for the Yankees any more. Maybe my early Jets years got me addicted to the uniquely charming brand of self-loathing that only they can provide, but I couldn't find it in me to love a team that won all the time. The best part of being a fan is sticking with your team through everything—the years, the losing, the injuries, the disappointments, the failures, and the times when you thought it couldn't get any worse—and then finally seeing them rise above it all. And at the end, you felt like you were a part of everything that happened. See, I never felt that with the Yankees. Even when I first started rooting for them, I felt like I was latching on to the coattails of a winner. Love them or hate them, the Yankees were winning either way. It was like rooting for the sun to come out. Yeah, there are cloudy days and even rainy days, but it'll happen eventually. Why? Because that's nature. The sun will come out and the Yankees will win.

Rooting for the Jets to succeed, on the other hand, is like rooting for a triple rainbow. And ultimately, I guess that's why I ended up getting sucked into loving them. I want to see something that hasn't happened in almost fifty years. I want to say that I was there to see the trade, the game, the throw, the moment that turned it all around. I want to love the Jets because a small, crazy part of me believes in miracles and omens and destiny and all the other sappy stuff that they write sports movies about. I want to be able to say that I was there for the whole thing and that I never lost faith, even when things were at their bleakest. I want to take the ultimate risk that every sports fan has to take: sinking time, care, and attention into your team with no guarantee of payoff, and stick around for the day when it finally does pay off.

You get what I'm trying to say, right? *I wanted to believe in something.* And as great and fun and successful as the Yankees were, they made it too easy to believe in them. I couldn't do it. So that's it. That's the full story of how I rejected the most successful franchise in the world just so I could keep living, dying, and dying some more as a fan of the New York Jets. But maybe I don't feel quite as strongly if not for baseball. Maybe I don't think as much, appreciate the games as fully, or cherish each moment like I do if not for baseball. And if I didn't stumble into baseball and the Yankees at the tender age of six, I couldn't have written this book.

Just another step on the long and winding journey through life for the average sports fan, if there is indeed such a thing.

TAKEOFF

By this point, I had become accustomed to supporting mediocrity. It wasn't unusual for me to try and slap a smile on playoff exists or 6-10 records and call it success. In fact, maybe I even enjoyed it. I felt like it was a badge of honor to be a Jets fan, to stick with a team that sucked so badly for such a long duration of time. For me, it was almost like the football version of surviving on a desert island or getting knocked out in the boxing ring, only to keep coming back and swinging away. I always held the firm belief that if the Patriots fans or the Giants fans had to go through the same exercise in futility as we did or had to live with the same legacy of losing that we do to this day, they'd quit watching football in five years, tops. They had no idea what being a real fan was. I thought this way because, on a visceral level, in a place that I never dared to acknowledge, I had already resigned myself to the fact that the Jets would be in the gutter forever. So, like all of those aforementioned first round playoff exits, failed draft picks, missed field goals, dismal records, and organizational failures, I tried to put a happy face on being a loser. After the collapse of 2008, I believed that we would never win a Super Bowl. Ever. Since I thought that we would never actually get off that desert island, I immediately created the defense mechanism of pretending that it was a laudable accomplishment to just survive there in the first place. In the immediate aftermath of the 2008 season, I had convinced myself that consistently supporting a team that got no results was a virtue.

A major component of being a fan that I really wanted to explore in this book is where the boundaries begin and end. If I completely lose faith in my team, yet continue to come to their defense and root for them the same way I always have, what does that make me? Am I still a fan for sticking with these guys week after week, or did I stop being a fan once I started believing that the Jets would always be the punchline of the NFL? And if I really believed that, then why was I still watching and, moreover, still caring?

I guess that I stuck with them because football was such a strong part of my identity by the time I was in seventh grade that it felt like heresy to *not* be fanatical about my team. Most people around school knew me as the kid who loved the Jets too much, the guy with answers about fantasy football, and the weird one who tried to wear every single piece of Jets apparel that he owned for Halloween. What was I going to do, completely disown the Jets after making them part of my life for almost eight years? Not a chance.

However, I resolved that I'd stop caring so much about them. I'd be a football fan first and a Jets fan second, somebody who just happened to like the Jets just a little more than everyone else. No more bawling after tough losses, no more staying up all night and staring at my phone waiting for score updates, and no more pacing in front of the TV when they were playing. I was too old for all that stuff. Maybe it took awhile, but I had finally learned to appreciate football and put my fanhood in its proper place.

This new, enlightened stance on my relationship with the Jets lasted for about one offseason month. Then, Rex came to town.

My first impression of new Jets' head coach Rex Ryan was much the same as my first impression of Eric Mangini; which was something along the lines of, "Who the hell is this guy?" In fact, the first time I even heard his name was when I watched the press conference that announced his hire. Look, there's no politically correct way to say this, so I might as well just lay it out there; the guy was huge. He must have weighed over three hundred pounds at the time. At that age, I had a certain preconceived notion as to what a great head coach had to look and act like. I wasn't quite sure what that notion was, but I knew that Rex didn't fit it. Looking back on it, I probably wanted some stern, gruff, fifty-five year old ex-football player with a permanent frown and a kickass circle beard leading my team into battle. Whatever my unclear standards of what a great coach were supposed to be, I can tell you that Rex Ryan certainly didn't live up to them. He almost looked like a cartoon character as he ambled his way up to the podium. In the days immediately following the press conference, I jokingly told my friends that the New York Jets had just hired Santa Claus as their next head coach. Little did I know that in just a few short months, Rex would transform the Jets into the bullies of the NFL.

For the first time in a while, the Jets started throwing around money. For the first time in an even longer while, the Jets started throwing that money at the right guys. We traded up in the draft for Mark Sanchez, our quarterback of the future. (Hey, stop laughing.) We dropped an eight million dollar per year contract on offensive guard Alan Faneca, a seven-time pro bowler who had made a name for himself in Pittsburgh as the best run-blocking guard in the league. We got Bart Scott, a trash-talking tackling machine from the Baltimore Ravens. We managed to snag safety Jim Leonhard from the Baltimore Ravens too, and he became the brains of the defense, a guy who ranked as one of the best on-field communicators in the league. The Jets were actively seeking out tough, physical players who came from teams that had success, then showing them both money and the opportunity to play on a team with other like-minded individuals. One of the main drivers behind this influx of was Rex. As it turned out, the guy I derisively referred to as "Santa Claus" was one of the most beloved coaches in the league by his players, and guys were lining up around the block to come play for him when the chance arose.

Then, Rex started raising a few eyebrows around the league. He did an interview on WFAN, the biggest sports talk radio station in New York, and was asked about Bill Belichick and the Jets' rivalry with the Patriots. Now, there's a very well-demarcated line between what a coach is supposed to say to such an inquiry and what Rex Ryan said. Let me illustrate that difference for you:

> **What you're supposed to say**: *I'm just worried about what we're doing. Obviously, I have a lot of respect for Bill Belichick and the Patriots. All I can do is get my guys ready to play the best I can and then hopefully we have a good enough team to compete with them. I can't worry about what Bill Belichick is doing with his team because my focus should be on the Jets.*

Good answer, right? It shows deference, professionalism, and "respect for the game of football", as every holier-than-thou announcer would like to say. You're not saying anything that would fill writers' columns or give other teams bulletin board material. That answer (or something reasonably close to it) is what thirty-one out of thirty-two coaches in the NFL would have given in response to that question. If only there were some coach out there who would break convention with an honest response. I wonder what *that* answer would sound like . . . .

What Rex Ryan said: *I didn't come here to kiss Bill Belichick's, you know, rings. I came here to win. Let's just put it that way. So we'll see what happens. I'm certainly not intimidated by New England or anybody else.*

Uh-oh. That comment was the alarm clock that woke up a giant, sleeping monster, otherwise known as everybody in the media who valued the "sanctity of the game." Suddenly, Rex Ryan was arrogant, a braggart, and somebody who needed to shut up. If you were ever involved with the NFL and thought that Rex's declarations were "shocking" and "disgraceful", somebody was bound to give you a few minutes on air or some column inches to chronicle your opinion. He became a "distraction" that needed to "tone it down" before his team "lost its focus." Everybody was acting as if new starting QB Mark Sanchez had an increased chance of throwing an interception in Week 7 because Rex took a shot at Bill Belichick three months earlier. (We now know that he was gonna throw that interception either way.) Perhaps worst of all, Rex Ryan was branded with the pompous football announcer's version of the scarlet letter; the dreaded "doesn't show respect for the game" label.

Me? I loved this. People were talking about the Jets again. Eric Mangini stumbled through his press conferences and shut the media out at every juncture. Very few people worked harder to give the media less than Mangini. In fact, only he and Brett were even allowed to talk to the press. Now, our coach was actively seeking out and engaging with the media and, by extension, the fans. I felt like Rex was talking to me when he publicly declared that he wasn't going to bow down to Bill Belichick. He was setting the tone for the team he wanted; a physically dominating squad that wasn't afraid to speak their minds and would back up that talk by punching their opponents square in the jaw every week. The bluster, the new availability to players that was granted by Ryan, the public declaration of war on the Patriots, it was all part of establishing the atmosphere that he wanted to establish.

Besides, as I pointed out at the time, the only time the Jets ever won anything significant was with Joe Namath at the helm and Namath was the most controversial and talked-about sports figure that the NFL ever had at the time. He talked a lot, had a larger than life presence, and acted as a sponge that soaked up all of the media criticism when the whole team did poorly. Namath was a uniquely talented person who helped to aim the spotlight on the Jets for all of the right reasons. He was a winner, an important figure, and somebody who could say or do anything at any time. Just like Rex.

See, I've always believed that in order to win Super Bowls (or even advance deep into the playoffs), you need a few big personalities (or one big personality) that will set the tone for everything that your team is trying to accomplish. You should be able to pick out one or two guys that everybody's going to rally around; the one or two guys who are going to be in the middle of the pre-game huddle. For the 2012 Ravens; it was Ray Lewis and his "last ride." For the 2011 Giants; it was Tom Coughlin and Eli Manning who spurred the whole "everybody's writing us off and we should be pissed about it!" movement. 2010 Packers; Clay Matthews and Aaron Rodgers. 2009 Saints; Drew Brees and the "Who Dat?" mantra. You get the idea. Part of creating an identity as a team is having that emotional backbone and knowing exactly what the group dynamic should be. And for the first seven years of my Jet fanhood, they didn't have a personality. But suddenly, they found one. After all, amid the pile of criticisms that were aimed at Rex Ryan, things like "his team just doesn't respond to him" and "he can't really inspire confidence" were definitely *not* among them. He had a winning mentality and an unapologetically humongous personality, which is something that everybody he coached loved and the fans quickly adopted.

So it goes without saying that the Jets were ready to stick it to the rest of the league when Rex came to town. They started with a 24-6 win over the Houston Texans on opening day, a win that showed exactly what the new look Jets were all about. Every single time that Houston quarterback Matt Schaub dropped back, a Jet was in his face. In fact, there was one time where Schaub took the snap from center and didn't even get to turn around before linebacker David Harris' hand dragged him down to the turf by his jersey. Whenever Houston was on offense, two or three Jet defenders were somewhere in the vicinity of the football at all times, as if they were somehow magnetically attracted to it. Eventually, Houston started bringing in two tight ends, calling conservative running plays, and only utilizing routes under ten yards or so. All while being down by more than a touchdown. (For anyone that's not familiar with football, the last two sentences described the offensive equivalent of shaking your head, throwing your arms up in the air, and saying "I give up.") On the other side of the ball, the New York offensive line pushed the Texans further and further back over the course of the game. Jet running back Thomas Jones went untouched for the first two yards or so of almost every run just because guys like Alan Faneca were bulldozing Houston off the ball time after time. Mark Sanchez looked sharp, Rex looked like a genius, and the Jets looked like a legitimately frightening team for the first time in a long time. Fans were beginning to get cautiously optimistic.

A week later, fans would ditch that cautiously optimistic mindset and go completely overboard in one of the best ways possible. Why? *Because the Jets beat the Patriots.* Actually, that's understating it. The Patriots were favored by three points and picked by over seventy percent of the country, even though they were on the road and all-world Tom Brady was rehabbing from an ACL tear. This was the type of game that could potentially deliver the validation that Rex and the Jets needed; an upset victory at home over a hated rival that had been declared public enemy number one in Jets nation. Case in point, Rex declared three former Patriots who now played for the Jets (including third-string QB Kevin O'Connell, who had been on the practice squad for about two months) team captains and sent them out to midfield for the coin toss. It was on from that point forward.

Not only did the Jets win, but they kept Tom Brady and the Pats' offense from even reaching the endzone. Darrelle Revis, the same guy that Randy Moss had taken to task just two years earlier, played fantastic coverage on the Pats' superstar wide receiver this time and earned some sorely overdue "Whoa, this Revis guy is pretty good!" conversation. Once again, the offensive line turned in a stellar performance, allowing Sanchez to be hit only three times all game and opening up running lanes for both Thomas Jones and backup running back Leon Washington. However, this day, like so many others to come, belonged to the Jets' suddenly hellacious front seven. (For people who don't speak fluent football, "front seven" refers to a team's defensive line and linebackers, who are usually the seven people on defense that are closest to the line of scrimmage.) The pass rushers repeatedly slammed Tom Brady to the ground and denied him the opportunity to get comfortable in the pocket. It seemed like every time the Pats' franchise QB took more than a second or two to decide where he wanted to throw, he would promptly be knocked on his ass by a Jet defender. By the fourth quarter, Brady wore an expression that I'd never seen from him before and certainly never expected to see in my life; complete confusion. *How do we stop these guys? What am I supposed to do when I'm getting killed back here on every single play? What plays do I call? And how the hell are we getting beaten by the New York Jets?*

On the Patriots' last drive, Tom Brady faced fourth and ten with just over a minute left to go and his team down by a touchdown. It was at this juncture that Rex felt like he needed to send one final message before calling it a day. Late in the game, you're supposed to keep at least seven or eight of the eleven defenders away from the line of scrimmage and back in coverage to eliminate the possibility of a deep pass. It's called a Prevent Defense, and it's the order of the day for when you need to prevent a quarterback like Tom Brady from completing an eighty-yard touchdown pass during the final seconds. But words like "passive" and "prevent" and "no pass rush" aren't known to be found anywhere in Rex Ryan's lexicon. So he blitzed. The three down linemen rushed the QB, as they usually do late in the game, but the linebackers, who were supposed to drop back into coverage, instead sprinted forward and overwhelmed the Pats' line. Brady was forced into an incompletion which gave the Jets a 16-9 win. It was possibly the most fun I've ever had watching a game of football.

In his postgame press conference, Rex went so far as to say that the fans were "huge in this victory" and that he "thought they were the difference." I'd never heard anybody, coach or player, say that before. Fans spend so much time and energy supporting a group of people that are often so distant and detached from everyday life. It's not necessarily by choice; their profession and the realities of the modern day simply demand it. Coaches aren't going to necessarily spend a lot of time doing things specifically to win the fans over when they're already working sixty-hour weeks. Their focus is on the team. Players have film to study, practices to attend, commercials to shoot, and other events that keep them insulated (at least to some degree) in their own world. And fans have learned to accept that. They're partaking in a business that requires their full attention and their job is to win games, not fans. But when somebody drops that barrier, even for just a little bit, and tells the fans that they matter, then that person wins the respect of the entire fanbase almost instantly. I'm not talking about the pre-prepared bits on the JumboTron that tells the crowd to MAKE SOME NOISE!!!!!! Nor am I referring to the paid autograph sessions or season kickoff events that some players are required to do. I'm talking about athletes that take little moments to acknowledge the people who spend so much to come support them. That's all it takes to make the fans happy. Just one or two unguarded, unscripted moments where a guy says something like Rex said after the New England game.

He even went a step further in the game ball presentation. For the readers out there who aren't familiar with football, it's often customary for the coach to give out a game-used football as a sort of trophy after a win to whoever he feels is the most deserving of it. Now, after a significant win like that one, Rex had no shortage of people he could have given the ball to. He could have given it to Sanchez for logging one of the biggest wins in recent Jet history in only his second game as a pro. Maybe Revis would garner the game ball for shutting Randy Moss down all day long. Ryan had the option of giving it to the entire defense, who repeatedly stonewalled a Patriots' team that strongly resembled the feared 07 squad in terms of personnel. Heck, he probably could have given it to the owner, the GM, the entire team, or even himself, and nobody would have voiced a single bit of dissent. But Rex didn't choose any of those options. Instead, he gave the game ball to none other than Ed Anzalone, better known as Fireman Ed. Yep, the same Fireman Ed from back in Chapter 3, the superfan that had shown up to every single game for twenty-some years and led the J-E-T-S cheer. Ryan sent him the game ball in the mail to thank him for firing up the crowd. As soon as I heard that, I knew that Rex Ryan was one of the rare sports people who truly understood the psyche of his fans. He was one of the only ones who not only acknowledged the fans, but went the extra mile to make sure they were a significant part of whatever the team was doing. Little things like giving the game ball to Fireman Ed and constantly bringing up how much we meant to him in press conferences endeared him to the Jets' fan base almost immediately.

It showed in the Jets' ensuing 24-17 victory over Tennessee, which moved their record to 3-0 and doubled as my annual family trip to Giants Stadium. First of all, it was the game where I ran into HEEERE WE GOOOO!!!! guy. (See Chapter 3 if you need/want to be reminded of the details.) More importantly, though, I could see the crowd had a spark that I had never seen before. Everybody just seemed deliriously happy that there was something they could believe in. People were overreacting to everything that was happening on the field, both good and bad. I saw more current Jet jerseys and green face paintings in fifteen minutes than I had over the course of the entire game in previous years. Win or lose, the Jets mattered again. And everybody that watched them knew it.

And that's what made their ensuing swoon so painful. Suddenly, they started losing again. They lost in New Orleans, where two Sanchez turnovers were returned for touchdowns. They lost in Miami on Monday Night, when Dolphins' running back Ronnie Brown scored a game-winning touchdown with under ten seconds left. They lost at home to Buffalo in a game that featured five Sanchez interceptions, all of which managed to cancel out running back Thomas Jones' 210 rushing yards. They lost another game to Miami after offensive coordinator Brian Schottenheimer called three straight passing plays that fell incomplete from the Dolphins' nine-yard line on a potential game-winning drive while Jones, one of the NFL's best rushers at the time, stood idly by in the backfield. They lost to the Jacksonville Jaguars on a last-second field goal. They lost their undefeated record and showed me how quickly 3-0 could turn into 4-5. They lost most of the goodwill that had been accumulated over the first three weeks. They lost their "Ground and Pound" motto and the ability to claim that they weren't "the Same Old Jets." These were *precisely* the same old Jets. Why? Because they lost.

Those games were probably some of the lowest points in my time as a Jets fan. Let's just say that it got a little bit dusty in the Goldstein household when the final seconds ticked off the clock of some of those games. I still hadn't learned how to put the games in perspective yet and everything still meant way more than it should have. If somebody made me choose between getting a prom date and the Jets making the playoffs, I would have chosen the Jets making the playoffs without even thinking about it. (I was a terribly misguided youth, as you can probably tell.) Just when I thought I had something to believe in for the first time in years, when I thought that my dream of going to the Jets' victory parade might have a ghost of a chance of coming true, they collapsed again. It wasn't fair.

Apparently, Rex shared my sentiments. After the Jets' loss to Jacksonville and with a potentially season-ending game against New England looming, Rex teared up in his postgame press conference. As he spoke, you could clearly see his eyes repeatedly blinking and watering over, as if to hold back tears. Like everything that Ryan said or did over his as-of-yet short tenure with the Jets, CryGate immediately became eleven o'clock news. The ESPN comments section on the "Did Rex Ryan cry?" story had to hold an impromptu roast of the embattled Jets' coach. (Come to think of it, is there really any other kind of Jets' coach?) Most people in the media, the Jets' fanbase, and the general football landscape took CryGate as another Rex Ryan theatrical device that showed how over the top he was. Everybody told him that he needed to turn off the waterworks, admit that he talked too much in the preseason, and go about his business. True to form, Rex responded to his critics by making light of the situation. The first thing he did during his Monday press conference was plop a box of Kleenex down on the podium.

That was really the quintessential Rex being Rex moment. I mean, the guy just cannot hide what he thinks or feels whatsoever. Happy, sad, angry, he can't help but show it. Here was a guy who cared a little bit too much and wasn't afraid to admit it, just like all the fans did. The unwritten coaches' code of conduct says to do just the opposite. It says to be tight-lipped, treat the press like they're actively trying to destroy you, keep the unguarded moments for after the cameras have been put away, and to always say as little as possible. But the fans, the players, the media, the other parties that make the wheels of sports turn, they just don't exist like that. If they have an opinion, they say it. If they're dissatisfied with something, they put it out there for public consumption. They're provocative, emotional, and go overboard for their sport. Watching Rex cry after the Jacksonville loss and then poke fun at himself afterwards helped bridge that disconnect. Yeah, he might have been a little bit of a blowhard but he was *our* blowhard. Finally, we found a guy who understood what Jets' fans were going through and seemed just as disappointed about the latest swoon as we were. Every time the camera cut to Mangini's emotionless stare on the sidelines while the Jets were in the process of blowing yet another game, everybody got the impression that he didn't care. Was that the correct conclusion to come to? Of course not, but we came to it anyways because Mangini never threw his headset or cried in a press conference. Rex visibly cared like very few others did, and that endeared him to Jets' fans in ways that nobody really ever had.

Unfortunately for the Jets, Rex seemed to be the lone bright spot in a season that was quickly falling apart. Gang Green pretty much eliminated themselves from the AFC East divisional picture the next week by losing to the Patriots in Foxborough by a score of 31-14. We were now 4-6 and would probably need to win the remaining six games on the schedule to assure a playoff berth. 5-1 would be the bare minimum record that the Jets would need to attain in order to even be in the discussion for the postseason. Everything that defined the team in their first three games seemed to fall completely by the wayside. Have you ever had a moment where your favorite team is completely over-performing? It feels so great, but you're also constantly worried about when the wheels are going to fall off. And then, when the wheels eventually do fall off, you have that mix of slight disappointment coupled with the sentiment of, "Oh well, I can't say I was surprised; at least this is something to build on." Well, that didn't happen to me. Those first three games completely and totally roped me in, and I should have known better than to be roped in. I honestly thought that we were going to the Super Bowl that year. Yeah, I know it was unrealistic to expect that much from a team with a new head coach and a new quarterback, but I thought it could happen. Instead, I was watching the Jets throw another season off the GW Bridge. If I knew anything about the Jets, they were done. Finished. Just End The Season.

Well, as I found out over the next six weeks, there really was something different about this team. They proceeded to win their ensuing three games in short order (home vs Carolina, in Tampa, and in Buffalo) to boost their record from 4-6 to 7-6. Suddenly, everything from the first three games came rushing back. The vaunted Jets' defense became the modern Steel Curtain again, dropping ballcarriers at the line of scrimmage and blanketing receivers all over the field. Every run started gaining four yards once more, two before contact and two after. None of the wins were glamorous. None of them would make it into the first half of *NFL Gameday Final*. However, they typified what the new Jets were supposed to be about; grind it out, get key stops, wear the opponent down, win by a score of 17-7, and call it a day. Granted, the three teams they beat were undoubtedly below average teams. Even if the Jets made the playoffs, it was seemingly quite clear that they weren't advancing past that first weekend. I didn't care. I just wanted to see my team play one game in January, just for the sake of feeling what it's like to really care about a playoff game again. For a Patriots fan, just getting to the playoffs didn't really mean anything; they had to go to the Super Bowl and win it. That's the expectation that was set early on in the Brady era. But all I wanted was for an announcer to say, "the Jets will be going to (insert city here) for their first-round matchup in the 2009 playoffs!" New York had been mired in this state of limbo for so long that I was desperate to see some kind of progress, some sign that the organization was moving forward. Maybe, if I just kept the faith a little while longer, I'd get it somehow.

I immediately regretted my choice to keep believing when the Jets dropped a disheartening home game to the Atlanta Falcons by a 10-7 final score. As usual, Gang Green was right there, in perfect position to take the game from Atlanta and climb their way into a playoff berth. And, as usual, they kept finding innovative new ways to make sure that didn't happen. Shaky kicker Jay Feely, the latest in a long line of shaky Jet kickers, missed two field goals and couldn't kick a third because of a botched snap. Atlanta scored three points for roughly fifty-eight minutes of the game, but engineered a last-second drive down near the Jet goal line. On third down, Falcons' QB Matt Ryan gunned the ball into the endzone and hit Darrelle Revis right in his mitts. Because these are the Jets, Revis dropping the ball would have made total sense, which is exactly what happened. The next play, Ryan fired a pass directly to his Hall of Fame tight end, Tony Gonzalez, who snagged it in between two defenders for the game-winning touchdown. Drive home safely everybody.

Fortunately, I was in the car to go to my Aunt Evelyn's Christmas party when this happened, otherwise I almost certainly would have had a conniption. I was sitting in the backseat and relying on ESPN score alert text messages to keep me informed because I had a crappy phone with awful 3G internet that would work once every leap year. There are very few things that are more agonizing than having no information about your favorite team when they're in the middle of playing an important game. And when I say no information, I don't mean the "I'm refreshing the espn.com play-by-play page every ten seconds to see if something happened" scenario. We're talking absolutely NO information, except for when somebody scores. You're just imagining everything that *could* be happening and can't decide whether you want to find out the score by any means necessary or avoid any information at all costs until there's an Internet connection. Every time somebody talks about something other than football, that "mhm, yes, OK, how nice" mode kicks in because all you can think about is what's happening with your team. It's like opening your email inbox on April 15th of your senior year and seeing all the decision emails from the colleges you applied to back in the Fall. You're ready for anything, nervous about clicking on them, scared about what might pop up after that click, and yet you know that you *have* to do it.

When I got the text message that read, "Ryan to Gonzalez, 6 yard TD, 10-7 Atlanta", my heart sank. I weakly snapped the phone closed and let it drop to the seat. It was probably a good thing that there weren't any ways that I could have watched the game. In retrospect, the fact that my parents were in the car and driving me to a family gathering, thus forcing me to remain mostly normal, was also somewhat of a saving grace. It was beyond belief and yet totally believable at the same time. I kept opening and closing the flip phone—remember when they were all the rage?—periodically to see if another score alert would pop up. This went on for another five minutes or so until my phone buzzed. My mom, who takes a deep interest in my social life, leaned back in her seat and cavalierly asked, "Who's texting you?"

I paused for a second to read the text message. "FINAL", it read. "ATL 10, NYJ 7." I then took another moment to internally debate whether I should speak about the Jets' game or just lie and say it was Matt so I could continue my abject denial over what just took place. She was eventually going to find out that the Jets lost, so I told her that it was a score alert from the Jets' game.

"Did they win?", she asked hopefully.

I sadly shook my head. Mom, who is usually immune to caring about this stuff, looked a little bit forlorn for a few minutes also. Poor Mom. Whether she admits it or not, I totally roped her in to this lost cause. In that moment, I felt a little bit guilty for doing so. Usually, it's the other way around and the parent feels bad for dragging the kid into the world of sports fandom. Every sports fan parent remembers the first time that sports broke their kid's heart, but I remember the first time that it ever really affected my Mom. Of course, she didn't break down crying like I used to do because she's an adult, but I could tell that she'd passed the invisible threshold into fandom. It took seven or eight years, but she started caring about this stuff. Not nearly as much as I did (which is probably a good thing), but she *did* care. I'm still not sure whether that's a good thing or a bad thing.

Even the boisterous Rex Ryan, the champion of the new-look Ground and Pound Jets, seemed to be throwing in the towel and declaring the 2009 season officially lost. A sullen Ryan stood before the assembled press after the game and told them, "We're obviously out of the playoffs, and that's unfortunate. It ain't going to be this year." Technically, the Jets were not eliminated from the playoffs; they were still in the playoff picture with a 7-7 record. If they won their last two games, then there existed a slight chance at claiming the last playoff bid. However, it looked like Rex Ryan had finally joined both the Jets' fanbase and the rest of the football world in the realm of reality. Absolutely nobody, myself included, had any expectations beyond 8-8 and a draft pick in the mid to high teens. Quarterback Mark Sanchez, the model of efficiency for those three fleeting games in September, had crashed back to Earth in a big way. Fine efforts by the defense were wasted by turnovers and failed possessions by the offense. Only one of the Jets' seven wins came against a team with any playoff ambitions whatsoever; the other teams that they beat ranged from "decent" to "complete and utter dung." I had finally reached the obvious conclusion that my team was nothing more than half-decent.

They were going to be destroyed by the undefeated Indianapolis Colts in their next game, and that would be that.

But things had almost never gone according to the pre-determined script over the previous three months anyways for Gang Green, so why start now? For two and a half quarters, the Jets stood toe to toe with the Colts, desperately trying to hold on to their dying playoff hopes. Colts' quarterback and future Hall of Famer Peyton Manning was limited by an aggressive Jet defense that played well in coverage for most of the day. Rex unleashed everything in his bag of tricks that he hadn't already used; blitzes, unique coverage schemes, people switching positions, just anything that could slow down the Colts' offensive juggernaut. To some extent, it worked. The Jets trailed only 15-10 midway through the third quarter. If the Jets had lost by that score, I would have been satisfied. Maybe a little bit disappointed, but satisfied nonetheless. My team decided to go down swinging, and there was no shame in losing a close game to an undefeated team. When you're a Jets' fan, you learn that moral victories are almost as good as the real ones. Finally, I was willing to accept a moral victory.

As the Colts took over possession of the football deep in their own end of the field, I noticed the Colts' quarterback jogging on to the field. On the back of his jersey was the name, "Painter." Since I spend an inordinate amount of time learning things about football, even and especially irrelevant things, I recognized him as Curtis Painter, the Colts' backup quarterback. Shortly afterwards, the camera zoomed over to Peyton Manning on the sidelines, wearing a headset and holding a clipboard. See, the Colts had gone 14-0 up to that point in the season and had only two games left. They essentially had two options: go for immortality and try to win those final games, or rest their starting players to avoid injury. Colts' coach Jim Caldwell had chosen the latter. The Colts' collective Elvis had left the building.

And let me tell you folks, this Painter was no Picasso. (Thank you! I'll be here all week! You're a great crowd!) I thought I knew what bad quarterback play looked like, but Sanchez on his worst day could not top this Painter guy. On his first possession, the Colts went three plays before being forced to punt. When the Jets had to punt the ball back to him late in the third quarter, he dropped back to pass from his own twenty yard line on the first play afterwards. Unfortunately for the Colts, Jets' linebacker Calvin Pace had gotten by his blocker and was bearing down on him. The hapless Painter just stood there like a deer in the headlights as Pace ripped through the second-string blocker that was assigned the task of blocking him. BOOM! Pace clobbered Painter, the ball popped free, and the Jets recovered it for a touchdown and the lead. The ensuing two-point conversion was good, the score rose to 18-15 Jets, and the result was never in doubt after that point. Gang Green ended up winning 29-15.

I really didn't know how to feel about the game. On the one hand, I wanted a Jets' Super Bowl and I cared very little which teams or players they had to go through to get it. For God's sake, they hadn't won one in forty years; I wasn't looking for an eight from the Russian judge to validate how difficult their competition was. But on the other hand, it feels a little bit dissatisfying when you beat a team that isn't at their best. All of your friends can give you the "You only won because (insert players/teams here) handed the game to you" argument to rebut any success your team might have. And the worst thing is that it's true. Of all the teams that had no incentive to give anything but their very best, the Jets stumbled into the one that *did* have a reason to "go easy" on them. There was a moment, maybe a split second after the game ended, where it almost felt like we didn't deserve to be on the precipice of making the playoffs. That moment, however, quickly passed and was replaced by inner jubilation. Within a day or two, I chalked it up to a lucky break for a franchise that had gotten very few of them over the years. Besides, who's to say that the Jets wouldn't have won if Manning were still playing? When you really love your team, it becomes easy to overlook the faults, very similarly to when you love anything else in life. We were a home win over the Cincinnati Bengals away from the playoffs, and that was that. The Colts' game was just an asterisk.

Bengals' wide receiver Chad Ocho Cinco (yes, the guy actually changed his last name from Johnson to Ocho Cinco) stoked the fire by talking trash to all-pro cornerback Darrelle Revis. He said that Revis "couldn't cover me in a brown paper bag on a Manhattan street corner inside a phone booth", whatever that's supposed to mean. Ocho even proclaimed that when he scored (not *if,* but *when*), he was going to imitate Fireman Ed, complete with his own Bengals' fireman hat.

None of it mattered, though. The Jets were on a mission when they ran out for that game, Ocho or no Ocho. After being left for dead two weeks ago, the chance to clinch their fourth playoff berth in ten years was right in front of them. And unlike the Jet teams that had come before them, this particular team took advantage of the opportunity. The Bengals did not gain positive yardage in the entire first quarter. New York dominated Cincinnati in every aspect of the game, so much so that they led 27-0 by the end of *the first half.* Much like the Colts before them, Cincy had already clinched a playoff spot. But unlike Indianapolis, they chose to leave their starters in the game until the outcome was already decided. So not only did the Jets make the playoffs with a rookie head coach and a rookie quarterback, they kicked the shit out of a playoff-caliber team. I'm not ashamed to say it was one of the best nights of my life.

I was in eighth grade at the time and still a few years away from regulating my own sleep schedule, so I had to acquiesce to my mom's request that I hit the hay at halftime. That I did, fist-pumping and chanting J-E-T-S all the way. But before I entered my room, I was able to discreetly slip my phone under my pillow. For about another hour and a half, I stayed awake, worriedly glancing at it for updates about a game in which the Jets were winning 27-0. It couldn't really be helped. Even when they were up by twenty-seven points, I still felt the need to check my phone for updates. They weren't totally trustable yet. Eventually, even though I had only gotten two score alerts (a Jet touchdown and a Jet field goal), I decided that I *had* to go downstairs and see this one out to the end. Stealthily, I crept down the stairs and turned on the TV, being sure to quickly press the mute button. As the screen sprung to life, Mark Sanchez took a knee as the final seconds ticked off the clock. Then, there was the wide shot that showed the Jets taking a victory lap around the field, playoff-bound once again. *New York Jets 37, Cincinnati Bengals 0,* read the CBS graphic. Gang Green had rallied back to claim the last Wild Card playoff berth. They would play their first-round game on the road in . . . . .Cincinnati.

This game was like Christmas Eve crossed with the Super Bowl plus a dash of July Fourth in the Goldstein household. Dad made wings, ribs, grilled chicken, and whatever the hell else you can put on a grill. Mom, who was fully dragged into loving the Jets at this point, bought a Jets' t-shirt. It seemed like we were talking about the game every single day. And, in a move that I still have mixed feelings about to this day, I told Ray, one of my best friends, that I was too sick to go to the movies with him, even though I was perfectly well. The Eagles, his favorite team, were playing later that night and the movie would eat up some of that game, so "the Jets are playing!" wouldn't have been a valid excuse. So I lied. Yes, I felt and still feel like a total scumbag because of that. All I can really say in my defense is that *the Jets were in the freaking playoffs!* Who knew when I was going to see that happen again? I faked a cough over the phone, told him that I had the common cold, and then spent the next twenty minutes debating whether I did the right thing. After all, if ever karma existed upon this Earth, then the Jets would have lost 42-0 and the Eagles would have won handily. These are the things that you think about when your team makes the playoffs.

Thankfully, karma did not come back to haunt me. The Jets ended up beating the Bengals 24-14 in a sloppy game that featured, among other things, nine Jet penalties and two missed Cincinnati field goals. But a win is a win, and I was willing to take it any old way I could get it. Especially since Gang Green had meager time to celebrate its victory before their appointment ritual sacrifice to the San Diego Chargers in the next round.

See, the best two teams in each conference are granted a hiatus in the first round of the playoffs. While the other eight playoff teams engage in a make-or-break struggle to keep their seasons afloat, these four teams get to rest up, drink a Mai Tai, and prepare for their next opponent. What's more, that opponent is usually an inferior team (at least on paper) that must travel to the better team's home stadium to try and keep marching towards the Super Bowl. So yeah, you might say that the visiting team is engaged in an uphill battle. Or, if you're putting it more bluntly, the team who just slogged through the Wild Card matchup is up a creek without a paddle before game time even rolls around. *Especially* if you had to play San Diego that year.

The Chargers started the 2009 season with a lackluster 2-3 record before going on a little winning streak en route to their first-round bye. Specifically, an eleven game winning streak. They had LaDanian Tomlinson, a future first-ballot Hall of Fame running back. Their offense was among the most feared in the league. Philip Rivers, their quarterback, made his name as a renowned deep-ball artist that could throw a sixty yard touchdown strike at any time. They had just won their division for the fourth straight season and the fifth time in six years. And to put the nail in the Jets' coffin, the Chargers got to play them at home after a cross-country flight. Vegas had San Diego favored by over a touchdown against the lovable, stumblebum Jets. Nobody was giving the Jets a shot in hell.

Personally, I loved it. Because of the lack of attention paid to this particular game by the national media, it became Jets against the world. On one side, there was the tortured New York Jets and their fanbase, quickly becoming the Delta Tau Chi of the NFL. And then there was everybody else aligned behind the Omegas and Dean Wormer; the San Diego Chargers. (By the way, if you got the semi-obscure Animal House reference, big props to you.) Everybody picked the Chargers, almost without exception. Chris Berman, Keyshawn Johnson, Michael Wilbon, Dan Marino, Terry Bradshaw, really, just about anybody with two arms, two legs and a brain. The only person that I can remember picking the Jets was grantland.com writer Bill Simmons, and he admitted that it was more than partially to jinx them into losing. I'm tellin' ya, it was Jets' vs World.

And for one of the only times in New York football history, the Jets shocked the world with a 17-14 road win over the Chargers. The teams played to a nearly scoreless impasse through the first three quarters, with San Diego holding a slight 7-3 advantage. Gang Green was aided by a bizarre Darrelle Revis interception that stopped a long Charger drive. The receiver cut in front of Revis downfield and appeared to catch a long pass, but Revis' hand knocked it out at the last second. The receiver fell to the ground, but the football did not. Instead, the football bounced off his heel and into the hands of Revis, who laid on the ground beside him. As always, you need to be a little bit lucky with this stuff.

At this point, I was in full-fledged, "I'm just happy to be here" mode. Really, they could have lost by that score and I would have happily taken the Revis interception and everything else that happened in the '09 season to the bank. I really and truly would have. But the best was yet to come. (And just writing that made me want to start singing some Sinatra, but I'll restrain myself.) After Sanchez fired a touchdown pass to tight end Dustin Keller to take the lead, the Jet defense stopped the Chargers on their next drive, which meant that Gang Green had the ball with a three point lead and ten minutes to go near midfield. That Jets' drive quickly culminated when the ball was handed off to backup running back Shonn Greene, who had played brilliantly in Cincinnati. At first, it looked like nothing more than a solid ten yard run for a first down. But then, *wait a second! He just ran over the safety! Go! Go! Come on, you're almost the-TOUCHDOWN! YEEEAAHHHHH!!!* Greene stopped in the end zone and flipped the ball to the ground while holding one hand behind his ear, mocking Tomlinson's famous "Teardrop" touchdown celebration. The camera panned around the stadium to show shots of all the San Diego fans, and they had that classic "slumped over, both hands on the forehead, exaggerated painful grimace" look of a loyal fan base that had been kicked in the groin. I know that look and that posture very well because I'd experienced it at least a dozen times before this particular Sunday, if not more. Now, Jets nation celebrated and it was somebody else's turn to get the water balloon thrown in their face. What can I say; it's the circle of life. A couple minutes later, the game was in the bag. Jets win, 17-14. My most vivid memory of the aftermath was logging on to espn.com twelve hours later and seeing a blogger named Tim Graham write that "twenty-eight other teams wish they were the Jets right now." *Nobody* ever wished they were the Jets. But these weren't the same old Jets anymore.

The Jets ended up losing the AFC Championship game 30-17 to the Indianapolis Colts (this time with all of their starters) after holding a slim lead at halftime. I guess I wasn't that surprised; the Colts clearly had the better team. Besides, a year after the Jets had collapsed from 8-3 to 9-7, two months after they fell to 4-6, and one month after their own coach mistakenly eliminated them from playoff contention, the Jets had taken the league by storm and nearly completed the unthinkable. This is the stuff you dream about, the hopes that get you through the losing seasons.

More than anything else, though, I'll remember the Empire State Building, standing starkly above the city, the same monument to the urban sprawl that was bedazzled in blue for the Giants' 2007 Super Bowl victory, lit up in green and white. I'll never forget all of the shots of the Jets' fan rally and that massive, green tribute to what my team did that season. Just like the Giants always meant something to the city of New York, now so to did the Jets.

Gang Green mattered again.

ASCENT

After going to the AFC Championship game for the first time since 1997, the Jets were ready to throw their weight around in the offseason. They were the most successful team in town, everybody was talking about them, and it seemed like every single player in the league wanted to play for Rex, so why not take advantage of the circumstances? In the Jets' case, taking advantage meant throwing around some more money.

Since most of GM Mike Tannenbaum's bets paid off the season before, he had a mandate from the fans to go and make more of those bets. He re-signed offensive linemen D'Brickashaw Ferguson (six years, sixty million) and Nick Mangold (seven years, fifty-four million) to long term deals. Then, he went about acquiring free agents. Running back LaDainian Tomlinson, the winner of the NFL MVP award in 2006, found his way onto the Jets, as did longtime Miami Dolphins linebacker Jason Taylor. Steelers' wide receiver Santonio Holmes was up on the trade block because of drug charges, so the Jets managed to take him from Pittsburgh for the price of a fifth-round pick. Former Pro Bowl cornerback Antonio Cromartie found himself in the doghouse with coach Norv Turner in San Diego, but the Jets were more than happy to part with a third-round pick and eight million dollars per year for him.

The two key departures from the team were running back Thomas Jones (signed with Kansas City) and Hall of Fame offensive guard Alan Faneca (retired). The keys to the Jets' running game were officially handed over to second-year running back Shonn Greene and the lead-blocking responsibility was given to another second-year player; sixth round pick Matt Slauson.

The Jets were the kings of New York during that offseason. Suddenly, everybody was talking about *them* instead of the Giants for the first time since the Bill Parcells era. You could hardly find a person that didn't have an opinion on the Jets or a tabloid that didn't have a Jet on the cover of the sports section. Fan expectations were at an all-time high and it was made clear in the offseason that anything less than a Super Bowl would be an objective failure. 2009 was the honeymoon season, a stretch of time in which Jet fans didn't expect much and were ultimately stunned at how much the team achieved. I can't speak for other Jet fans, but the AFC Championship game against the Colts couldn't have been more of a "happy to be there" experience for me. We were a somewhat overmatched squad that clawed our way past the first two rounds and approached the Super Bowl's threshold in our quarterback's rookie year. I was happy with being a half away from victory because I knew that the Colts were truly the better team. No longer. This time, the Jets *had* to be the better team. They *had* to get back there and finish what they started. And now, the whole league was on notice.

Fittingly enough, there were a few other notable changes to the Jets besides the contents of their roster. Their end-of-season victory over the Cincinnati Bengals ended up marking the last game ever played at the old Giants' stadium. On February 4th, demolition crews began to destroy the iconic spires of the stadium that had housed both the Giants and Jets for over thirty years. Four months later, the last remnants of Giants Stadium had been either disposed of or sold to sports memorabilia agencies. In its place, a new and imposing goliath rose. Both the Jets and the Giants would, from then onwards, call New Meadowlands Stadium their house.

With the grand opening of the new stadium around the corner and the Jets' popularity growing quickly, an opportunity to make tons of money suddenly presented itself to owner Woody Johnson. That opportunity was quickly maximized in two ways; raising ticket prices and introducing personal seat licenses.

The 2010 offseason saw the Jets surpass the Patriots and claim the league lead in the Most Expensive Average Ticket department. ($120.85 for the Jets and $117.84 for the Pats, according to USA Today. And if you'd rather *see* some of the game than be stuffed in what may as well be the janitor's closet for four quarters, be prepared to put an even bigger dent in your checking account.) That $120.85 average going rate for a ticket was a 31.8 percent increase from 2009's average ticket price. Here's the thing about fans and high ticket prices; it's not as big of a deal as it used to be *provided that the team is winning.* We have high-definition, 54 inch TVs now. We have all the highlight shows we could ever want. Most of us watch the game under better conditions from home than we would if we went to the stadium. No lines for anything, it's temperature controlled, there's a comfortable couch to sit on instead of a hard-backed folding chair, you can flip between games and instantly get the best view, etc. Many of the people that do have tickets are people who have had them in their family for a few years or are part of a company that bought seats. So it's not that big of a deal if the team is winning. If the team is losing, then big ticket prices become symbolic of a greedy owner that prioritizes profits over putting out an enjoyable product for his fans. Even if that's not true most of the time, that's how it's perceived. Fans forgive a lot when they're winning and they forgive very little when they're losing. Ticket prices are no exception.

Raising ticket prices as sharply as the Jets chose to raise them is a risk. Sure, the team will be worth more and the owner can line his pockets with significantly higher amounts of cash. But it's also a declaration to the fans that a substantial increase in the quality of the team will follow. For the first time in Jet history, "Super Bowl or Bust" was the dominant organizational mentality. Anything less would be considered a disappointment, given the new players and substantial price hikes. Rex Ryan poured a gallon of gasoline on the already-galvanized fanbase by publicly guaranteeing, a month before their first game, that the Jets would be the Super Bowl champions. This kind of brash declaration would raise hackles all over the football world no matter who said it or where it was said, but having Rex say it in New York took things up several notches. He even put it in writing when the NFL Live bus came to Cortland, New York for Jets' training camp. At every other stop, the head coach just signed his name. Rex wrote, "Soon to be Champs."

This wasn't the first time that the Jets fielded a competitive team, far from it. However, it was the first time that they truly *knew* what was possible. The ticket prices, the sense of "swaggerliciousness" (an actual term used by linebacker Bart Scott to describe the team), the hype; it was all building towards an atmosphere where winning was supposed to be commonplace, something that happened all the time. And this was all *before* Rex invoked the most famous moment in Jet history by guaranteeing that his team would win the Super Bowl for the first time in forty years. So, yeah. No pressure or anything.

Game one was on Monday Night against the Baltimore Ravens, the team that employed Rex on its defensive coaching staff for a full decade before he left for New York. All of a sudden, the Jets found themselves in another unfamiliar place; the first ten minutes of just about every football show in the country. Maybe this is just me, but I always find a certain sense of pride when the analysts on these shows talk about the Jets first. After all, there's so much going on around the league at any given time. Whatever they discuss first has to capture the viewer's attention for the rest of the show, which means that if your team is being talked about in the A Block (AKA the timeslot before the first commercial break. I thought I'd use the industry term to sound smarter.), then your team matters. Occasionally, they matter for the wrong reasons, but they matter nevertheless. Before Rex came to town, the Jets were almost *never* in the A Block. Ever. Nobody outside Jets Nation really paid that much attention, probably because there wasn't a whole lot to pay attention to. After all, an up-and-down team with limited upside and no identity isn't really an eye-catching story to splash across the TV monitor behind Chris Berman on *NFL Countdown*. But everything was different before the Baltimore game. "Rex returns to face his old team" was *the* storyline in the NFL, and that Monday Night matchup was a must-watch for football fans, thus marking one of the few times that "New York Jets" and "must-watch" have been included in the same, un-ironic sentence. When your team is irrelevant for so long, it feels *fantastic* when they finally get the top billing. Of course, in typical Jet fashion, they would go on to lose that game after a fairly lackadaisical showing on offense, but I didn't really care. The old Jets would have gone into a tailspin after losing a big game like that. Not the new Jets, though. They'd find a way to punch back.

And punch back they did, winning five games in a row, three of them coming over the three other teams in the division. (New England, Miami, and Buffalo.) Somewhere along the way to that AFC East-leading 5-1 record, the 2010 Jets seemingly found the one thing that earlier Jet teams had sorely lacked; stability. The frustration of loving a team that you can't predict is totally maddening and possibly dangerous to one's health. For so long, that was the Jets. First they'd lose horribly, then they'd win a game, then they'd lose horribly again, maybe they'd have a two-game winning streak before another loss, and so on and so forth. In a way, that's more agonizing than having a purely crappy team. At least when you love a bad team, you know exactly what you're getting on a week-to-week basis and are reassured by the knowledge that there's nowhere to go but up. The Jets, on the other hand, tortured their fans by occupying that middle ground, threatening to go both up and down before running right back towards the mean.

This, however, seemed to be at an end. In just one short year, Rex and GM Mike Tannenbaum built something substantial on the wrong end of New York. Through smart free agent signings, cultivation of existing talent, and savvy drafting (three things that aren't particularly commonplace throughout Jets' history), a Super Bowl-caliber started to take shape. I was more attached to that team than I ever had been or ever will be to another one. After spending so many years waiting for the Jets to lay some kind of foundation, they finally did it. The term "playing Jet football" had no definition for ten or fifteen years, but now it stood for toughness, physicality, and winning the battle along the offensive and defensive lines. Everybody did their jobs well, generally liked each other, hustled out every play, and played with a certain bravado that nobody else in the league seemed to have. That's what endeared me to this particular team the most. Constructing a good team is the easy part, plenty of good Jets' teams have existed over the years. Building that organizational framework is the difficult thing. Getting continuity at the highest levels, assembling talent that meshes well as a unit, having everybody embrace their role on the team, tinkering with the formula to get it *just* right while still maintaining what you've built; *that's* the most difficult challenge in sports. Maybe, just maybe, the Jets were starting to conquer it. I was watching, for the first time, a sustainable and unique team that could deliver the same performance week after week. This was the team that I'd been waiting for.

After a slight hiccup immediately following their bye week (an embarrassing 9-0 home loss to Green Bay that featured the most sardonic crowd I'd ever been a part of), the Jets reeled off four more wins to boost their record to 9-2. Moreover, the way they won these games gave me hope that the Jets were the team of destiny for 2010. In the words of Michael Scott, I'm not superstitious, but I am a little bit stitious. Fans can't help but look for some kind of sign of what's to come. We're constantly searching for the moment that defines a championship team. Most of that stuff becomes clear in retrospect, and very few people realize that moment when it happens. But it doesn't stop any of us from searching for it. And when your team starts getting breaks like the ones I'm about to describe, then it's impossible to not think like that, no matter how hard you try. The way that the football gods kept bailing the Jets out was plain uncanny, and it happened three weeks in a row.

By all accounts, the Jets should have lost the first game of this stretch to the last-place Detroit Lions, who led Gang Green by a score of 20-10 deep into the fourth quarter before botching their defensive schemes/clock management enough for Mark Sanchez and the offense to tie the game. The score actually would have been 21-10, thus requiring the Jets to score a touchdown instead of kicking a field goal on the last drive, but the Lions' kicker was injured during the game and their 330 pound defensive tackle missed the extra point when he was sent in to replace him. As for the clock management, Lions' QB Matt Stafford threw an incomplete pass on third down late in the fourth quarter to stop the clock and give the Jets forty more seconds to put together the drive that ended in a game-tying field goal. Once in overtime, Santonio Holmes caught a seventeen-yard up-and-in pattern from Sanchez around midfield and took it roughly thirty more yards due to the Lions' safety being horribly out of position. Nick Folk kicked the game-winning field goal a few plays later. The Jets had just won a game that they had absolutely no business winning. But still, that was one game. Everybody gets lucky now and again, right?

Fast forward a week to when the Jets march into Paul Brown Stadium to take on the mighty Cleveland Browns . . . . . . just kidding, they also occupied the cellar of their division. For sixty minutes, the two teams played to an uninspiring 20-20 draw. (Is it just me, or does reading/hearing the phrase "sixty minutes" instantly prompt you to make ticking sounds like the pocketwatch on the show? *Deafening silence* Really? Just me?) By all accounts, the Jets deserved to lose this game as well. Browns' QB Colt McCoy, a man who would not hold down his starting job for a full year after the game, engineered a game-tying touchdown drive in the final two minutes of regulation. New Jets' field goal kicker Nick Folk, more colloquially known as The Grim Reaper around my living room, missed three field goals over the course of the game, one of which was in overtime and would have given the Jets a victory. Cleveland even took possession of the ball with a minute and a half left in overtime when Sanchez threw a butterfly straight into the hands of a Browns' cornerback. Cleveland could have just taken three kneel-downs after getting the ball and forced the Jets to settle for a tie: AKA the only thing worse than a loss.

But lo and behold, the Browns decided to run three plays deep in their own end of the field, one of which was an incomplete pass. Suddenly, the Jets somehow stumbled their way into another possession on Cleveland's 37 yard line with twenty-four seconds left. Just the perfect down and distance for The Grim Reaper to shank one last field goal before we could all call it a tie. Before he did, though, the Jets had enough time left to run a play or two. Sanchez strode up to the line and lined up in the shotgun formation with Santonio Holmes standing to his left, near the sideline. (For the readers out there who don't watch football, "shotgun" denotes any situation where a quarterback is lined up five to seven yards behind his center instead of right on top of him.) The ball was snapped, Sanchez scanned the field for the briefest of seconds, and then chucked it right at Holmes, who had gained the inside track on his corner with a slant route and was about five yards upfield. *Thud.* The ball landed right in Holmes' outstretched arms as he began to turn towards the endzone. Because Cleveland assumed that the Jets were going to try a route along the sidelines so they could get out of bounds and stop the clock, they never thought to defend the inside slant route, a pattern that took Holmes away from the sidelines. Now, there was only one man in his way; a Browns' safety that was already ten kinds of twistified from the unexpected play-call. As Holmes ran by the cornerback, it was all the safety could do to even lay a hand on the Jets' number one receiver as he ran to daylight. 26-20, Jets win in overtime. Well, this is starting to get a little bit weird. Maybe Santonio Holmes really is the greatest thing since life's bread. Or maybe it's just a weird coincidence or something. Yeah, that's it. A really, really fortunate coincidence. Until . . . .

One week later, the Jets played host to a formidable Houston Texans team. And by "formidable", I really mean "another freaking last place team that the Jets should have destroyed by twenty points if they were really that great." Common misconception, I know. At least this time, the Jets created the illusion of business as usual. They dominated the Texans through the first three quarters and jumped out to a 20-7 lead. Pure Jet football, let me tell ya. They controlled the lines at will, gained the yards in bunches of four, and engaged the other team man-on-man up front every single play. Have you ever played a game of tug-of-war on the side that was clearly stronger? You can feel some resistance, you're aware that the other team is there, but it doesn't matter because the rope keeps going steadily in your direction, bit by bit. And you know that there's nothing the other side can do about it. That's what the Jets were built on, and that's what it felt like against Houston. But it didn't last for long.

Suddenly, out of nowhere, everything started going wrong in the fourth quarter. After both teams were able to put a field goal on the board (thus making the score 23-10), the Jets began to engineer a drive of their own to put the game away. It was all going so darn well until Shonn Greene fumbled the ball near midfield, a stupidly happy gift that the Texans were all too glad to take. On the very next play after Greene's miscue, Texans' quarterback Matt Schaub threw for a forty-three yard touchdown. It was now 23-17 Jets with just under ten minutes to go in the fourth. Instantly, that all too familiar "*Oh, shit*" feeling kicked in, almost purely by reflex. There are certain fan bases that have had so much baggage associated with their team over the years, so many heartbreaks endured, that they collectively go into the fetal position when something bad even has the possibility of happening. They assume the worst because their team has offered them no reason to assume otherwise. I can't speak for other Jet fans, but I know that I chewed every single fingernail that I had down to barely a nub, just like I did during that Steelers playoff game when I was seven. This was where the luck would run out. It *had* to be.

It looked like my suspicions were about to be confirmed. Gang Green couldn't do a thing with their ensuing possession, which meant that they had to punt it back to Houston. Did the Texans proceed to drive down the field for a touchdown? Of course they did. The Jet defense that had been stingy for most of the day seemed to completely wither away on that last drive. I mean, it was disheartening to watch. Not just because of the game, but because it's a microcosm for the entirety of Jet history up to that point. Yeah, we've had some nice moments over the years, but when it really counts, when you really need someone to come up big, it never happens. That's what was going through my head as the Houston extra point sailed through the uprights to give the Texans their first lead of the day. As I wondered if I could possibly feel worse about my choice of favorite team, Sanchez threw an interception on the next drive. Texans' football with under two minutes left and deep in Jets' territory. Game presumably over.

The Jets held Houston to a field goal on that drive and burned all of their timeouts in order to get the ball back at their own twenty-eight yard line with fifty-five seconds left to go. Things looked just about hopeless. Sanchez was able to march the offense downfield to approximately the fifty-yard line, but that ate up another thirty seconds of clock. The Jets had twenty-four seconds to cover half the field against a defense that was clearly expecting a deep pass.

Sanchez took the snap from shotgun, surveyed the defense for a second, and then flung it as far as he could for wide receiver Braylon Edwards down the right sideline. *This is it*, I thought. *The Texans are going to intercept this thing and put me out of my misery.* Edwards had gotten behind his cornerback and was chugging his way down the field, his eyes fixated on the ball. As the pass began its downward trajectory, the Texans' safety closed in on Edwards. If the safety played it the right way, he would have a chance for an interception or a big hit on Edwards that would surely cause the ball to pop loose. That never happened. The safety closed in on the football, ready to deliver the big hit, but he misjudged the ball's flight path. Instead of connecting with the front of Edwards as soon as the ball got there, he hit Edwards' left side a split second after the receiver stuck his hands out to haul in Sanchez's long throw. Down the football fluttered, straight onto the fingertips of Edwards, who caught it and absorbed the hit. Forty-four yards in eight seconds. On the next play, Sanchez lofted a pass into the back left corner of the endzone for—who else?—Santonio Holmes. He caught it, tapped both of his feet in bounds, and the Jets pulled yet another game out of their ass. 30-27, Jets win.

What you have to understand to appreciate how improbable this was is that these were *always* the games that the Jets would lose. Always. The "miracles", the improbable last second comebacks, the "wait a second, something's really different about these guys" feeling, they all happened to *other* teams. When you wait and wait and wait for so long to get that team and those moments, you start to lose faith that it's ever going to happen. And that's how I felt after only eight years of hopeless addiction to the Jets, so I can only imagine how people who have been lifelong Browns or Cubs fans feel.

Part of the reason why being a sports fan stops being so important after awhile is because that sense of idealism, the whole "anything can happen at any time" shpiel starts to lose its initial luster. Just like how transitioning from childhood to adulthood slowly removes the rose-colored glasses from your eyes, so too does being a sports fan. Winning the lottery, watching a favorite team go undefeated, starting the next Facebook, being in the stadium when your favorite team wins it all, these are the things that happen to a select few *other* people. So we often alter our expectations to match reality. I guess a part of me was dumb enough to neglect to do that, which probably explained why every excruciating Jet loss caused me to react like it was the first time it had ever happened. Which, of course, is why this particular team took on far more significance than it should have for me. I don't want to give you the whole English teacher "this particular event is a metaphor/motiff/symbol for something because blah blah blah" speech, but I am afraid I have to, because those three wins symbolized something greater, something that I thought I'd finally learned to let go of. Having a team capture your imagination like that, take you to the brink of despair only to pull you back into euphoria, it's one of the greatest experiences that can ever be had by a fan. So when it starts happening to you, amid all of the wild comebacks and "can you believe they did it again?" storylines, there begins to emerge a tiny glimmer of hope—because most people that support teams like the Jets refuse to allow themselves any more than a glimmer—that this is the year.

Or . . . . all of that high-minded writing was an attempt to distract you from the fact that the Jets needed to pull off improbable comebacks in the final seconds in order to beat last-place teams by the narrowest possible margins. It's open to interpretation.

After a relatively drama-less win over Cincinnati that advanced the Jets' record to nine wins and two losses (seriously, nine and freaking two! It actually happened! Look it up, they were at 9-2 at one point in the not-too-distant-past!), they cruised in to Week 13 riding a five-game winning streak and a giant wave of hype. More importantly, they were also hanging on to the AFC East divisional lead by the slimmest of margins.

The Hated New England Patriots ("hated" has practically become a part of the Patriots' name around the Goldstein household) also held a 9-2 record, with the Jets' advantage over them coming from the 28-14 Gang Green win back in Week 2. So, conveniently enough, guess who was up next on the Jets' schedule?

(If you seriously can't guess after *that* obvious of a build-up . . . .)

Yes, the Jets would have to travel into the ~~seventh circle of Hell~~ Gillette Stadium in Foxborough, Massachusetts to defeat ~~Satan~~ New England once and for all. (I don't actually have anything against Gillette Stadium, Foxborough, or Massachusetts in general. If it isn't clear by now, I just really hate the Patriots.) Even though the Jets had made it to the AFC Conference Championship just a year ago, this was the closest that Gang Green had ever been to a Super Bowl. The future of the rivalry between the two teams, how everything that had happened over the last couple of years would be viewed in retrospect, the Patriot dynasty, the legacies of both Rex Ryan and Mark Sanchez, four decades of tortured Jet history, whether or not I would be forced to bring shame upon myself and my family by wearing a Patriots' jersey due to an ill-advised bet I made with Matt, the AFC East divisional winner, home field advantage in the playoffs, and the future of NFL offenses (among other things) all rested, in some part, on the outcome of this game. But seriously, guys, just go out there and have fun with it.

There was no doubt in my mind that the Jets were going to win this game. I wore a Jets shirt to school every day during the week before the game. Not only that, but I went out of my way to mention, every single chance that I got, that they were going to win. Why not? The Patriots had looked somewhat beatable going into the game because, well, the Pats almost never really mash the accelerator down until December. But instead of rationally thinking about it that way, the fan in me allowed the wish to supercede the thought. I kept needling Matt about how the New England dynasty was over. Over and over, I openly invited the wrath of karma by calling Tom Brady "washed up" (inaccurate), teasing him about SpyGate like it was sixth grade (old news), and even stole his planner to write my prediction for the game in big, bold letters across a whole week's worth of dates (kind of a jerk move.) Matt, in his infinite wisdom, said very little in return. He fired a few retaliatory shots, but he mostly stayed quiet because he knew that he supported the better team. Well, and he figured out that if he stayed quiet, Mrs. Dunham would yell at just me for fooling around during English class instead of being mad at both of us. Either way, he played it smartly.

For the way I annoyed Matt that week, maybe I deserved what was about to happen to the Jets. I couldn't help it though; I was like Kevin Garnett screaming, "ANYTHING IS POSSI-BLLLLEEEEEEE!!!!" all week because of the way the season had gone so far. The hype, the comeback wins, the 9-2 record, it was all so unfamiliar to me. It would have been stupid to not be overly excited about it. But what went down on that Monday Night in Foxborough, well, let's just say it was all *very* familiar territory to me. Even so, I had no idea how bad it would really get.

From the moment the Jets stepped on the field, they were outclassed. New England went over, under, around, and through New York in every single aspect of the game. On offense, they struck with such speed and precision that the Jet defense was left completely flummoxed. Between every play, Jet defenders practically had to sprint off the field as their substitutes sprinted in. Anything less than a full-blown "running from a burning building" level sprint resulted in people being horribly out of position when the ball was snapped. I have no idea why I even wrote that last sentence, because it didn't really matter whether or not they were in position. Brady just completed the damn pass anyways. The Jet offense wasn't much better than their defense. Here's a quick summary of how their first-half drives went; missed field goal, punt, field goal, punt, punt, end of half. They weren't that terrible (I had certainly seen worse from them), but in no way, shape, or form could the offense even dream of matching New England point for point. The score at the end of the first quarter was 17-0, Pats. By the end of the half, that lead grew to 24-3, New England. I don't think I had ever been as depressed after watching thirty minutes of football as I was on that night.

And somehow, in the second half, things managed to get worse. The Jets got the ball at the beginning of the third quarter and put together a five-minute, sixty-four yard drive that looked like it would end in a touchdown . . . . right until Sanchez threw an interception on the goal line right over the middle of the field to Pats' linebacker Brandon Spikes.

It would have hit Spikes directly in the helmet had he not put his hands up to catch it. The outcome of the game was never in doubt after that play. But just to be sure, New England scored another touchdown on their next possession. 31-3, New England.

Meanwhile, I'm sitting on the couch watching the carnage unfold, totally transfixed in what can only be described as sheer horror. I guess I was in too much shock to cry, get mad, or really do anything worthwhile. So I just sat there, probably looking as pathetic as my team was, trying to wrap my head around what was happening. This had to be some kind of bad dream. There were several moments where I expected to wake up in bed, sweating, heart pounding, relieved to find out that it was all some kind of nightmare. Sadly, this was all very real. The Jets had roped me in. Again. I invested so much hope in this group of bums when I should have known better than to do so. It honestly felt like a small part of me died that night as I watched the Jets roll over in their biggest game since Super Bowl III. I'm well aware that non-sports fans will think I'm being way over-dramatic, but this is something that you have to love a particular type of hopeless team to understand. You feel this mix of anger, hopelessness, sadness, regret, envy, and foolishness, seasoned with a pinch of despair. The first time you feel it, you're surprised that you even feel it at all. That was me after the Doug Brien game in 2004. I had no idea how much I cared about my team, and thus had no idea how much it would hurt when they let me down for the first time. I'm guessing that I cried for a good half hour that night, not to mention the fact that I swore to never watch football again. But as the Pats were pulverizing the Jets, I'd become somewhat numb to the pain. Eventually, I had to turn the TV off when it got to New England 38, New York 3.

Now, at this point, the clock had almost struck midnight. The bus for school left at 6:50 the next day, which means that I usually had to be up by at least six o'clock. And I had yet to take a shower, change, and do half of my homework, so the best case scenario would be that I'd drag my sorry, tired behind into bed for about four and a half hours of the least satisfying sleep of my life. I ended up doing none of these things. Instead, I went on the computer and mindlessly browsed the Internet for an hour. Then, still not feeling tired, I tried to lie down in bed, hoping that I could salvage sleep of some kind. But how on Earth could I sleep after what just happened? Staring up at the ceiling and replaying the game over and over in my head would have to be an acceptable substitute. That whole night I spent fidgeting around, trying desperately to get to sleep and ultimately failing. There was just no letting go of the overwhelming feeling of awfulness that stemmed from the game. I was angry at them for rolling over to New England, angry at New England for being better than we were, angry at myself for ever picking the Jets as my favorite team, angry at the TV for functioning properly on that evening, angry at everything. Eventually, around 4:30 in the morning, a wave of exhaustion hit me and I finally went to sleep for about an hour and a half. I somehow woke up on my own at six o'clock with the previous day's clothes still on, most of my homework undone, my hair a complete sweaty mess, and my alarm clock blaring "American Woman." (I've since deleted that song from my iPod.) Just another Tuesday in the life of a Jet fan.

At school the next day, everybody treated me like one of my close friends had been hit by a bus. People who I had never talked to in my life came up and gave me a pat on the back. Random classmates, most of whom I'm pretty certain had never watched football for more than an hour in their lives, asked me if I was still feeling OK. Some, who had watched sports before, half-jokingly inquired as to whether or not I was alive. Every single sad smile or "Hey, sorry about the game, man" comment made me realize how far the reach of sports extends, and in how little time. After only a week of annoying everybody I saw about the game, and in spite of me offering average onlookers every reason to root for New England so I'd finally shut up, a small part of all these people sympathized with me. Even the people who usually teased me about the Jets kept a respectful distance. I'm forever indebted to these people for helping me get through a legitimately dark time in my life, even if it was only a day or two.

Despite these strangers' well-wishings (which I sincerely appreciated), I didn't want to be in school. I kind of wanted to crawl back in bed and mope some more. The unbearable knot in my stomach only grew larger when Matt walked into first period English class with a huge, shit-eating grin on his face. With the way I had antagonized him over the course of the previous week, very few people in the history of sports were more entitled to this day of schadenfreude than was Matt. He reached into his backpack and tossed me the Wes Welker jersey. I had lost the bet, so I had to suffer the humiliation of wearing the other team's colors. For the day, I was set to become a human trophy. In a moment of extreme weakness, the coward's way out of the bet presented itself to me. I took my sweatshirt off and tossed the Pats' 83 jersey on. Then, with all due haste, I threw the hoodie back on and zipped it up to conceal the Welker uniform that lay beneath. With that, I'd probably lost all respect, both from Matt and from myself. But in the moment, respect was the last thing on my mind. I just wanted to go home.

Somehow, the week passed by and the pain of the loss eventually passed. However, karma wasn't done sucker-punching me quite yet. Gang Green followed up the pitiful New England loss with an equally uninspired 10-6 loss to Miami, a defeat in which Santonio Holmes dropped what would have been the game-winning touchdown. Even worse, the one arrow still left in the anti-Patriots quiver (dredging up SpyGate) quickly vanished because of Jets' strength and conditioning coach Sal Alosi. During yet another Jet punt, Dolphins' cornerback Nolan Carroll was running along the Jets' sideline to make the tackle when he mysteriously fell. The video replays showed no other players in Carroll's immediate vicinity, nor did it show any indication that he might be injured. In fact, he seemed to get up and immediately look back to see why he fell. A couple more rewinds of the tape showed a man dressed in Jet-green apparel, later identified as Alosi, stick his knee out as Carroll ran by in an effort to trip him up.

So, just to review, in the span of two weeks, the Jets had gone from *Rudy*-ish title contenders to ineffectual, bumbling, blustery, cheating, overmatched, and underhanded losers. Rex's usual bravado, instead of lifting both the team and the fanbase up, instead contributed to the sense of comical arrogance surrounding Gang Green. We were suddenly like the villains from a bad Saturday morning cartoon or PG-rated comedy; complete with empty threats, a penchant for tripping on our own shoelaces, a boss that served as a caricature of himself, totally incompetent underlings, people that bent the rules to get ahead, and a predefined stigma of sucking. *Duh, the Jets lost to the Patriots. I mean, what the hell else did you expect? You didn't honestly think that they were going to start winning, did you? Come on, they're the Jets!*

Losing like that, coupled with my subsequent reaction, made me take a good, long look at why I cared about sports in the first place. There had to be more to being a sports fan than waiting for your team to stab you in the back again. And if there wasn't, then why did I even bother rooting for anybody? Why not just pour the effort involved in loving a team into learning a language or doing something useful with my life? Those miserable two weeks, when I really took a good look at why I loved sports, was the beginning of my move towards some kind of normalcy. Before the New England and Miami losses, I'd always thought that letting losses ruin your day was just part of being a fan. Sadness and dissatisfaction were just the price of doing business. If you wanted the highs, then the lows were inevitable, or so I always believed. This was before I realized that the Jets could only really ruin my day if I let them do it. If I just stopped caring so damn much, then maybe football could be fun again. Someday, when my kid becomes a fan, I'll tell him/her what I realized at that moment, but wouldn't put into practice until at least a year later: never let sports become anything bigger than they ought to be.

After those two tumultuous weeks, things took a turn for the (slightly) better. Gang Green emerged victorious on the road against a very good Pittsburgh Steelers team after a last-second Pittsburgh pass into the end zone fell incomplete. A close road loss to the Chicago Bears and an easy win over the Buffalo Welcome Mats capped off a season that the Jets finished with an 11-5 record, their best in over a decade. For that, they managed to procure the final AFC playoff spot, which meant a trip to Lucas Oil Stadium, where Peyton Manning's Indianapolis Colts were poised to eliminate the Jets from the playoffs once again.

With the way everything went down at season's end, I wasn't particularly hopeful about this game. When Rex injected his usual bravado into the game by proclaiming that things were "personal" between him and Peyton Manning, it felt like the first half of Bluto's *Animal House* speech. Just ol' Rex in the middle of a room, screaming about how "NOTHING'S OVER UNTIL WE DECIDE IT IS!!!" while everybody else blankly stares at him. (*Two* Animal House references in this book? Sometimes I amaze myself.) Head coaches in football tend to fizzle out over time because they run out of new cards to play, in both the technical and motivational departments. When a coach can't outfox the guy on the other sideline anymore and he isn't extracting the very best out of his own players like he once was, then he has passed the peak of his usefulness. My point is that it seemed like both Rex and his team arrived at that point. The "it's personal" comment felt more tired than anything else, much like certain comedians repeat the same jokes over and over again in different forms because they can't think of new material.

But in a way, going into the playoffs like this was the best possible outcome. Almost as quickly as it had appeared, the target on Gang Green's back shifted to their opponents. After all, losing 45-3 tends to put a damper on the "Super Bowl or Bust!" rhetoric. If the Jets lost in the first round, then so what? It's the Jets; they're supposed to lose in big games, a fact that was made abundantly clear on that night in New England. They were back to being the same old Jets in the eyes of the public, which is fantastic because the few times in their history that they've ever really done anything of significance were when absolutely nothing was expected of them. Indianapolis, though, was a whole 'nother story. Peyton Manning had (and, as of this book's publication, still has) a reputation for choking in the playoffs. Whether that reputation is deserved or undeserved is another debate, but the dreaded "chokes under pressure" label is prominently attached to him by many people. If he ended yet another promising regular season with a first round loss at home? To the Jets? Well, that might put a little bit of a blemish on his legacy. And if he won? Big deal. Unless the Colts completely blew the doors off New York and won by forty points, winning this matchup would be nothing out of the usual for Indianapolis. They were the favorites in this game (albeit by only three points), picked by almost every single one of CBS' analysts to win. The New York Jets were playing with the house's money, and just about everybody knew it.

For most of the game, things stayed relatively calm, save for a fifty-five yard touchdown pass from Manning to wide receiver Pierre Garcon. Indy held on to a slim 10-7 lead as the game entered its final quarter and I tried to desperately convince myself that I didn't care about whether the Jets won or lost. Based upon every single thing you've read in this book and all of the various Jet-related neuroses that I'd contracted over the years, the realistic chances for success in that endeavor were relatively low. Even though I fully expected another soul-crushing loss, I found it nearly impossible to stop caring. And if that doesn't give you at least some idea of what being a fan means, then I really need to give up this writing thing. But once again, I'm digressing.

Most of what happened over the course of the fourth quarter escapes my memory, to be perfectly honest with you. Things really weren't that exciting until the clock ticked down to about four minutes and thirty seconds left. The Jets had taken a 14-13 lead by that point on the strength of a Mark Sanchez-led touchdown drive. Now, the ball would be in the hands of the savvy comeback artist Peyton Manning, who would attempt to dissect a Jet defense that had stood tall all day. Manning won that battle. He marched the Colts down to the New York thirty-three yard line before the drive stalled. Colts' kicker Adam Vinatieri then drilled a fifty-yard field goal right down the pipes. 16-14, Colts with fifty seconds left to go.

Well, that's it. Another promising Jets' season down the tubes. But, true to form, I resolved to stay and watch to the bitter end because miracles do happen every once in awhile. Not to the Jets, but they do happen. That's what flashed through my mind as Antonio Cromartie caught the kickoff from a yard deep in the endzone for the Jets and began to veer to the right. Somehow, after running about twenty yards, he managed to squeeze his way through the tiniest of gaps between two Jet blockers and book it down the sideline. Suddenly, the Colts realized that Cromartie was about to take this thing all the way if they didn't do something quickly. He was finally bumped out of bounds at the New York 46 yard-line, about twenty yards away from field goal range. First time for everything, I guess.

At this point, my calm, rational routine was dropkicked out the window. No longer am I reclined on the couch with a pillow under my back. Rather, I'm standing with my hands affixed to my temple. It was one of those rare *"No way did that just happen"* moments, the kind that every sports fan lives and dies to see. That's part of the payoff of investing so much time in sports, enjoying moments like this on a week-to-week basis. Seeing the improbable comebacks and game-turning, once-in-a-lifetime plays is one thing, but when they happen to *your* team? You completely and utterly lose your mind. It's weird; just when you think you've got sports all figured out, it produces something like the Cromartie return that makes you rethink everything all over again. I'm never going to forget that distinct, *"Oh my god, I cannot believe I just saw that"* feeling that came over me when Cro broke loose down the sideline. The Jets were alive once again.

Sanchez immediately followed the big return by firing a quick eight-yard pass to Braylon Edwards near the right hash marks. Colts' safety Antoine Bethea immediately slammed into Edwards, dropping him to the turf . . . . along with the football, which had dislodged itself from Edwards' grip. Indianapolis picked it up and the ref signaled that the Colts had successfully taken possession of it. Game over . . . . . that is, until the replay booth buzzed down for a review of the fumble. Video evidence showed Edwards' knee dropping to the turf before the pigskin did. Down by contact. Jets still had the ball with about forty seconds to go and ten yards left to gain for field goal range.

After the close call, Sanchez completed two significant passes, one a shallow out route to Holmes and one a deep fade to Edwards. This left the Jets sitting on Indy's 14 yard line down 16-14 with three seconds left in the game. The entire season was about to come down to kicker Nick Folk. If he missed this kick, he's the newest in a long line of goats throughout Jet history, a source of anguish for the tortured years to come. But if he made it? Then, the Jets would finally best Peyton Manning and, more importantly, get to square off against a team they knew all too well.

I HATE THE PATRIOTS

Every sports team has rivals and most fans have at least one team that they hate as much as they love their own. The New York Jets are certainly no exception. Over the years, Gang Green has developed healthy rivalries with a few different teams. These rivalries have been lost and renewed as the teams involved in them rise and fall from prominence and instigators are either added or subtracted from the equation. All of these rivalries throughout over forty years of football are brought together with one very evident common bond; the Jets get their asses thoroughly kicked in almost all of them.

Obviously, there's the "rivalry" with the New York Giants that goes along with sharing both a stadium and a city. However, that one never really felt like a real rivalry because the Giants play in the NFC and the Jets play in the AFC. Can you really keep a serious rivalry going when the teams involved only see each other in a meaningful game once every four years? Besides, the Giants have achieved infinitely more success over their existence than have the Jets. They've won four Super Bowls to the Jets' one, have nineteen Football Hall of Fame members as compared to the Jets' five inductees, and have won 54.9% of their games as opposed to the Jets' 45.9%. In summation: the two teams rarely meet in meaningful games, there is little real animosity between the two teams, and one has achieved drastically more success than the other. Just like Lakers vs Clippers was never considered a rivalry purely because the teams "shared" the city of L.A., Giants vs Jets shouldn't be considered one either.

That leaves the three teams the Jets share a division with: the Bills, the Dolphins, and the Patriots. Personally, I've never had anything against the Bills. In fact, I've always felt a certain kinship with Bills fans because of how much both of our teams suck. In fact, they're one of the few football teams that have the Jets outdone in the "punching their fans in the stomach" department. I mean, they went to the Super Bowl four years in a row during the 90s and lost each time, for goodness' sake. Plus, they've only had one winning season in the last thirteen years, not to mention zero playoff appearances in that timeframe. I don't want to spend energy scuffing my shoes on the doormat, especially since I know what it feels like when my team is the doormat.

The Miami Dolphins are a little bit different. There's some legitimate history there with the Fake Spike, linebacker Jason Taylor calling Jet fans "ignorant" and "classless", the Monday Night Miracle, and the A.J. Duhe game, among other things. Plus, the 49-44-1 record (in favor of the Jets) actually suggests a somewhat even matchup over the years. Sounds like rivalry material to me.

However, there was always something missing for me with Jets-Dolphins games. For some reason or another, I never felt like they were different than any other team the Jets played. Besides, the Dolphins weren't really successful enough to warrant hating. Sure, they made the playoffs now and again, but they seemed to struggle just like the Jets did. Sports rivalries make the other side seem somehow less human when the game is being played. I'm not saying it's healthy or right to think that way, but it's a fact. And the Dolphins seemed, both on a personal and organizational level, human. They had ups and downs from year to year, they could never find a consistent cornerstone on offense after Hall of Fame QB Dan Marino left in the early 2000s, and they were plagued by some disastrous offseason moves. I couldn't really hate them because I looked at that team and saw a little bit of the Jets. The Dolphins were relatable.

Then, there were the New England Patriots. Trust me when I say that for most of my childhood, I hated nothing in the world as much as I hated the New England Patriots.

Clad in silver helmets and navy blue uniforms (white if they were playing a road game), the Patriots would run out of the tunnel, the smoke from the fog machines billowing around them as they ran past. By late October or early November, the weather at their home stadium in Foxborough, Massachusetts would turn cold enough that you could see the players' every breath hanging in the early evening air. The roar of the crowd permeated through the TV and into my living room as everybody began their last minute stretching, the wind whipping in from the gap in the stands on the stadium's north end.

Now, the weird thing about the Patriots is that they don't necessarily look different from any other team before the game starts. Anybody who has ever been to a Bulls game during Michael Jordan's prime will tell you that everybody in the crowd, without exception, could tell that MJ was the best player on the floor just by watching him shoot before the game and watching the way his teammates reacted to him. He was simply a force of personality that you couldn't ignore. The Steelers of the 1970s had physical freaks of nature like Mean Joe Greene and generally *looked* like a team that was all ready to kick your ass. They were bigger, meaner, tougher, and carried themselves like the schoolyard bullies ready to take the league's lunch money.

But it was never like that for the Patriots. Tom Brady would always go through his pre-game preparations with the same emotionless stare etched on his face. There was never any pre-game video of drill sergeant speeches or elaborate handshake rituals or chest bumps. You see, the Patriots had a system in place, something that the media and several members of the organization dubbed the Patriot Way. It was the blueprint for how New England was able to win three Super Bowls and dominate the 2000s. Non-coincidentally, a large part of that system involved shutting up whenever cameras were around. New England was always content to let you do your talking while they let their own play say everything. And when it was time to play, the Patriots hit you upside the head like a ton of bricks.

Trying to defend against New England's offense was like trying to defend against Muhammad Ali in his prime. The Patriots just moved at such a breakneck pace that it became impossible to adequately stave them off unless you disrupted their flow, sort of like how nobody could effectively stave off Ali when he was throwing three punches per second. Both the Patriot offense and Ali usually left opponents in the same condition by the end of the day; confused, knocked down, exhausted, and unable to totally discern what the hell had just happened to them.

I'm telling you, the New England hurry-up offense was absolutely murderous for a defense. First of all, you never knew exactly when it was coming. If the Patriots decided to destroy you from the outset, it would come on the first drive. If they were playing a better team next week and decided not to show too much of their gameplan, maybe it would only make sporadic appearances. More often than not, it came in the second or third quarters when the score was still close, maybe within ten points.

Then, I can only assume that somebody on the New England sideline pulled the whole offense together and said, "OK, enough screwing around. We're gonna run them off the field starting right now."

Then, quarterback Tom Brady takes the field. He might complete a short pass, maybe five yards or so. Instead of going back to the huddle, the Patriots would then reset their formation in about eight seconds. Brady would bark out a few orders, snap the football, and then complete another short pass for a first down. After that, the Pats would march right up to the line and Brady would zip another pass to an open wide receiver for ten more yards. At this point, the defensive coordinator of the opposing team has seen enough. He signals a few players to come out of the game and for the players standing beside him to quickly run in. That is, he begins to signal the switch until he notices the Patriots at the line of scrimmage once again, ready to snap the football.

Let's skip a few plays ahead. New England is now at the opponent's twenty-five yard line after moving the ball almost sixty yards in eight or nine plays. Massive beads of sweat are dripping down the face of every single defender as they desperately try to get in position, stunt, audible, do *anything* to force an incomplete pass and get fifteen seconds of rest. The measured and sharp postures of the drive's beginning are a relic of three minutes ago, now replaced by inattentive slouches indicative of players whose minds and bodies are both reeling. Six yard gains have gradually turned into eight, ten, and fifteen yard gains. The haymaker has to be coming soon.

Brady takes another snap out of the shotgun formation with two wide receivers on either side of him as the cornerbacks hurriedly assume their positions five yards in front of the wideouts. The receiver to Brady's immediate right runs a quick out route. Brady quickly eyes him, starts to wind up for the throw . . . . and then pulls the ball back. The beleaguered outermost corner on the right side of the field, seeing a chance to jump the route for what was sure to be at least an incompletion and a guaranteed rest of at least fifteen seconds, breaks towards his teammate's responsibility for a split second before realizing that he has been duped. Before anybody else can pick up the receiver that the corner who screwed up had unwittingly left all alone, Brady calmly lobs a pass to him in the corner of the end zone. Touchdown. The defense is drenched in sweat and keeled over with their hands on their knees, gasping for air. Brady trots back to the sideline, looking as if he just returned from the supermarket as opposed to the football field.

Such was the nature of the Patriot Machine, a combination of eleven imperfect human beings into a seemingly flawless unit. They mercilessly attacked defenses every Sunday, probing and prodding them until they found just the right spot to attack. When they finally found that weak spot, they assaulted it for all it was worth until the defense could take no more. Week after week, they'd win by scores like 34-17, 41-20, and an occasional 52-7, just to remind everybody that they could do what nobody else could.

At the head of this unstoppable juggernaut were two men, Tom Brady and Bill Belichick. Brady was the field general that could read and interpret the ever-evolving chess game on turf with a surgeon's precision and just a few milliseconds ahead of everybody else. Every necessary pre-snap adjustment was made before anyone knew it needed to be made. Every ball was delivered on the fingertips of the wide receiver. Every move, every scheme, every plan that any defense could possibly come up with, Brady knew how to beat.

Brady was the poster boy of the Patriot Machine. He had everything that you'd expect a star quarterback to have. The commercials, the huge contract, the mansion, the supermodel wife, the everlasting respect of everyone who ever played with or against him, he had all of that and more. The media swarmed around his stand at the postgame press conference and fans clamored outside of Pats training camp in the sweltering August heat, hoping to catch a glimpse of one of football's greatest quarterbacks ever.

If I'm going to get dorky and compare the Pats to the empire in Star Wars, then Brady was like Darth Vader for me. He was the public figure, the first thing that popped into anybody's mind when they thought of the Patriot Machine. Just like everybody remembers Darth Vader rather than The Emperor even though he's not the main villain, you'll always hear people laud Tom Brady first and foremost when they talk about the 2000s Patriots.

Even though I hated Tom Brady, the Darth Vader comparison doesn't really work with him. He was a little bit too likable to be a villain. His only crime from a ten year old Jets fan's perspective was being good at his job and playing for the Pats. Looking back on it, maybe I hated what he stood for more than I actually hated him. After all, I was disposed to hating anybody who knifed the Jets in the front, back, and sides as much as he did. I didn't like him, but I probably wouldn't say that I despised it. However, Bill Belichick, the Patriots' head coach, was a different story. He *was* The Emperor.

Belichick stalked the Patriots' sideline every week, pacing back and forth with a menacing scowl forever plastered onto his grim complexion. That visage was usually at least partially hidden under the cowl of his trademark hoodie, emblazoned with the Patriots' colors and logo. His expression never seemed to change, either. Didn't matter whether he was up by thirty, tied, or losing by thirty, he always looked like a father who was angry at his kid or something.

His stance toward the media fell somewhere between nonchalant dismissal and outright antipathy. At times, I genuinely wondered if Belichick was competing against himself to try and set a new record for least information given in a fifteen minute press conference. To illustrate that point, here are a few questions that I made up, along with the type of answers that Belichick would typically give.

Q: How do you plan to improve your defense's performance for next week's game?
A: They've got to give up less points.

Q: Do you think that Tom Brady can continue to succeed like this over the course of an entire season?
A: He's a good quarterback.

Q: Do you ever plan on answering any of our questions?
A: No

Another thing about Belichick is that he never pulled back when the Pats were up big. In fact, it became a well-established Belichick tradition to send a receiver deep to try for a late touchdown bomb when the Pats were blowing somebody out in the fourth quarter. He'd go for that long touchdown even if his team was up 35-0, just to prove a point. One time, he even tried a fake spike play in those very circumstances. The fact that Belichick was offered the Jets' head coaching position in 2000 before spurning them made him seem all the more villainous to me.

Together, Brady and Belichick were my personal axis of evil. They symbolized everything that I so desperately wanted for the Jets: success, stability, and fundamental soundness. I was on the good side, the side of the lovable Davids against the unstoppable New England goliaths. My anger towards New England came from an overpowering sense of my team's inferiority coupled with the painful wait for the day that we'd finally flip the script on them. Did the Pats ever do anything to me? No, I was just able to pretend that they did. Does any fan who hates another team hate them because they did something other than be better at their jobs than the players on that fan's own team are at theirs? 99.9% of the time, no. Will that dose of rational thinking stop anything from becoming a rivalry? Absolutely not. Would any fan, myself included, want it to? Hell, no.

Of course, I'm using the term "rivalry" a little bit loosely in this case because for most of the 2000s, Pats vs Jets was a rivalry the same way that the guillotine vs King Louis' head was a rivalry. Between 2001 (the Pats' first Super Bowl Year) and 2013, the Patriots have eighteen regular season wins against the Jets and only six losses. They've beaten the Jets in close games (17-16 in 2001), blowouts (45-3 in 2010), through the air (Brady has eighteen touchdowns and five interceptions all-time against the Jets), and on the ground (Kevin Faulk, Corey Dillon, Shane Vereen, Stevan Ridley, and Lawrence Maroney are just some of the Pats' ballcarriers that have killed the Jets over the years.) The Patriots have won the division title eleven times in that span and the Jets have won it once. New England has accumulated eleven playoff appearances, five Super Bowl appearances, and three Super Bowl titles in those thirteen years. The Jets have appeared in the playoffs five times and have zero Super Bowl appearances or wins.

When you develop such a hatred towards another team and you constantly get stepped on as much as the Jets have, you start to develop the sports fan's version of an inferiority complex. In my case, I started thinking about absolutely everything that the Jets did in the context of whether the Patriots would have done it or not. *Well, we just re-signed our wide receiver, Laveranues Coles, but would the Pats have done that? I like the Eric Mangini hire; he was a New England guy before he came over to the Jets. Oh, New England has their equipment manager on the trading block. Maybe we could snag him for a sixth round pick.* Think about how much of a loser's mentality that is. Would the Yankees ever measure themselves by how they did in comparison to the Red Sox? If the Yankees just signed a marquee player that the Sox didn't want, no Yankees fan would ever think, "Nice signing, but I'm kind of concerned that the Red Sox never showed much interest in him. Is something wrong with that guy?" No, a Yankees fan would never think that because they're the Yankees, they do it their own way, and they have the twenty-seven rings to prove that their way works. The Jets don't have that validation, which is why I found myself measuring them not against the rest of the league, but against the one team that they saw every year who *did* have that validation. Anything less than a World Series title would never satisfy the Yankees, but finishing with a better record than the Pats was enough to declare a particular season a huge success in the eyes of a pre-teen Jet fan. Of course, we never actually got a better record than the Pats had, either.

The only thing worse than trying and failing to measure up to a team that you absolutely despise is not being on their radar whatsoever. Maybe some of the seasons were just so long ago that I don't remember what happened, but I can't ever remember a time when a Pats' player or coach offered the slightest opinion on the Jets. In a way, it's almost more insulting when the other team doesn't even take notice of you. It's like that one scene in *Mad Men* where Michael Ginsburg condescendingly tells Don Draper that he feels bad for him and Draper replies, "And I don't really think about you at all." That's what it was like. I would have preferred that the Patriots talked trash to the Jets, bragged about their wins, and did all the stuff that the victors do in other rivalries because it would have at least given the impression that the Pats cared about beating the Jets in the first place. It's degrading to know that your favorite team's biggest games of the year are seen as just another unremarkable game on the schedule for the other guy. Only another date on the calendar.

Even though SpyGate reinvigorated the rivalry and knocked the Pats down a peg, it felt underhanded. Sure, it made the Pats seem like the evil empire, but the victory was something of a hollow one for the Jets. New

England had just finished raking the Jets over the coals again on the field, so a Jets' employee who happened to work with the Pats used his insider info to call out something that may or may not have been cheating. Don't get me wrong, I was definitely basking in the poetic justice of the whole situation at the time. But after awhile, it became meaningless to me. We *had* to whistleblow on them because we couldn't beat them between the lines. It was like when a WWE wrestler loses a match and then swings a chair at his opponent after the fight is over. It was the NFL's version of the Pine Tar Game in baseball and while it may have hurt the Patriots, it changed absolutely nothing. They were the model for how to build a franchise, we were the Jets, and SpyGate didn't convince a single person to circle the Jets-Pats game on their calendars.

Everything changed when Rex arrived, though. He announced that the Jets weren't going to settle for being second-class citizens in their own city. He publicly declared that he wouldn't stand for a legacy of losing. And, in his now infamous "not here to kiss Belichick's rings" interview, he sent a warning to the Pats that these Jets were different. That message would be vindicated a few months later when the Jets' defense kept Tom Brady out of the endzone in that 16-9 win in Week 2 of 2009. The win represented a massive shift in the rivalry. Instead of trying to emulate the Pats, instead of beating them with technicalities, we were going to punch them in the face.

And that's the way it was after the first year and a half of the renewed Jets-Pats rivalry. Coming into December of 2010, the Jets went 2-1 in their three games against New England. The Pats laid an egg against Baltimore at home and lost big in the first round of the 2009 playoffs while the Jets came within thirty minutes of the Super Bowl. When the preseason previews came out, the Jets were the sexy pick to win it all, not the Patriots. Both teams were 9-2 through the first twelve weeks of the season. New England was well-positioned for the next two or three years, but the Jets were seemingly in good shape for the next decade. And, for what it's worth, New York was just so much *cooler* than New England ever was. We had a coach that you'd want to grab a beer with, players that weren't restricted from speaking their minds, a unique identity, and a brash persona that made the Jets the NFL's bullies.

In fact, you know what it was like? It was a little bit like the rivalry between Larry Bird's Celtics (the Pats) and Isaiah Thomas' Bad Boy Pistons (the Jets) in the 80s. The Celtics represented everything that was "right" about basketball. Their team was a stable dynasty that was built around putting the good of everyone first and executing fundamentals perfectly every time. It was mostly a team filled with extremely likable players who had somewhat boring public personalities, with the exception of Kevin McHale. (I love Larry Bird and Robert Parrish as much as the next guy, but they weren't exactly people who would rival Charles Barkley or Joe Namath in the "I want to spend a weekend partying with that guy" category.) Both the 2000s Pats and the 80s Celts were the good guys, the teams that people who were neutral couldn't help but respect, if not immediately like. The success of both teams hinged on the once-in-a-lifetime talents of superior players (Bird and Brady) who were surrounded by Hall of Fame sidekicks (Kevin McHale and Randy Moss), not to mention a cadre of criminally underrated all-star players that covered everything that the stars couldn't do. (Dennis Johnson, Parish, Wes Welker, Vince Wilfork, etc.) Both teams were the firmly entrenched establishment and the new model for future dynasties.

Meanwhile, the Jets were like the Pistons. They were both the villains, the arrogant and brash young upstarts who refused to be intimidated. Every single person who loved the Pats/Celts absolutely hated the Jets/Pistons, mainly because the two sets of teams were antipoles when it came to persona. Both the Jets and the Pistons had a mix of volatile personalities that did plenty of talking off the field and, for good measure, did some more talking once the game started. *Everybody* had an opinion about both teams, and those opinions usually fell on either one end of the spectrum or the complete opposite end. The Pistons forced Larry Bird to push himself to another level in order to defeat them, much like the Jets made Tom Brady work for every single yard he gained. Unlike the elegant and sophisticated offenses of the Pats/ Celts, the Pistons/Jets relied on incredibly stingy defense and winning physical, low-scoring contests. Both the Pistons and the Jets had people involved with them that were universally maligned and depicted as classless cheap-shot artists, both fairly and unfairly. (Bart Scott, Bill Laimbeer, Rick Mahorn, Antonio Cromartie, etc.) Detroit and New York were both seen as the second wheel to both of the Boston teams, and it felt like that reputation gave both teams something of an inferiority complex. As a result, *everything* was about beating Boston. Everything was about finally shattering that glass ceiling and winning a title just like they did. Of course, therein lies the biggest difference between the Jets and the Pistons. Detroit eventually broke through that ceiling during the gap between the Larry Bird era and the Michael Jordan era, winning the 1989 and 1990 NBA titles. The Jets, as of today, haven't been able to do it.

That's what hurt so much about that demoralizing December 2010 loss to the Pats. 45-3 wasn't just another loss on the Jets' schedule. It was a complete and utter domination, in every sense of the word, by our only real rivals. After a little while, it hardly seemed like the Patriots had to try any more. Every gut-wrenching flick of Tom Brady's risk, every maddening swing of Stephen Gostkowski's leg, increased the degree of the Pats' thorough ass-kicking of the Jets. It's like the Jets were stuck in a rip current for the whole night; the harder they swam and the harder they tried to get out of the situation that they placed themselves in, the faster they were routed. The Jets weren't just beaten; they were outclassed. They looked like they didn't even belong in the same league as the Pats did. I guess the most painful thing about it is that I watched every game leading up to the fiasco. I was convinced that the Jets' time to take the reins had come. I knew that they were good enough to beat the Patriots. I would have bet anything that the Jets would either win or come damn close. And it turned out that the 9-2 record, the new-look defense, everything that I thought the New York Jets now stood for, wasn't enough. The Patriots brutally stripped the facade away and laid the Jets' shortcomings out for the world to see. Nobody would ever question whether the Patriots were better than the Jets for a long, long time. Our fight to be taken seriously, to supplant New England, was over for the time being. Or so I thought.

Then, Mark Sanchez completed that pass to Braylon Edwards and Nick Folk trotted out on to the field for a thirty-two yard field goal that would end the Colts' season. The Indianapolis crowd was on their feet, half of them screaming and half of them probably unable to look. Folk's eyes glanced down towards his holder's outstretched hands a second before the ball arrived and the laces were spun facing outwards. The embattled kicker took two strides forward and swiftly swung his foot into the football. As the ball fluttered through the air, the roar of the crowd dropped to a low murmur. I heard Nick Folk scream "YEAH!" and the next thing I knew, the oblong piece of leather hit the net behind the goalposts.

Six weeks after I thought it was over, it began again.

THE PINNACLE

A second after Nick Folk's game-ending 32 yard field goal attempt sailed through the uprights, it hit me. *We're going back to New England.*

This was it. The 2006 Playoff loss, Spygate, the Pats' 16-0 season, Mangini, Rex Ryan's bluster, the 45-3 game on Monday Night in December, it had all come down to this. Only a month or so after the Pats had beaten the Jets in every way possible and turned them into a league-wide punchline again, New York had a chance for revenge.

It's one of the most unique experiences that you can have as a fan to take in the atmosphere of a game like this, not to mention the game itself. I don't just mean a playoff game or an important late-season battle for a Wild Card spot. I mean a game with some bad blood behind it, a game between two good teams that actively despise each other. (Even though the Patriots didn't show it as much because of Bill Belichick's influence over how his players dealt with the media, let there be no doubt that they hated our guts as much as we hated theirs ever since Rex came into town.)

Well, if you haven't been a part of something like that, then let me try to describe to you what happens and what it feels like. First of all, there's a week-long chorus of bulletin board material, hype, predictions, rumors, and trash talk that builds to a deafening crescendo as game time draws closer and closer. If you have any friends that root for the other team, you start to feel a certain unspoken distance developing between you for that whole week. When you see people wearing your team's baseball cap or sporting the jersey of your team's star player, you feel like you *have* to acknowledge them in some way. Everybody's in this one together, after all.

By about Wednesday or Thursday, the game starts to take over your thoughts. You memorize the betting line, you think about what happened the last time the two teams met, you start to remember, word for word, exactly what the other team's middle linebacker said about your quarterback. The adrenaline that normally courses through you when it's kickoff time starts to take effect ninety-six hours beforehand. You're *ready* for something to happen.

If your team is the heavy underdog, like the Jets were on that Sunday, then that adds a whole new dynamic. Remember when I said in the last chapter that I was able to viscerally convince myself that the Pats had done something to me, personally? When you're the underdog in a situation like this one, everything that the other guys do becomes a personal affront to both you and your team. You just get an overwhelming sense that something you're going to remember for the rest of your life is going to happen in just a few days. There is no *if*, you positively *have* to win this game. Losing is simply not an option.

It didn't take long for shots to start being fired on both sides. Actually, it didn't even take until the end of the Jets-Colts game. During the first half, Twitter was abuzz about Tom Brady's whereabouts during the game. As it turns out, he was watching *Lombardi* on broadway for a good portion of the contest instead of staying home and scouting the team he and the Patriots would be playing next week. A normal, sane person might say, "Well, the guy just led his team to the best record in the league, a first round bye, and is enjoying his first week off in months. He deserves a little bit of a break." Brady's excursion didn't sit too well with Jet fans, though, who felt collectively slighted that the great Tom Brady apparently didn't think that extra preparation time was required for us. Had Brady actually done anything particularly significant? No. But were we able to convince ourselves that he had. Oh, it was *on*.

Of course, Rex Ryan just couldn't help himself after that. First, he reaffirmed that this rematch was a "personal" thing between him and Bill Belichick, just like it was "personal" between him and Peyton Manning. You know, just in case anybody had any doubts about whether this was a grudge match or not. He then started needling ~~Darth Vader~~ Brady through the media, talking about how "nobody studies like Peyton Manning" and how "Peyton Manning would have been watching our game." Cut to me enthusiastically nodding.

Still, it wasn't anything too out of the ordinary. Rex Ryan was just doing what Rex always did, which is to try to draw pressure and media focus away from his players and on to his own shoulders. He has always been outspoken and with the most important game in Jet history since Super Bowl III less than a week away, it made sense that he would be fired up. So, par for the course, no love lost, Rex had his moment, blah blah blah. So now we're done with the trash talk and ready to play, right?

Jets' defensive end Shaun Ellis: "Any time [Brady] gets a chance to rub it in our face, he's going to do it. For us, it's just a matter of we want to see him on the ground as much as possible."

Antonio Cromartie: "[Brady's] an asshole. *** him.

Well OK, then.

So naturally, somebody from the Patriots had to fire back. Enter Wes Welker, who dropped no less than eleven mentions of the words "feet", "toes", and "foot", a not so subtle dig at a leaked video of Rex and his wife. (I'm not going to describe the video in this book. Just Google it if you're curious, although Google at your own risk and be advised that it's not safe for work.) And of course, after hearing that, people on the Jets had to fire back. Nick Mangold dug up the Spygate scandal in a press conference the next day and Bart Scott went so far as to say that Welker's days in a uniform were "numbered."

Well, glad to see that there are no hard feelings here.

After Friday, though, everything died down. Nobody said a thing on Saturday. Even the espn.com message boards, which give Youtube's comments section some healthy competition for the least intelligent debate on the Internet, calmed down significantly. It was as if a tacit and mutual understanding fell over the players, coaches, and fan bases of both teams that the time for talk was now over. Every angle that could be taken by the press had been taken, everything that could be said by the parties involved had been said, and there was nothing else to do but play.

Now, before I begin to describe the events that took place on January 16th, there's something that you need to understand. Absolutely *nobody* thought that the Jets had anything resembling a chance against the Patriots. Nobody. A few analysts here and there thought that the Jets might get beaten by a touchdown, but that's the most optimistic outlook I saw. After all, New England had just crushed this team in the 45-3 game a month and a half ago, so why on Earth would anything be different this time? Not only did everybody pick against the Jets, everybody relished picking against the Jets. They were the annoying loudmouths and arrogant braggarts that needed to be shut up once and for all. It wasn't like Yankees-Sox in 2004 where you *wanted* the Sox to finally be the ones who came out on top. It wasn't even like rooting for a fifteenth seed in March Madness, where you want a team to win just to inject as much absurdity as possible into a situation. The Jets were hated by the majority of other teams' fans, were despised by the "they don't respect the game" people in the media, were told that they needed to be quiet by their critics, and gleefully discounted by all.

And why not? The Patriots had Tom Brady, one of the greatest quarterbacks to ever play in the NFL. The Jets had Mark Sanchez. The Patriots had assembled one of the best offenses in NFL history that year, and the Jets had assembled one of the worst. (At one point in the season, they went ten consecutive quarters without scoring a touchdown.) The New England Patriots forced turnovers, held their blocks, and never missed the chance to finish opponents off when they were on the ropes. The Jets committed penalties, lost games that they had no business losing, and generally had a knack for committing turnovers at the worst possible times. New England won three Super Bowls on their way to being the team of the decade. The Jets' only Super Bowl appearance was in 1969. The Patriots let the Jets have their moment in the spotlight. They let the Jets talk, and now they were going to destroy them with the same brutal efficiency that they'd displayed on that Monday Night in December. That was the only way this could end. Or so we all thought.

The game was the last one of Divisional Weekend and was put in the 4:00 P.M. timeslot, which is usually reserved for the most intriguing matchup of the weekend. Even with the trash talk and the bitter feud between the two teams, it would not have garnered that all-important timeslot if CBS or the NFL thought that the game would be a blowout. So that was the first sign that the Patriots might have to break a sweat.

As the two teams trotted out to midfield for the coin toss, I could see that LaDainian Tomlinson and James Ihedigbo, two Jet captains, were carrying a jersey with them. Upon closer inspection, one could see that the jersey had been cut and scuffed up quite a bit. Stretched across the back of the jersey was the number 90 and the name, "Byrd."

Dennis Byrd, number 90, was a defensive end for the Jets until he was paralyzed on the field in 1992 after a brutal collision with his own teammate, forcing him to re-learn how to walk. Since that date, no member of the Jets had ever worn the number 90. During that volatile week which preceded the game, Byrd had sent a package to Rex Ryan. That package contained a letter and the jersey that was carried on to the field; the one that he was wearing on the day he was paralyzed. Byrd had hung on to the jersey for eighteen years and felt that now was the right time to send it back to the Jets. Ryan was so moved by this that he asked Byrd to come in to the locker room and speak to the team.

Now, I'm not superstitious. I've never believed that anything fans can do at home will affect the outcome of the game. But before that game, I was looking for some kind of sign that we were gonna win. Maybe football drove me insane for that week (that's a lie; football drove me insane long before then), but I wanted to hear about an Inches speech from *Any Given Sunday* or a "Coach stays" moment like there was in *Hoosiers*. That turning point just *had* to happen at some point in that week. The Byrd speech and the jersey at the coin toss was it. I knew, after seeing and hearing about what happened, that the Jets were going to shock the world. Sometimes, fans just randomly get this sixth sense about games where they just *know* that their team is going to win or lose. I can't really explain when or why it happens; it's just one of those weird things that come with rooting for a team over a prolonged period of time. That sixth sense was triggered for me after seeing Dennis Byrd's jersey, a symbol of hope and courage throughout the organization, come out with the Jets to battle at the time where they needed it the most. They were going to win. It was that simple.

The Jets started with the ball and hung on to it for about three minutes before punting it back to the Patriots. Tom Brady then started driving the Patriots down the field, all the way from the New England sixteen yard line to the Jets' twenty-eight yard line. The vaunted Jet defense looked confused and out of place against the Patriot Machine. They were losing the battle up front and Brady was getting all the time he would ever need to throw the ball. Somebody, anybody, would need to make a big play to change the complexion of the game.

On first down and ten from the Jets' twenty-eight, Brady took the snap from under center. Pats' running back BenJarvus Green-Ellis approached the line of scrimmage and Brady faked handing off to him. Receiver Wes Welker ran behind Brady and he faked the reverse handoff to him too. Green-Ellis then swung out into the right flat for a screen pass. Ninety times out of a hundred, Brady completes that pass and it goes for at least a few yards. Nine times out of a hundred, Green-Ellis drops it or Brady throws it at his feet for an incomplete pass. Neither happened on this play. Brady, still backpedaling, lofted a wounded duck a foot over Green-Ellis' head. This thing just stayed in the air for what seemed like forever. It was the throw that you never, ever expect from Tom Brady. Jets' linebacker David Harris, who was running up to the line to make the tackle on Green-Ellis, suddenly found the ball floating right into his hands. After the catch, Harris streaked down the left side of the field before he was finally brought down at New England's twelve yard line. The Jets' sideline, which had previously stood paralyzed as Brady marched the Pats down the field, became a sea of raised fists and arms that furiously motioned towards the Jet end zone. New York had caught their first break of the night.

Naturally, they wasted that break when Nick Folk pushed a 30 yard field goal wide left on the ensuing drive. New England was able to tack on a field goal of their own near the end of the quarter to make the score 3-0 Pats at the end of the quarter. Still, gone was the dominance that the Patriots had exerted in the 45-3 game. Their offense looked apprehensive, cautious, maybe even a little bit confused. That first quarter was when it really dawned on me, "Wow, we're standing on even ground with the Patriots. We can do this."

After the two teams traded three and outs to start the second quarter, the Jets got the ball back. After two plays, the Jets faced third and six from the New England 45 yard line. Sanchez then lofted a beautiful pass to Braylon Edwards along the left sideline, who hauled the pass in with cornerback Darius Butler clinging to his jersey from behind. A few plays later, LaDanian Tomlinson caught a swing pass out of the backfield and dove into the endzone to give the Jets their first lead of the night. The ten point underdogs were now up 7-3 on the road against the Patriots.

The rest of the second quarter played out much the same way as it started; with the Patriots' offense being repeatedly stonewalled by the Jet defense. Since New England no longer had a guy like Randy Moss who could stretch the field vertically (he was traded mid-season that year), the Jet corners were getting up in the receivers' faces and jamming them at the line of scrimmage. Safeties crept up into the box. Cornerbacks immediately leaped to within inches of their receivers. The blitzes were coming from every direction and slowly confining Brady in an ever-shrinking pocket that began to look less like a pocket and more like a jar to which the Jets were simply sealing the lid.

In their December meeting, the Jets' defense sent only three or four rushers at Brady and dropped their secondary back in zone coverage, which fell right into the hands of the timing-reliant, highly precise Patriots' receivers. The Patriots might not have gotten that big fifty yard touchdown bomb, but they were able to pick up all of the nine yard digs and twelve yard curls at will. The Jets' defense was playing not to get beaten, and they ended up getting obliterated play by play. This time, they were playing like what they were; confident, ten-point underdogs with absolutely nothing to lose and everything to gain. All night long, Patriots' receivers were getting bumped off of their pre-designed routes and arriving at spots a second too late. The Jets had figured out how to beat the Patriots. We finally had the answers, and they couldn't change the questions.

It went on much the same way for most of the second quarter until a New England drive stalled at their own thirty-eight yard line with a minute and a half left before the intermission and they were forced to punt with the score still standing at 7-3. Suddenly, the ball was snapped not to the punter, but to punt protector Patrick Chung, who promptly dropped the football. Chung tried to run away from the Jet pursuit and towards the first down marker, but he was promptly swarmed under at the thirty-seven yard line. To this day, I don't know if the call was an accident or done on purpose. It was such an unbelievably lucky break that I didn't totally care at the moment. The Jets now had the ball back.

Unlike the last turnover, the Jets made the most of their opportunity. Mark Sanchez led the team down the shortened field and punctuated the drive with a slant route to Edwards, who caught the ball at the eight yard line and then started trudging towards the end zone with cornerback Devin McCourty hanging onto his back. I felt like I and everybody else in Jet nation was silently willing him towards that goal line. *"Come on, Braylon, you can do it, buddy. Just stay upright a little while longer . . . . just a little more . . . . almost there . . . . YEAAAAHHHHH!!!!!"* 14-3 Jets going into the break.

All throughout halftime, I couldn't sit still. I got up from the couch and walked around the house a little bit. I paced back and forth across the kitchen floor just thinking over and over again, *"We're about to beat the Patriots. It's going to happen."* That halftime felt like forever. I kept glancing back at the TV, hoping against hope that the game was back and I could finally stop waiting for something to happen. Finally, the ad for "Blue Bloods" started playing. Blue Bloods was a CBS show and networks always place the ads for their own shows right before the game is about to come back in order to rope in the "we used the commercials for a bathroom break/food run/beer run/ etc" people. Thirty minutes. That's all that stood between the Jets and the biggest win in the franchise's history since Super Bowl III. All they needed to do was hang on for thirty more minutes.

The first five minutes of the quarter passed uneventfully as both teams failed to move the ball past the fifty yard line and were forced to punt it away. On the Pats' second possession they faced second and ten at their own thirty-three yard line. As Brady dropped back to pass, Jet linebacker Calvin Pace began his rush into the backfield on the right end of the offensive line. He was working on Pats' tight end Alge Crumpler and was gradually pushing him back. Finally, he dipped his shoulder under Crumpler's outstretched arm and bore down on Brady, whose eyes were fixed downfield and to his left side. He had no idea that Pace was there. As I watched the play unfold, I knew that unless Brady got rid of the ball in the next second, he would get sacked. And since he didn't know that Pace was coming and thus wouldn't know to tuck the football in towards his chest, it was going to come out. That ball *had* to come out. Pace kept taking strides in Brady's direction as he continued to search for an open receiver downfield. Brady began to step up into the pocket as Pace launched himself at the exposed football . . . .

BAM!!!!

(I was channeling my inner John Madden for that one.)

Pace connected with Brady's shoulder and crashed to the ground on top of the helpless quarterback. The ball dropped to the grass like it had an anchor attached to it. Within a half-second, two Pats' offensive linemen dove for the football that was now bouncing around at their feet. Two Jets' defenders happily joined the scrum a quarter-second later. It looked like the ball bounced just out of the reach of the first Jet defender to have a play on it. After several seconds of pile-clearing, the ball emerged . . . . in the hands of New England running back BenJarvus Green-Ellis. For the first time, the Pats' crowd looked genuinely worried that their team would lose.

Most of the third passed uneventfully until the Patriots got the ball back with four minutes left in the quarter. Suddenly, Brady began to go to work. On the first play from scrimmage, Brady stood tall at his own twenty yard line and fired deep down the left side of the field for all-star tight end Rob Gronkowski, who had been relatively quiet for most of the day. Gronkowski made the catch amid two Jet defenders and rumbled all the way to the Jet 43. Suddenly, Gillette Stadium roared back to life. Fans started jumping up and down. Deafening chants echoed throughout the stadium as everybody began to believe in a New England comeback. Brady continued to give oxygen to the suddenly raging fire that was the Pats' crowd by completing more passes and driving his team closer to the end zone. He finished that drive with a two-yard touchdown pass to Alge Crumpler, followed by a direct snap to running back Sammy Morris for a two-point conversion. The crowd was going out of its mind. Gillette Stadium seemed to sway back and forth, rocked by the seemingly never-ending sea of fans in Pats' jerseys that enveloped the field. And that would be the way that the fourth quarter ended; with the Jets desperately clinging to a 14-11 lead, the Pats on the comeback trail, the crowd going bonkers, and me sweating bullets on the couch, desperately hoping that the Cardiac Jets would hold on for one more quarter.

The first thing that I noticed after the Jets trotted back onto the field for the fourth quarter was how calm Mark Sanchez looked. His face bore a blank expression and his body language was relaxed and nonchalant. He cavalierly strode to the Jets' huddle, barked out his play call, and took his place in the shotgun formation like it was any other play.

This may not sound significant, but there's absolutely nothing worse than being a fan of a team that's in a pressure-packed situation and then having the camera cut to your team's best player/coach, who looks just as terrified as you do. As soon as players and coaches start projecting that "Oh shit, I'm in way over my head" persona, a chain reaction is triggered that drags everybody's morale down. The psychological game is arguably more important than the physical one, and when you see team personnel openly showing signs that they lost that psychological battle, then the entire attitude of the team is changed for the worse. That can't happen. Especially not now. Little did I know that the greatest quarter in Jets' football history was about to unfold.

Mark Sanchez took the first snap of the fourth quarter on second down and six from his own twenty-nine yard line. To his left, wide receiver Jerricho Cotchery dodged the linebacker who was trying to jam him at the line of scrimmage and worked his way over the middle of the field in a wide pocket between two New England defenders. Sanchez stepped up into the pocket and delivered a perfect spiral to Cotchery, who caught the ball a few yards past the first down marker.

If he had been tackled after that catch, I would have been satisfied. Just pick up the first and continue the drive, right? But after a split second, I noticed that Cotchery had about twenty yards of open field ahead of him. After he caught the pass, he began running diagonally toward the right sideline. Around midfield, a Patriots' defender dove at Cotchery in a desperate attempt to bring him down, but Cotchery neatly sidestepped him and continued running. He would run all the way down to the New England thirteen yard line before finally being shoved out of bounds by Pats safety Brandon Meriweather. Gillette Stadium suddenly fell silent. It was like the stadium had an on/off switch that was just switched back into the "off" position.

Meanwhile, I'm going crazy on my family room couch. I'm running around the room with my arms outstretched like Santonio Holmes always did. (Yes, I would grow up immediately following the conclusion of this season.) It was finally starting to sink in that the Jets were no longer "hanging in there"; they had a legitimate chance to knock off the Patriots. It was something that I would have never imagined happening at any point before the Dennis Byrd moment at kickoff. My team was *right there*. Now, they just needed to close. And they did.

The Jets ended up facing third and four on the New England seven yard line. Sanchez took another snap from the shotgun and immediately turned to his left. Holmes, who was matched up one-on-one outside the numbers with Pats' corner Kyle Arrington, immediately began taking strides towards the back corner of the endzone. Sanchez lofted the ball up and in front of Holmes, who was being pressed up against the sidelines. The angle of Arrington's body relative to Holmes' position blocked him from being able to see the football. This one would have to be all timing. As the ball began its downward descent and the amount of space Holmes had to work with rapidly diminished, he extended his arms and leaped towards where the ball was coming down . . . .

For a second, I wasn't sure what had happened. Arrington also leapt for the ball and crashed down on top of Holmes as he went to the ground. Both players skidded a foot or two across the turf and stopped near the pylon in the back left corner of the endzone. And as Arrington rolled even further into out-of-bounds territory, Holmes' entire body was now visible . . . . up to and including the football that was tucked against his chest with both hands. But was he in bounds? Holmes immediately sat up and looked over to the ref for his signal. The ref slowly walked over to Holmes, both of his arms outstretched above his head. Holmes then looked up to the sky and slowly raised two clenched fists high above his head. He then let out a huge "YEEEEAAAAAAAHHHHHH!!!!" that was clearly audible even through the TV set. Every single Jet on the field came over to greet him in the endzone as he held both arms out, mirroring an airplane's wings in celebration as he'd done so often for that whole season. After about a minute of high-fives and chest bumps, the Jets' offense trotted back to the sideline. Ten point lead, thirteen minutes to play.

Meanwhile, I was going absolutely out of my mind. Jumping up and down, yelling, doing the Jet right along with Santonio Holmes, yelling "M-V-P!" for Mark Sanchez (in retrospect, I'd like to take that one back), and doing all of the other nonsensical things that fans do when their team is finally winning. *This is it*, I thought. *This is the Jets' time*. We were beating; no, *humiliating* the New England Patriots. We were bouncing back from 45-3, from Sal Alosi, from not scoring a touchdown for ten consecutive quarters, from forty-five years of almost perpetual futility. That was the kind of game that fans of every troubled team dreams of having, the moment when your team suddenly turns the world of sports upside down. We were in the process of doing just that. The minute Santonio Holmes' right knee hit the turf in bounds, the fortunes of the Jets were forever changed. Or so I thought.

Nothing eventful happened for the next ten minutes, really. The Pats took the ball after the Santonio Holmes catch and were able to put together a forteen play, forty-eight yard drive that took almost eight minutes off the clock and ended in a punt. That was the entire night for the Patriots in a nutshell. They played well, perhaps even well enough to win. Not once before the clock ticked down to 0:00 did the Jet players feel in any way assured of the fact that the Pats would fall. New England bent the Jet defense at several points throughout the game and looked like they were on the verge of breaking them. If David Harris doesn't intercept that Brady pass in the first quarter, if that fake punt is never called, if the Patriots would have only had a few plays unfold differently, then maybe they would have won. But after that failed drive, it became clear that they weren't going to.

The Pats were able to get the ball back with just over three minutes left and were able to advance far enough into Jet territory to kick a field goal, which made the score 21-14. They would have to try an onside kick in order to try and get the ball back before regulation ended.

Pats' kicker Shayne Graham set the ball on the tee to kick to a Jet formation that featured six players on the left side of the field, one in the middle, three on the right side, and one in the endzone in case the Patriots tried to kick the ball deep. Graham, whose body was aligned diagonally facing the left side of the field, raised his hand and began striding up to the ball. As his stride gradually turned into a jog, Graham suddenly swung his body towards the center of the field and gave the ball a little tap that sent it bouncing in between the hashmarks towards the lone Jet who stood in its path. The entire Patriots' formation ran after the ball and I'd say that seven of them got there within one second as compared to only two or three Jets. Uh-oh.

To pull off a role-reversal of this magnitude, you need a bounce or two to go your way. You need to start getting the breaks that your team has never quite gotten over the course of their history. Simply put, you need to be a little bit lucky with these things. When everything starts going your way, when every wayward pass falls incomplete, when you consistently win that game of inches for a first down, that's when you know that it could be your year. And so it was that the ball bounced around in a pile where Pats outnumbered Jets two to one, where it seemed natural for the Patriots to come from behind and the Jets to lose in the most agonizing way possible, where it made sense for the Pats to pull it out in the end. The ball stayed in that pile for about two seconds until a stray hand or foot knocked the ball out of the crush and towards the fifty yard line . . . . where a waiting Antonio Cromartie snatched it off the ground a fraction of a second before a Patriot defender got there.

If he had just fallen down right there on top of the ball, I would have been ecstatic. The Jets, for all intents and purposes, had won. But Cromartie didn't fall. Instead, he was able to run along the sidelines for twenty-three more yards while desperate Patriots tried to detach themselves from the pile after realizing that Cromartie had the ball. After he was bumped out of bounds, Cromartie faced the Gillette Stadium crowd and held his index finger to his mouth. Not that it was necessary, of course, because the entire stadium had fallen silent anyways.

Two plays later, running back Shonn Greene would stick the final dagger into the back of the Patriots and run for a fifteen yard touchdown to make the score 28-14 with under two minutes left to go in the fourth quarter. Greene, upon entering the endzone, placed the football on the ground and laid down, his head resting on the football. Immediately, the entire Jets' team crowded around him in celebration. Rex, who was standing at least twenty yards from the end zone on the sidelines, began huffing and puffing his way over to the celebration. The guy ran all the way downfield just to slap Greene on the back and be part of the big group hug going on in the endzone. The ref charged the Jets with a fifteen-yard unsportsmanlike conduct penalty for excessive celebration, as if anybody on either team actually cared. And, in the irony of ironies, the hand motion to signal an unsportsmanlike conduct penalty is outstretching both arms with the palms down to your right and your left. Just like Santonio Holmes' celebration. Yep, even the refs were doing the Jet. As was Greene. In fact, as was almost every single person on Gang Green's sideline. People were running up and down the sideline with their arms outstretched to their right and left, flying like Jets.

The Patriots were able to score a garbage time touchdown after that play to make the final score look a more palatable—a 28-21 loss looks a little bit better than a 28-14 loss—but the outcome was the same. New York lined up in the victory formation after recovering an onside kick with under a minute left in the game and took a knee. I counted the final seconds as they ticked off the clock, my mouth agape in disbelief. Everything that it took to get here . . . . *10, 9, 8,* all the years of believing . . . . *7, 6, 5* . . . . it was all worth it for this . . . . *4, 3, 2,* this one night . . . . *1.*

0. We beat the Patriots. The Jets just beat the Patriots.

Wait a second, did that actually happen?

Holy shit, we beat the Patriots.

I realize that using "we" throughout this book might seem a little bit ethically questionable. After all, *they* did all the work while I just sat on my couch and yelled at them through my TV set as if they could hear me. But when you go through a decade of futility, which was preceded by thirty-some years of more futility, hoping all the way that *something* magical would happen, and then it actually happens when you least expected it, how do you not feel like a part of everything? When you never stop hanging on, when you see just a little bit of light at the end of that tunnel and keep having faith that it's *not* just a figment of your imagination, that it *does* exist, you begin to feel like you're tied to your team for life. And to attain the ultimate validation as a fan, the knowledge that the little light you see is real and in front of you, is one of the greatest feelings in the world. So, yeah, I felt somewhat compelled to use "we" instead of "they" for such a personally significant moment.

On the field, bedlam was breaking out. Braylon Edwards did a backflip on the sidelines. Half the Jets' team stormed the field with their arms outstretched, flying like Jets after playing like Jets. In typical Jet fashion, some players took to trash-talking fans and other New England personnel. Linebacker Bart Scott was in the process of needling the Patriots' mascot when he was asked to do an interview by ESPN's Sal Paolantonio. He proceeded to run over in the Jet pose, take a knee in front of Paolantonio for his "landing", and then talk to him. The following italicized section is the transcript of that brief conversation.

Bart Scott: To all the non-believers! TO ALL THE NON-BELIEVERS! Especially you, Tom Jackson! Way to have our back, Keyshawn! ANYBODY CAN BE BEAT!

*(Tom Jackson and Keyshawn Johnson are both ESPN football analysts who
    picked the Patriots to win.)*
Sal Paolantonio: So how did that just feel?
*Bart Scott: It felt great; poetic justice. We know that we're a much better
    team and we came up and represented ourselves. And we were—we were
    pissed off. We were ready to come back and show what kind of a defense,
    what type of team this was, what type of character we had, we took a lot
    of slack. People gave us no chance like we barely made the playoffs, but
    we're a good football team!*
Sal Paolantonio: It looks like this team played with anger all day. Why, Bart?
*Bart Scott: Because of all you non-believers, disrespecting us, talk crap about
    the defense, and we're the third best defense in the league! All we hear is
    about their defense and they can't stop a nosebleed! 25th in the league,
    and we're the ones that get disrespected!*
Sal Paolantonio: Congratulations. See you in Pittsburgh.
Bart Scott: CAN'T WAIT!

That interview put the perfect exclamation point on the entire
evening. The Jets wanted it more than the Patriots did. They came out
pissed off and emotionally ready to win at all costs. Nobody gave the
Jets anything resembling a chance, but they beat the odds. I'm in no way
ashamed to say it was one of the ten greatest nights of my life. I ended up
watching TV for two and a half hours afterwards because I was so happy
that I had no idea what to do with myself. I think I ended up walking my
dog at like 12:30 that night for a little while just to burn off some steam
and try to process what had happened. Ultimately, I couldn't do it and
just had to settle for shaking my head and smiling.

You know, after that game, I would have imagined that anything was
possible for the Jets. We had crossed that unspoken threshold, the one that
every burgeoning Super Bowl contender needs to cross. We could win the
Super Bowl that season. We could take the AFC East from the Patriots. We
might be the next team of the decade. *Anything* was possible. Anything.

Little did I know that the night of January 16th, 2011 was the
pinnacle of the Ryan era. They would never be any better or come closer
to the ultimate endgame during my childhood than they did on that
evening in Foxborough.

CARDIAC MARK

After the meltdown of 2008 and the inevitable exit of Broadway Brett, one thing became immediately apparent. We needed a quarterback. We needed somebody who we could take into battle against Tom Brady and the Patriots, somebody who would elevate the team to the next level, somebody who we could toss the keys to and be 100% sure that he wouldn't crash the car. We wanted somebody that would finally carry on the legacy of Joe Namath, somebody who would take the Jets back to being world champions and establish a dynasty in New York. So, we traded up to the 5th pick of the 2009 draft and took USC quarterback Mark Sanchez.

Yes, I know, it's really funny for all of you non-Jet fans in retrospect. Come on, stop laughing, you're making me feel terrible: even worse than I did while writing the last paragraph . . . . O.K., ten more seconds of laughing and that's *it*, you hear me? 10 . . . . 9 . . . . 8 . . . . 7 . . . . 6 . . . . 5 . . . . 4 . . . . 3 . . . . 2 1

Alright, we're back. This may sound a little bit strange coming from somebody who has been consistently frustrated by Mark Sanchez over the last five years, but I don't think that bringing him to the Jets was a bad move. It turned out badly, which I guess is all that really matters, but I can appreciate that the process and logic behind it was fairly sound. The Jets desperately needed a QB, there were no good ones on the free agent market or up for trade, and Brett Favre was never coming back to New York after the season that he had just gone through. I'm not so sure that the fans would have even wanted him back anyways. That meant the only recourse the Jets had was the draft. Now, the three starting-caliber QBs available in that draft were Matt Stafford, Mark Sanchez, and Josh Freeman. Stafford was going with the first pick to the Detroit Lions and there was nothing anybody could do about it. This was the draft immediately after they went 0-16, so there was no chance they were giving that number one pick up. I mean, they just went winless for an entire freaking season. They needed all the help they could get. That left trading up for Sanchez or staying at pick number seventeen and taking Kansas State product Josh Freeman as the Jets' only options if they wanted a QB.

I've always believed that there are two very distinct ways that people can screw up. The first way is the kind of decision where it's easy to say what should have been done after the fact, but it was explainable at the time. The second way is the kind that make you scream, "Wait a second, what the hell is going on?" as the situation is unfolding. The move to bring in Sanchez is definitely the former, and not the latter. I'm a big fan of teams who take the initiative and leverage all of the assets that they have to make significant moves. As much as I have, can, and will complain about the Jets throughout this book, their willingness to take chances and spend both money and assets (occasionally) is something that I have to commend them for. I took another look at the video of Mark Sanchez being drafted, and Jet fans were beside themselves. There were some assorted boos from the healthy minority of Patriot fans in attendance, but almost every single camera shot of the crowd in the ensuing five minutes shows Jet fans applauding, starting "J-E-T-S" chants, and generally losing their minds. I hold former GM Mike Tannenbaum accountable for a lot of stuff that contributed to the Jets' collapse, but this is not one of them.

Actually, I wasn't even watching the draft on TV. In fact, I usually try to change the channel when the Jets are up because watching them draft is like watching in horror as a drunk surgeon grabs a scalpel and tries to perform a triple bypass. I was in the car and going to my piano recital (shout-out to my piano teacher, Mrs. Marsh!). My Grandpa was in the passenger's seat and he heard the news from my Uncle Jamer, who is always armed with his iPhone and readily available updates. The Jets had traded up and picked Mark Sanchez. Grandpa then relayed that message on to me and I was immediately hit by a wave of . . . . .not much. I just kind of shrugged my shoulders and said, "Oh, cool, we have a quarterback now." Considering how much I would think about, worry about, analyze, scream at, defend, and generally try to figure out Mark Sanchez over the next four years, it seems comical in retrospect. It was almost like I was in the eye of what would soon become Category 5 Emotional Hurricane Mark.

His first season certainly started out well enough. The Jets won their first three games of the season, in Houston, home against the hated Patriots, and home against the Tennessee Titans. He became the first rookie quarterback to ever start and win the first three games of his NFL season. He even won Rookie of the Week in all three of those weeks. The Jets were starting to form a strong identity that was spearheaded by a physical running game, a murderous defense, and a poised rookie QB. He was unflappable, on point, and read all of his progressions correctly. If I had no clue who he was and I just watched those three games, I would have guessed that he had played in the league for at least five or six years. I was in heaven for the whole month of September in 2009. We had a good QB in one of the cushiest possible situations. We had a team that looked like it could win both now and in the fairly distant future. Perhaps most importantly, we had a guy who would finally carry on the banner of Joe Namath and lead the Jets to a title. After those three weeks, I would have bet absolutely *anything* that Sanchez was the one that the Jets had been waiting for all of these years. He was our franchise quarterback, and the New York media had already given him their blessing with a catchy new nickname; the Sanchise.

And then, the Sanchise started to become unglued as the Jets lost their next three games. In those three games, Sanchez completed 45% of his passes (ouch), threw one touchdown and eight interceptions (ew), averaged 143 yards per game (currently sobbing), and averaged a 41.0 passer rating (I.. I don't even know what to say). As Sanchez's statistics eroded, so did his confidence. He looked abjectly terrified to come back out on the field after throwing an interception. After every single one of his bad throws, I would immediately begin hoping that the camera wouldn't show a close-up of his face because then I'd see how utterly helpless he looked. I felt bad for the guy; he was trying his best to make something happen and he was doing and saying all of the right things, but for whatever reason, he just couldn't make anything work.

After the Jets seemingly got back on track with a 38-0 evisceration of the Oakland Raiders (incidentally, the game that featured the now-infamous moment where cameras caught Sanchez eating a hot dog on the sideline), the Jets dropped their next three games to the Dolphins, Jaguars, and Patriots. At that point, I was ready to give up hope both on the Jets and on Sanchez. There were whispers that he had come out of college too early, that he didn't work as hard during the season as he did back in March when the eyes of scouts were on him, that he didn't have the arm strength to make it in the NFL, and that he was really a local pop warner quarterback in disguise. (OK, that last one was slightly exaggerated.) His TD-INT numbers at this point were 10-16 and he missed wide open receivers at least three times per game.

Before the Jets' next game against the Carolina Panthers, word came out that the Jets were going to use a color-coded system to simplify the playbook for Sanchez. He actually trotted out for that game wearing a red, yellow, and green colored play-coach on his wrist. The meaning of these colors, from my hazy recollection of the New York Daily News story, were essentially:

Red Play: Whatever you do, don't turn it over. Seriously, take a knee for all we care, just don't effing turn it over.
Yellow Play: Please, please, please don't turn it over.
Green Play: Ah, what the hell, we're either up or down by so much that a turnover won't make any difference. Go ahead, bomb it forty yards downfield into double coverage.

It was hilarious and sad all at the same time. Our rookie QB, the savior, the Sanchise, was so inept at on-the-field decision-making that we had to reduce our playbook to the football equivalent of See Spot Run just so we would get to hold on to the ball for more than three minutes at a time.

Whatever was in that Baby's First Playbook, it must have worked. The Jets recorded a 5-1 record in their last six games, propelling them into the playoffs. Over those last six regular season games (and the ensuing playoff contests, which would make nine games total), Mark Sanchez had thirty or more pass attempts in exactly two of them. Take a step back and try to appreciate how absurd that is. In today's hurry-up, spread formation, shotgun, can't-destroy-receivers-when-they-cross-over-the-middle-anymore era, quarterbacks' pass attempts regularly go into the forties. Some QBs average almost fifty pass attempts per game. Yet there were the Jets, going the complete opposite direction with their young QB.

On the one hand, it was great that the Jets were winning and I didn't care how it happened, given their tortured history. But in retrospect, it probably wasn't a great thing that the Jets' offensive game plan which led to their most successful stretch in the last decade was largely based around having their "franchise" QB do as little as humanly possible. Between allowing Sanchez to throw the ball only twenty times per game, running the ball two plays out of three, and generally prevailing in the most boring way possible, the Jets were perfectly suited to win the 1972 Super Bowl. All because Mark Sanchez couldn't be trusted in the least.

As anybody who read my last book knows, I love Football Outsiders. They probably have the best football site on the entire Internet and they really should have gotten co-author credit on my first book. Well, the first column ever written on that site debunked the myth that teams need to "establish the run" in order to win. Essentially, they asserted that teams are running because they're winning (in order to run the clock down or to make it less likely for a turnover to occur) and not the other way around. The public and the football media, they argued, were putting the effect before the cause.

Why do I mention this? Because a similar phenomena occurred with Mark Sanchez over those last nine games. At the beginning of that stretch, everybody rightfully denounced Sanchez as unfit to be a starting NFL quarterback. He was frustrating, wildly inconsistent, and a guy that made me shield my eyes and say, "please, dear God, just not an intercept—whew, only an incomplete pass." (Browns fans can relate.) But then, the Jets pulled off that 5-1 run and went deep into the playoffs. Suddenly, Mark Sanchez's stats moved up from "abysmal" to "below average" and everybody was commenting on how much more focused/relaxed/in control/(fill in complement here) he looked. Because the Jets were jumping out to early leads on some bad teams (Carolina, Buffalo, Tampa, an overrated Cincinnati squad, etc), they could afford to yank the ball out of Sanchez's hands sooner and give it to the competent half of the Jets' backfield; the two-headed running back attack of Thomas Jones and Shonn Greene. And because Sanchez had dramatically fewer chances to screw things up, he didn't screw things up nearly as much. That's it. He didn't really contribute anything more to the Jets' chances of victory, but he sure looked better because his name was attached to it. Thus was created the delusion that Sanchez was a "winner" who "delivered when it counted" and possessed the necessary "intangibles" to succeed. In the middle of a Jets' winning streak, who was going to bring up that his tangibles still sucked? Certainly not fans who needed hope and writers who had column inches to fill. Oh, and least of all, me.

After the end of the 2009 season, I was one hundred percent back in on Mark Sanchez. When your team hasn't been a serious contender for at least a decade and they've made exactly one Super Bowl in your fifty years of existence, you start believing in anything. Anything at all. Which is why I asked for a Mark Sanchez t-shirt jersey for my birthday and started developing convoluted arguments for why he was something greater than what he was; an average quarterback. I looked past just about every glaring flaw and tried to make excuses for twelve touchdowns and twenty-three interceptions.

He's young. He's just learning the system. Maybe the offensive scheme was way different at USC. His receivers were at fault for at least half of his interceptions. Rex is entirely focused on the defense and doesn't spend enough time developing him. He'll get there.

And every single time I made this argument to anyone other than a Jets fan, they remained utterly unmoved. The polite people dismissed it with a "well, we'll just have to wait and see" or a "let's hope so." The people who decided to speak a little bit more freely about Sanchez told me that I was an idiot and vehemently rebuffed my argument. And by "people who decided to speak a little bit more freely", I mean every single one of my friends.

Twelve touchdowns, twenty-three interceptions. Awful mechanics. It's like he doesn't see the defense at all. Overrated. The Jets won in spite of him, not because of him. Had one of the worst QB ratings in the league. He's never going to get there.

In retrospect, they were one hundred percent right. But that's what fans do when we really want a particular player to succeed; we talk ourselves into him. We distort facts and twist logic around in order to make a guy seem better than he is, hoping against hope that he'll live up to what we want him to be. We build him up as much as possible and pray that we never end up breaking him down. Even with modern society's extreme tendency towards cynicism (especially in sports), a little part of every fan wants to believe that this player will be The One. So we hold on and hope, often longer than we should. Sometimes, it ends up paying off. In Mark Sanchez's case, it didn't.

Still, for a brief window of time, it seemed like it would. Sanchez entered the 2010 season much improved. He didn't look scared anymore. Instead, he looked like everything that you'd ever say about a run-of-the-mill starter: competent, not that bad, capable of throwing footballs for a decent team, fairly good mechanics, average, and a guy that you could start at QB without getting mercilessly ripped to shreds in the press. He looked like he finally learned to step into his throws and drive through the ball on deep passes. His pocket presence and ability to handle defensive pressure was, if not good, at least passable. There were some 300 yard games, three touchdown performances, and other measurable things that would indicate a solid NFL starter. Maybe he wouldn't be the next Brady or the next Manning, but he looked like a guy that the Jets could win a Super Bowl with *if* the rest of the team was good enough. At the very least, he was no longer seen as a liability to the Jets' Super Bowl chances, contrary to the overwhelmingly well-supported offseason opinion that the Jet defense would have to drag him by his hair into the playoffs.

Of course, since the Jets were 9-2 and the average New York City resident had at least *heard* of Mark Sanchez, he instantly became plastered on the cover of every single tabloid in town and the subject of sportswriter's columns the world over. The "Sanchise" moniker that had been declared over just one year prior was suddenly revived from the dead by the substantial groundswell that had begun to grow for the Jets. They were the league's most popular team and Sanchez was the most recognizable face of all of them. He was the one who dated Jamie-Lynn Sigler. He was the one who made cameos on *Saturday Night Live*. When the local news played the clips from Jet games on Monday, his postgame interview was the first (and often the only) interview they showed. People, especially casual fans, gravitated towards the guy, and the media followed with headline after headline.

Still, I couldn't shake this nagging feeling that he wasn't the one we were looking for. Your franchise QB shouldn't make you hold your breath on every single throw. He shouldn't be handing it off more times than he throws it, especially not in 2010, the most pass-happy year in the history of the league. And why exactly were announcers clamoring for Jets management to "take the training wheels off Mark Sanchez" and let him throw the ball more? (This was a popular cliche at the time.) I mean, shouldn't it say something fairly substantial that those training wheels were still on in the first place? So even though I would never, ever admit it to my friends (and *especially* not to Matt), I had a sneaking suspicion that he would never be what everybody touted him as; a franchise quarterback. However, he still needed a nickname for me to scream with joy at my TV whenever he came through in the clutch as I pretended to have never doubted him. The 1980 Cleveland Browns were known as the Cardiac Kids because they won several games that were decided in the final seconds, so I just ripped off that nickname and gave it to Sanchez. And thus was born unto the world my enduring name for one of the most up-and-down, enigmatic, and bewildering quarterbacks in the league: Cardiac Mark.

Cardiac Mark, although fairly mediocre, led the 2010 Jets (who ended up finishing 11-5) to five wins that were only decided in the game's closing seconds. Every throw from Cardiac Mark could go for an eighty yard touchdown or an eighty yard pick-six the other way. Nobody ever (and I do mean *ever*) felt good about putting the ball in his hands with two minutes left and the game on the line, and yet he would always pull through somehow. He could throw a beautiful thirty yard go route to Santonio Holmes on one play and then fumble the snap or throw an interception into triple coverage only twenty seconds later. He was infuriating, frustrating, occasionally joy-inspiring, and never boring. (Mostly for the wrong reasons, but still.) Put it to you this way: If I was watching the Jets game with a bunch of friends and left to go to the bathroom, then came back and one of them told me, "You have *got* to see what Mark Sanchez just did", I would be in complete terror. *Oh no, what did he do this time?* That's the Cardiac Mark experience in a nutshell.

And yet, he just kept stepping in between raindrops. A game-tying and game-winning drive to beat the Detroit Lions in overtime. A game-ending touchdown pass to beat the Cleveland Browns in overtime. Another game-winning touchdown to beat the Houston Texans with under thirty seconds left on the clock. Three straight weeks, three games won courtesy of Cardiac Mark. Jets fans at this point were like Al Pacino in The Godfather Part III; just when we thought we were out, Mark Sanchez pulled us all back in. If you were to pose the "Two minutes left, down by a field goal, ball at your own twenty, who would you want leading the game-winning drive?" question to the majority of educated and impartial fans in 2010, Sanchez might not have made the top five on a single person's list. Yet, he continued to deliver clutch throws and big wins against all evidence pointing to the fact that he shouldn't be.

Most fans that I've met, no matter how hard they try to disguise it, are optimists. They can never stop believing, deep down, in the lucky breaks and little omens and the one perfect season where all the stars align and you win it all even though you have no idea how the hell it happened. Beneath all the naysaying and heartache and old hopes that disappeared as suddenly as they appeared, fans can never stop believing. It's why we're called fans, after all. And as Mark Sanchez's string of improbable competency grew longer and longer, both myself and many other Jet fans started to say, *"If the Bucs won the Super Bowl with Brad Johnson and the Ravens won the Super Bowl with Trent Dilfer, why can't we win it all with Mark Sanchez?"* When the Jets' win streak hit four (their second such win streak of the season), everybody was in "Screw it, we can *absolutely* win a Super Bowl with Mark Sanchez" mode. Yeah, he would probably never have his name mentioned in the same breath with the league's top-flight QBs, but it didn't need to be. All Mark Sanchez needed to attain was competency. All we needed him to do was make the occasional big throw and hold on to the ball, two things that he had shown he was able to do. So by the time of that December 6th Pats' game, I was ready to believe in Mark Sanchez again. I believed that we could go all the way with Cardiac Mark at the helm. Seriously, why couldn't the next Super Bowl-winning QB be Mark Sanchez?

Well, over the course of the 45-3 game, the Patriots showed us why it couldn't be Mark Sanchez. All of the old habits, everything that every single Jets fan was secretly worried would manifest itself at the worst possible time, ended up manifesting themselves at, wouldn't you know it, the worst possible time. Just like fans never stop believing, they also never stop worrying. In this particular case, everybody knew that Sanchez hadn't grown out of that terrified, inconsistent persona that he had assumed during his rookie year. The only two things that any Jet fan could do were hope and worry. Hope, desperately, that the old Sanchez would never show up again, and worry endlessly that he was going to. Very few things feel worse as a fan than worrying about your favorite player and having those fears come true. You know, kind of like they did in that Patriots game.

I can only attempt to describe the startling transformation that Sanchez underwent on that night in Foxborough. By the second quarter, the score was already 17-0 and the poor guy stopped looking for receivers downfield. Instead, his eyes danced from his offensive line to the Patriot secondary and back again. The guy was so obviously terrified of making a mistake that it began to take over his body language and play on the field. It turned into a sort of self-fulfilling prophecy; he tried so hard to do anything he could to avoid making mistakes that he was often forced into taking sacks which he had no business taking and throwing passes into non-existent windows as the Patriot pass rush closed in on him. Since fans (as well as players) often take their cues from the team's most visible player, I also reverted back to being abjectly terrified that he was going to screw things up. Every single scrap of confidence that Sanchez might have inspired in me vanished on that one night.

That game started a stretch where the Jets' offense was kept out of the end zone for nine straight quarters. Sanchez looked like he just wanted off the field in the worst way possible, and his receivers were happy to help any way they could. Once he snapped the ball and finished his dropback, he seemed to keep bouncing up and down in the pocket instead of setting his feet and stepping up, as if he didn't trust anybody around him. He didn't trust his offensive line to block, his receivers to run the correct routes, and least of all, himself to make a good throw.

Have you ever been a fan of a team or a player that, try as they might, just couldn't seem to get out of their own way? Or, to put it in non-sports fan terms, have you ever tripped and fallen on your own shoelaces? Well, the Jet offense (especially Sanchez) between the beginning of Week 13 and the end of Week 15 was like watching someone trip on their own shoelaces, fall down, get back up, fall on their own shoelaces again, and then get sucker-punched as they try to regain their footing. If you're a sports fan for long enough, you've undoubtedly experienced what I'm talking about. It's unbelievably agonizing to hope against hope that your streaky point guard remembers how to hit jumpers, that your closer can finish games the way he was just a month ago, that your quarterback will somehow regain the confidence to step up in the pocket and throw a decent spiral, and know deep down that it's not going to happen. For all you people who are reading this book to learn more about fans, *this* is the kind of stuff that makes us yell at TVs and invent new curse words on the fly. It all comes back to the greatest fear of sports fans, the ever-present spectre of getting no return on a tremendous investment of hope. So when Sanchez, a player that had been improving by leaps and bounds throughout the season, started looking like just another in a long string of disappointments, I completed the process of bailing on him once again. Never again would I ever be fooled into thinking that Mark Sanchez was anything but a mediocre quarterback on his best day.

Then, the playoffs happened and the Jets clawed their way to within two games of winning the Super Bowl. Even more shockingly, Mark Sanchez suddenly became the quarterback that the Jets had desperately needed him to be. He was assertive, smart with the football, and kept key offensive drives going on crucial plays. Every single throw that he needed to make was on point and accurate. Hell, he even had a few genuinely impressive playoff moments. There was the back-of-the-endzone throw against the Pats to Santonio Holmes. There was also the eighteen-yard out route to Braylon Edwards that set up Nick Folk's game-winning field goal to beat the Colts, a play that Sanchez himself called after dismissing whatever dumb play Brian Schottenheimer recommended. (Knowing what Jets fans now know about Schotty, it was probably a halfback draw or some such garbage.) He even played most of the playoffs relatively mistake-free.

For the first time in a long time, Jets fans poured every iota of faith that they could into something *and it actually happened.* Over the course of those first two games, it seemed like Sanchez had transformed his career and defined what he was going to be going forward. He would never be a fantastic statistical quarterback. Nor would he ever draw the praise from announcers that other QBs did. But if he just held on to the football and could make a play or two per game, then maybe it would all work out. Maybe he could still be Joe Namath. Maybe he could still be the guy that every single Jets fan thought they would get when he was drafted. Maybe he would finally be the one that the legion of Jets' faithful had wanted for so long. Maybe.

Still, though, we all approached him with a great deal of pensiveness. Sure, we all liked Sanchez. I mean, he was the quarterback of our team, a squad which nearly made a Super Bowl and was on the verge of potentially making a second. And on top of that, he seemed like a genuinely kind, well-spoken guy. How could you not love that? We all liked Mark, rooted for Mark, bought Mark jerseys, and generally convinced ourselves that he would be hoisting the Lombardi Trophy over his head in just a few weeks. But deep down, very few, if any, Jet fans ever totally trusted Mark. At the end of his second year, people were still holding their breath on every throw. Every Jet fan worried about whether the Sanchez that showed up last week was the same guy that would show up this week.

When you attach so much faith to someone who you don't fully trust and whose performance changes radically from week to week, you start seeing a similar pattern emerging within the team. Sometimes, you get the best from your team and it takes you to highs that you never thought possible. It's one of the greatest feelings ever, when a person or group of people who you desperately want to succeed actually succeeds against all odds.

But that's the danger in rooting for a team like the Jets and a player like Mark Sanchez; there's always a chance it could all come crashing down. And just as frequently as a situation brings out the best in your team, it could also bring out the worst. That's why it was emotionally dangerous to be a Jet fan; they're so unstable. No matter how much success you feel like you've helped them achieve, no matter how much you persuade yourself that Mark Sanchez was another Tom Brady, it doesn't change the fact that there's this little, nagging voice in the back of your head that tells you that it can't possibly last. The worst part is that after awhile, you start believing it.

And that's maybe the best way to describe what it was like to watch Mark Sanchez. I loved the highs and badly wanted them to last forever. Yet the lows would come so frequently and hit such depths that I knew that the highs were merely transitory. Cardiac Mark was really the perfect nickname for him. Just like the lines on a heart rate monitor, he would reach these fleeting peaks, and fall back down to Earth. And, if we're going to take the moniker a little more literally, he gave every single Jet fan at least one mini-heart attack at some point. But in the end, these weren't the same old Jets and this wasn't just another bad quarterback. No matter how many times he would lose the fanbase's trust, he would find some way to get it back, and it was usually when the Jets absolutely needed him at his best. He was inconsistent, but his best stretches came at the right moments every single time. After two years, I was convinced that I had finally figured out Mark Sanchez and the Jets had finally found the answer to their quarterback question, the one that had eluded them ever since Namath.

Well, I was wrong about both of those conclusions; something that would become readily apparent when the Jets took on Pittsburgh the next week.

TURBULENCE

Contrary to what the Jets' postgame celebrations and the tabloid coverage of the team would suggest, the Patriots game was not the Super Bowl. The Jets did, in fact, have to play another team after that. More specifically, they would have to play and win two more games to get to their ultimate goal; the first one being against the Steelers in Heinz Field for the AFC Championship game and, of course, their eventual Super Bowl opponent. They would never get to play that second game.

From the moment the Jets lined up against the Steelers on that frigid January Sunday, I could tell that something was different. There was just no *edge* to them. The Steelers approached the game with a strategy that was a little bit different than New England's air attack. This strategy mainly consisted of pounding the Jets into submission up front. The New York Jets' defense, the self-made bullies of the NFL, was suddenly getting driven backwards by the Steelers' offensive line. Pittsburgh running back Rashard Mendenhall was slowly, inch by inch, beating the Jets backward. Five yards here. Six yards there. Third-down conversion to keep the drive going. It was just demoralizing to watch your team's identity slowly being taken away. I knew that it would take one play-just *one play*—to turn the whole thing around. Looking back on it, I also knew deep down that it was never going to happen. The Steelers entered the locker room at halftime up 24-3, having bulldozed the entirety of the New York Jets.

But because they're the Jets, they had to dangle some hope in front of me. Sanchez threw a beautiful downfield strike to Santonio Holmes to make the score 24-10 as the third quarter ended. I decided that even if the Jets lost, I would still be naming my kid Santonio someday. (I've since changed my mind about that; more on this in a few pages.) The Jets continued their forward surge in the fourth quarter by getting the ball back and driving the ball all the way down to the Steelers' two yard line.

Now, let me paint the picture for you here. I'm a nervous wreck. I've been standing up in front of the TV since the half started. I can't find it in myself to relax to the point where I could even *consider* sitting down. I'm hyperventilating, have tossed a stress ball back and forth between my hands a couple hundred times, and feel unrelentingly nauseous.

Everything around me other than the game seems like white noise. Any sane person goes to bed at this point, especially with a history midterm the next day. Me? I'm not sane. No matter what happened, I *had* to know what would happen next. Hindsight being 20/20, brushing my teeth and bolting for bed would have been the correct choice.

On the first play from the Steelers' two yard line, Shonn Greene runs up the middle for a yard and a half. You practically couldn't get any closer to the end zone without being in it. Suddenly, the camera cuts to Sanchez running over to the sidelines towards Brian Schottenheimer, presumably to receive the play call. He had done this several times throughout the drive and he was doing it again. I'd estimate that he wasted at least two minutes of game time doing this, which isn't ideal when you're trying to come back from a two touchdown deficit on the road with limited time left. As it turned out, Sanchez's helmet headset had malfunctioned and he had to run back and forth between Schottenheimer and the huddle to get the play call and communicate it to his teammates. (I swear that this shit seems to happen to the Jets and *nobody* else. Yes, I fully believe that one of the Jets' employees was a double agent under orders from Bill Belichick to screw with the headsets. And yes, I'm a perfectly reasonable person; why do you ask?) But nobody knew that at the time. All we knew at the time was that Sanchez had thrown two minutes of clock or more down the drain. I often think about what could have happened if only the Jets had those extra two minutes.

Mark Sanchez was then forced to call two passing plays in a row, both of which fell incomplete. After all, what could he do? If he called a run and it couldn't get through to the end zone, Sanchez would have to take off another thirty seconds running back to the sideline. The drive would end one play later when running back LaDainian Tomlinson was stuffed at the line of scrimmage, mere inches away from scoring.

I felt my face reddening. My hands curled themselves into fists. I spent roughly a minute looking around for something to punch or throw that I wouldn't break. Because of the Jets' failure, something would have to endure my furious and terribly uncoordinated punches. Finding nothing else suitable, I ultimately decided that the pillow on the couch would have to do. Thankfully, my parents were smart and had left the room an hour ago. They'd learned, after all of these years, to evacuate when the Jets were losing a big game. The Steelers lined up for their first play from the one yard line just as I was about to go to town on that poor, innocent pillow. The next thing I knew, I heard Jim Nantz yelling something. I can't remember quite what he said, but I just remember hearing the word "fumble." I quickly flicked my eyes back towards the TV to see a pile-up of players fighting over the ball. Ben Roethlisberger had dropped the snap and the Steelers pounced on it in their own end zone. That's a safety; two points for the Jets and the football back. 24-12 Steelers with half of the fourth quarter left. We weren't dead yet.

Mark Sanchez proceeded to lead the Jets down the field on a ten play, fifty-eight yard drive that led to a four yard touchdown pass to Jerricho Cotchery. 24-19 with three minutes left to go. This was going to be it. We had finally gotten our version of Tom Brady's nullified fumble in the Snow Game with Roethlisberger's botched snap. We rallied from twenty-four down in Pittsburgh to the very edge of victory. Our embattled QB had constructed a nearly flawless second half and was finally becoming the guy that everybody knew he could be. The Statue of Liberty was adorned in green, just like it had been at this time in 2009, as uncountable thousands of Jet fans all hoped that the gears of football history would turn in the next three minutes. This should have been our moment.

The Steelers converted one first down early in the drive, but Gang Green used all three of their timeouts and every ounce of defensive integrity they had left to force the Steelers into a third down and six situation. If they converted that third down, the clock would wind down to zero. If not, then the Jets would have one last chance to make a miracle. Of course, right before this play, the most important play of the Jets' season, the two-minute warning happened.

Have you ever heard somebody say that waiting in line for the roller coaster is worse than the roller coaster itself? Do you remember what it felt like when you were a little kid and sat in the doctor's waiting room before a shot? This was a thousand times worse. I was *dying*. Mom, who had re-entered the family room, tried to tell me some kind of funny story about what had happened at work the previous week, but I couldn't hear a word she said. All I kept thinking was, *"Oh my God. This is it."* Those commercials seemed to go on forever, the tension growing by the moment. (Note to Dad, who had also come back into the room; this was decidedly *not* the best time to yell, "GO STEELERS!" Although, I probably shouldn't have expected anything else.) Finally, after what was surely a couple of hours, the CBS score graphic popped up and Jim Nantz welcomed the audience back to Heinz Field. At this juncture in time, I sincerely wanted my parents to leave the room, but I knew I couldn't say that. All I could do was watch.

Pittsburgh QB and prospective Jet-killer Ben Roethlisberger took the snap from the shotgun formation on third and six. He stood tall in the pocket, scanning the field as the Jets' pass rush began to collapse in on him. Inch by inch the defensive line closed ground as Roethlisberger began running out of places to go. Suddenly, at the last possible second, he dashed to his right and cleared the collapsing pocket. Jets' safety Eric Smith, fearing that Roethlisberger might try to take off running with the football, broke coverage. He dashed forward from eight yards downfield as Roethlisberger took huge strides toward the line of scrimmage, giving every indication that he wanted to run. All of a sudden, he pulled up, his feet skirting the line, and began his throwing motion. Pittsburgh wideout Antonio Brown, the man that Smith was covering, had become open immediately after Smith ran up to the line. Uh-oh. The ball elegantly spun its way directly into the hands of Brown, who nestled it against his chest and fell down to the ground. Game over. Jets' season over. It all took about four and a half seconds.

The look that immediately sprung to my face must have clearly told my parents that they should not even attempt to interact with me. I silently walked up to my room and closed the door. Once there, the waterworks started. I'm guessing that I must have bawled my eyes out for at least five minutes straight without stopping. Coupled with the river's worth of tears were childish and inane utterings of "Why?" and "It's not fair!" interspersed with various R-rated words I'd picked up over the years. If you walked into my room for those five minutes and knew nothing about me, you'd have probably guessed that somebody I knew had become seriously ill or died. Nope. All this was over the Jets' season. And I was a Freshman in high school.

The next morning, I woke up and said to myself, "This *has* to stop. I can't keep doing this." Yeah, what happened sucked. Big time. But at some point, I would have to move past the point of caring this much. And that's what happened. I never cried or even came close to crying over football again because I finally came to my senses and realized that sports are sports. Shit happens. In a way, I'm almost grateful for the loss because the lesson learned from it was one that needed to be learned at some point in my life. Besides, there's always next year . . . . right?

Well, not exactly. See, the NFL players' union and the owners have a collective bargaining agreement that governs how the league operates. Everything from salary caps to TV revenue splits to acceptable sock length is either directly or indirectly covered in the CBA. Well, before the 2010 season, the NFL owners decided to exercise their opt-out clause on the current CBA and wanted to negotiate a new one, mainly to ensure themselves a greater share of the ever-growing pool of television money. That didn't necessarily sit well with the players, who essentially told the owners that they can stick their new revenue-sharing proposal where the sun don't shine. With the two sides practically separated by the Snake River Canyon and *nobody* on either side particularly concerned about offending the fans, there was only one way to proceed after the 2010 buffer season ended. L-O-C-K-O-U-T.

More than every single loss, bad management decision, inexcusable draft screw-up, and calamity that I'd experienced as a die-hard fan of the New York Jets, this was the one event that put sports into perspective for me. Yes, the Jets made me want to tear my hair out and occasionally question my existence on planet Earth, but at least they always seemed to give a crap that they were losing. This one, the group of people that ran football wantonly disregarding every single supporter on the face of the Earth, hurt in an entirely new kind of way. After all, it becomes a whole lot easier to not care about somebody after watching them demonstrate utter indifference towards you.

You see, sports fans deservedly have a strong sense of entitlement when it comes to the player/owner/fan relationship. We're the ones that pour money, loyalty, reverence, and whatever else we have into what essentially amounts to glorified entertainment. Everybody, deep down, knows how fundamentally illogical it is to do this, to throw away hard-earned resources on a game, but we keep doing it anyways. And we're fine with that, as demonstrated by sports' ever-expanding financial and cultural reach. But in return, we ask a few things of these people. Namely, we ask that they care about us. Don't whine about having to sign autographs for fifteen minutes after you walk out of the locker room. Don't flip off the press after a loss. Always give a crap on the field. (And if you can't, then fake it.) Thank us after the season is over. If you see us in a bar, maybe even buy a round. For owners, be willing to sit outside the luxury box once in awhile. Perhaps even keep ticket prices at a semi-reasonable level. Essentially, we want the people who make money off of sports to always remember that the reason they can continue to do so is because the fans are willing to keep supporting them. Once that trust is breached, once a person shows or even proclaims outright that this tacit agreement means nothing to them, well, there's no going back. Ever. Both sides, over the process of labor negotiations, essentially announced just that. After a month or two of fruitless contract negotiations, the owners decided to lock out the players, putting the 2011-2012 season in jeopardy and flipping every single football fan on this Earth a nice, big middle finger.

I could attempt to drag you, kicking and screaming, through the five months of deliberation that eventually resulted in the lockout being lifted. Believe me, if my goal were to get you to throw this book in the trash can, light it on fire, and mistrust prominent sports figures forever, the lockout provided more than enough material. But I don't want to do that, out of respect for both your sanity and mine. (For information's sake, the lockout ended on July 25th of 2012, roughly two weeks before regular season games would have had to be cancelled.) Out of every single thing that has happened over the course of my life as a football fan, the lockout is the one that I've chosen to not process and place in context. To do so would be to shatter the comfortable and convenient illusion that being a fan provides. The whole point of fandom is that it's an escape from the real world into an alternate reality, one that provides you with the chance to devote your time and energy towards something you love. If I try to revisit that sordid moment in NFL history and examine what it really meant, then I'd probably realize how silly an idea this whole book was. The lockout would force me to look at what some of the people in sports valued, and if I did that, I'd come to the conclusion that teams and scores and all of the experiences woven into sports don't truly matter.

It's inevitable, and I don't want to face that inevitability. So I'll go on pretending that it never happened. Deep down, though, I've never looked at sports the same way since.

So the Jets reported for business in August with almost the exact same team and very similar Super Bowl aspirations. We all knew that, of course, because Rex came out and said it. Yes, he made another Super Bowl guarantee. At halftime of a Lakers-Knicks basketball game, he said in an on-camera interview, "last year, I thought we'd win it. This year, I know we'll win it." In the same interview, he also admitted to being a "major league dancer", so everything he said probably should have been taken with several oversized grains of salt. Still, the Jets entered the season with an air of certainty about their capacity to be among the NFL's elite. After all, Rex said he knew the Jets would win it. He just *knew*.

The season started out promising enough, with an emotional, come-from-behind 27-24 home win over the Dallas Cowboys that happened to come on the same day as the tenth anniversary of 9/11. Amid what would eventually become a disappointing slog of a season, that game and everything leading up to it was the one meaningful silver lining. If the lockout was sports at its worst, then the national anthem and the unfurling of the giant, field-long U.S. flag before kickoff had to be sports at its best. In the right context, sports can help people heal. They can unite an entire city after tragedy. Watching the camera pan around the stands on thousands of people wearing NYPD or FDNY baseball caps is something that I'm always going to remember. A simple, silly little football game was helping an entire city continue onward after the events of 9/11, with a heavy heart for all who had died. Rex, fully aware of what this game meant, said that he wanted to win this one for New York. Not to beat his brother Rob, who was the Dallas defensive coordinator. Not for the Jets, not for his players, not even for his fans. This one was for *everybody*. And the Jets played like it.

Gang Green followed up their big victory over Dallas by thrashing the Jacksonville Jaguars at home. They were now 2-0 to begin the season, and everything seemed to be working sufficiently. Mark Sanchez seemed to be taking strides and the defense looked like the same old ferocious Ryan squad that it had always been. Small sample size, I know, but I wanted to believe that everything was just peachy in Jetsland. There had been nothing in the first two games to suggest that they weren't. If only I knew how quickly the bottom would fall out of this whole thing.

In short order, the Jets dropped their next three games and, in the process, found new and inventive ways to completely botch even the best of situations. Week three saw the Jets travel to Oakland and get completely dominated by an average-at-best Raider squad. The box score says 38-28, but the Raiders' superiority over the Jets was a good deal more thorough than the score lets on, especially on the ground. Oakland running back Darren McFadden finished the day with 171 yards, two touchdowns, and a nine yards per carry figure, numbers which had to make a coach like Rex, who prides himself and his team on tough defense in the trenches, feel the urge to start convulsing right there on the sideline. I mean, this was just unbelievably out of character, to the point where I wondered if the real Jets missed their flight and they had to get lookalikes. It was like watching Mike Tyson lose a bar fight to the local angry drunk. So yeah, that was the first sign of trouble in paradise.

Gang Green followed up their sterling performance in Oakland by going to Baltimore, where Mark Sanchez and the entire Jet offense was put into a full Nelson and slammed to the turf by Rex's former employer, the Ravens. Sanchez especially brought his own uniquely facepalm-worthy brand of incompetence to the occasion. On his first play of the day, he was sacked and stripped by Baltimore safety Ed Reed. The ball was then picked up by linebacker Jameel McClain, who ran it back the other way for a touchdown. Sanchez ended up fumbling another ball early in the second quarter, which led to a Baltimore field goal. And, just for good measure, he held on to the ball far too long on a particular play later in the quarter, which allowed Ravens' defensive tackle Haloti Ngata to barrel into Sanchez like a freight train. Wouldn't you know it, the football came out again, flying almost all the way from the center of the field to the sidelines. Linebacker Jarret Johnson picked that one up and ran it in for a touchdown to make the Ravens' lead 27-7 as I shook my head in disbelief. What else can you do, really, in a situation like this? Even when the Jets battled back to make the score 27-17, Sanchez quickly sensed hope and immediately remedied that problem by throwing a horrible cross-field pass as he was being tugged to the ground once again. That pass was intercepted by Ravens' corner Lardarius Webb, who took a leisurely seventy-three yard stroll into the Jet endzone from there to make the score 34-17 Ravens, which would also serve as the game's final score. Most teams don't have three turnovers returned for touchdowns all year, but we had three run back against us in the same game. Suck on that, Super Bowl hopes and dreams. This Jets' season seemed to come with only two certainties so far; our quarterback looked like a bewildered Freshman starting in a varsity game and our coach looked like he wanted to strangle somebody. Neither of those events appear on the short list of things you want to see from your favorite team on a game-to-game basis.

In fact, the defining memory from that cesspool of football for me is bugging my mom all week to let me stay up late enough to watch the entire game, then immediately bolting for bed when the score got to 27-7. If this were 2010, I would have stayed. After all of the last-second heroics they pulled off the year before, there would have been no doubt in my mind that they'd find some way to make it close again. But I didn't have that same good feeling about the 2011 team, and I was not sticking around long enough to watch things spiral further out of control. That was really the difference between the 2010 and 2011 Jets; in 2010, I'm thinking, "Wow, how are they gonna pull this one out?" In 2011, I'm immediately saying, "Alright, let me just turn off the game now before things get worse." It's one of the most disheartening attitude transformations that a fan can undergo, and it happened in about four games.

And then the media sniping campaign started. After the Baltimore game, certain anonymous players began taking shots at various teammates. In fact, some players in particular didn't even bother with the umbrella of anonymity and started hurling insults out in the open. The Jets' top three wide receivers (Holmes, Plaxico Burress, and Derrick Mason) went to Rex Ryan privately before the game to express their disapproval with offensive coordinator Brian Schottenheimer's offense. Of course, Holmes took it a step further and publicly harangued the offensive line by saying that the Jets' struggles "started up front", a clear reference to the O-Line's ineffectiveness. Guard Brandon Moore fired back, publicly labeling Holmes' remarks as "disrespectful" and "divisive", among other things, which they absolutely were. It's true that the offensive linemen were essentially human turnstiles during the Baltimore game, but in the sports world, it's taboo to come out and say that to the press. In doing so, Holmes broke two fairly significant rules. First of all, you don't throw your own teammates under the bus publicly, no matter how badly they performed. That's just general good practice for sports or otherwise. The second rule that Holmes violated is especially sacred in football; don't interfere with the business of another unit on the team. Teams win Super Bowls when two things happen; everybody excels in their assigned role, and everybody on the team can at least tolerate each other from both a professional and personal standpoint. What went on after the Baltimore game (and would continue to go on over the course of the season) is the exact opposite of those rules. When Santonio Holmes suddenly becomes the offensive line coach, people openly question the offensive coordinator, half the team takes on the role of PR Director, and the people who *do* embrace their roles perform them with limited efficacy, then the entire system starts to collapse.

So it's no wonder that the Jets dropped their third consecutive game the next week, losing to New England by a semi-respectable score of 30-21. Pats' running back BenJarvus Green-Ellis, an undrafted rusher who was widely considered a league-average running back, gained 136 yards on only 27 carries and scored two touchdowns to boot. Once again, the whole "Jet football!" and "Ground&Pound!" rhetoric that had garnered so much league-wide attention over the last couple of years was based around being the one team that was still committed to winning the battle up front in a league where quarterbacking and the seventy yard touchdown bomb was beginning to rule the day. New England, in the eyes of Gang Green faithful, was the finesse team with a newfangled offense and a well-manicured quarterback that couldn't stand the thought of being hit. They weren't tough, like we were. They couldn't run the ball, they couldn't win games the old-fashioned way, and they would fold up like a tent if anybody so much as laid a finger on the dainty Tom Brady. So when an undrafted running back lights your prized defense up to the tune of 136 yards, it tends to poke a few holes in that mirage. Suddenly, you start questioning the foundation of the entire organization. Every good team, no matter the sport, needs to be able to point to at least one or two things where they can say, "If all else fails, at least we can do this particular thing better than just about anybody." Take away that one strength, and you really don't have a ton left. Run defense and the offensive line were the Jets' strong points, and they had both been abused over the course of those three games.

Of course, the inevitable "what's wrong with the Jets/how would you fix this team?" segments started on just about every football talk show in the country, which are always disheartening because it's basically just a group of people delivering a never-ending litany of everything that sucks about your team, laced with a hint of various sportscasting cliches and nicknames for variety's sake. *Coach, I think they need to have more leaders on that team. Well, Boomer, if you can't stop the run, you're not going to last very long in this league. Let me tell ya, pal, anytime you start out 2-3, that's not a good thing. What the Jets need to do is find a way to win games, and you can't win games if you're giving up big chunks of yardage. I think that the Jets are a good team, but good teams need great players to make great plays, and if you're the Jets and you don't have any playmakers, then the plays aren't going to be made.*

If you've had enough of that generality-littered analysis after five seconds, imagine how I felt listening to my favorite team being picked apart like this all week. It was not the most pleasant of times to be a Jet fan.

Fortunately, things reversed course rather quickly, as the schedule tossed the Jets a bone in the form of three relatively easy opponents, two of which they got to take on at home. They won all three of these games, thus setting up a showdown with 5-3 New England in Giants Stadium for control of the AFC East. Yep, another pivotal game between New York and New England, both of whom have the same record, locking horns for the inside track to winning the division. For some reason, the script seemed so familiar. Unfortunately, that script still included the part where New England ran the Jets off the field. Yes, again.

A 37-16 loss at the hands of the Patriots pretty much handed the AFC East to New England. The frustrating thing about the whole game, other than, you know, the Jets pretty much handing the AFC East to the Patriots again, was the fact that the game could have been won. The score at the end of the half was only 13-9. New York possessed the ball for roughly the same amount of time, gained about the same number of yards, and generally looked like a competent team at most points. But, as has come to be typical of the Jets over the years, they killed themselves with a never-ending slew of dumb plays. Namely, those plays came in the form of three Jet turnovers, one of which was a Mark Sanchez interception that New England linebacker Rob Ninkovich returned for a touchdown. Right tackle Wayne Hunter, through virtue of some truly atrocious blocking, gave up four sacks to the same New England defensive end over the course of the game. And then there were the Jet linebackers, who couldn't get in position quick enough to stop New England's no-huddle attack, just the same way that they failed to do so a year earlier.

By this point, I couldn't really get upset. I mean, what's the point, right? It's not like I was surprised in the least by any of this. Quite the contrary, in fact, I'd seen it roughly a million times before. Jets win a few ultimately meaningless games to rope the fans in. Jets have opportunity to make significant gains and become relevant. Jets are outplayed, shoot selves in foot, or do some combination of the two. Every time, the same old song and dance. Once your team has disappointed you a couple of times, you become somewhat numb to it. You learn to lower your expectations so that there's no chance of losing; if your team wins, you supported them all along, and if your team comes up short, then you never expected that much anyways. It's the ultimate defense mechanism, an easy out that can ensure the possibility of maximum return on the fan experience with only a fraction of the emotional and mental cost. I'd already embraced it wholeheartedly, to the point that I only felt marginally upset that the Jets lost. Yes, it felt like I was finally growing up and not letting sports affect me as much as I used to. It also felt . . . . wrong.

I didn't like the fact that I used to freak out over the Jets losing. I knew it was childish and immature as I was doing it. However, the one positive thing that those bouts of pouting *did* reinforce was that I cared, damnit, so much so that I was willing to make myself unhappy after they lost as a twisted form of self-punishment. Now, though, as the final seconds ticked off and I cavalierly clicked the off button and went to bed, something felt wrong. It felt like I'd given up on my team, on my entire life of being a fan, just because the Jets weren't good anymore. Sure, I was still watching their games, but no longer did I experience the peaks and valleys that should come along with all of those games. You know, when adults always told me things like, "Well, I used to be a Cowboys fan, but that was a long time ago. I don't really have the time to care about sports anymore", I always swore up and down that I'd never be like that. I would *always* love football and the Jets. Yet here I was, on the verge of becoming everybody else, the very thing that I didn't want to be. Circle of life, I guess.

After a crushing loss against the Denver Broncos the next week, one in which Denver QB and cult icon Tim Tebow led a 95 yard game-winning drive despite barely throwing a decent spiral all game, the Jets' record dropped to 5-5. Suddenly, they were in real danger of missing the playoffs and steadfastly clinging to the last wild card spot for dear life. The team that came oh so close to reaching the Super Bowl two years in a row returns pretty much the exact same core group of players . . . . and ends up falling short of even making the playoffs. For everybody else, calamity. For the New York Jets, Tuesday.

Just as Jet Nation began to panic, though, the random number generator that determines the order of opponents before each season flew through the window wearing a cape and tights, rescuing Gang Green from the lair of mediocrity. Once again, New York was gift-wrapped a three game stretch of well below average opponents (Buffalo, Washington, and Kansas City, for the record), and played two of them within the confines of Giants Stadium. They won all three, although the Buffalo and Washington games were a little bit close for awhile. Mark Sanchez even threw four—no, seriously—*four* touchdowns against Buffalo. After some uncertain times earlier in the season, everything was going to be just fine. There were three games left and we were 8-5, so the Jets would probably win one or two of the remaining three games, get the last playoff spot, and call it a regular season. Unfortunately for both me and the Jets, that previous sentence could not bear less resemblance to what actually happened.

The Jets' Week 15 road matchup with the Philadelphia Eagles pitted my tortured, long-suffering team against my friend Ray's tortured, long-suffering team. In fact, a paragraph in this book should be spared for poor Ray, who had watched the Eagles sign a bevy of top-quality free agents during that offseason and generate tons of Super Bowl hype . . . .

only to watch them fall flat on their face and go 4-8 in their first twelve games. In fact, after yet another disappointing Sunday a few weeks before the Jets game, Ray told me that he'd given up on that year's Eagles. He was no longer watching any of their games for the rest of the season, which I can't really blame him for saying. Of course, Ray remained suspiciously well-informed about the goings-on around his favorite team for the rest of the year, which was a clear indicator that he couldn't help but go back to watching his team. (Hey, at least his fantasy team was beating the hell out of mine. He was going one-for-two, at least.) Now, in the cruelest of football jokes, the Eagles had won their previous game by a hefty margin and were starting to put it all together, *after* they had already been eliminated from playoff contention. Still, both Ray and I remained fairly subdued in our trash-talking throughout the week. Believe me, I would have trash-talked with the best of them if I felt the least bit confident in my team, but I couldn't say that. I even turned down the token "if your team loses, you have to wear my team's jersey" bet offer from Ray, both because the Jets weren't that good and because Ray had an undersized (even for me), fairly cringe-inducing Terrell Owens Eagles jersey stuffed somewhere in the bowels of his closet. (For those who are not privy to 90s/early 2000s football, Terrell Owens was a fabulously talented, Hall of Fame caliber wide receiver that also happened to be one of the biggest a-holes on the face of the planet. Despite playing for five teams and making significant contributions to three of them, you will find very few fans who regularly wear his jersey.) Long story short, I did not have a great feeling about this particular Jets game.

And it was a good thing that I turned that bet down, because it was an absolute slaughter. The score was 21-0 Philadelphia before most of the second quarter had even been played. And then, a few minutes later, it became 28-0 Philadelphia after yet another Jet turnover. The Eagles gained nearly twice as many yards as did the Jets, and accrued twice as many rushing yards as well. The turnover, long a New York Jet specialty, was well-represented on this particular day; the Jets had four of them. I remember watching the game at my Aunt Evelyn's Christmas Party, surrounded by at least a few Eagles fans, all of whom were cheering and yelling and generally happy that the Eagles were *finally* being the team that they were supposed to be. In the middle of it all, there I stood, watching the Jets go the complete opposite way, a team that turned out to be far less than what they should have been. Uncle Pat had the Red Zone channel on his TV, and was bravely forsaking an entire half-Sunday of it for the good of all Jets/Eagles fans in the building by keeping the game on. After the score went to 21-0, Uncle Pat turned to me and asked, "Well, what do you think? Should we switch this thing to another game?"

I looked at the celebrating Eagles, the limp, lifeless Jets, and that damn scoreboard, and replied, "Yeah, I think we can change it." Just a year earlier, you would have needed the National Guard to drag me away from the TV when the Jets were playing, no matter the score. But I wasn't that guy anymore. I'd moved on already. (The Jets ended up losing 45-19, if you're really interested.)

I took a mild ribbing from Ray for the blowout loss, but my guess was that he lightened up on the gloating because, in their own special way, the Eagles were torturing him too. They'd started to put it all together only when it was far too late to truly go anywhere. Still, at least his team *was* moving in the right direction. The Jets, on the other hand, were not. Their record had dropped to 8-6 and, as it turned out, they would need to win the next two games in order to reach the playoffs. Game number one of those two? A "home" game against the crosstown rival Giants.

The Giants, at the time, were 7-7 and on the brink of being eliminated from playoff contention. All week, an air of desperation hovered over both teams, the players speaking as if their lives were on the line rather than their seasons. All of the tabloids and local media outlets in the tri-state area were abuzz over the game, running what seemed like every single sound byte that ever emerged from the collective mouths of either team. This, of course, was a prime opportunity for Rex to get in a couple of his own opinions about the state of the rivalry. During his Monday press conference—and please, keep in mind that this is not even a *single day* after the Jets were butchered by the Eagles—he stood at the podium and publicly declared that he "didn't come to New York to be a little brother to anybody" and that the Jets were "better" than the Giants. These comments, of course, reinforced remarks that he made about the Giants in his book, where he said the following:

"Some people like to say the Giants are the big brother team and the Jets are the little brother team . . . . I have news for you: We are the better team. We are the big brother." . . .

"When people ask me what it's like to share New York with the Giants, my response is always I am not sharing it with them—they are sharing it with me . . . It seems clear that right now we are the better team and we are going to remain the better team for the next 10 years. Whether you like it or not, those are the facts and that's what is going to happen."

The Giants players responded, mostly, by staying tight-lipped. Some assorted Giants returned fire, though. Two such players were running back Brandon Jacobs and offensive lineman Kareem McKenzie, who perfectly encapsulated the Jet-Giant relationship with their reactions to Ryan's tough talk. Jacobs said that Ryan's bravado may have been an attempt to "put something in people that may not be there", while McKenzie responded to a reporter's question about the remarks by asking said reporter which team had won the Super Bowl more recently. With that, the point, the set, and the match were already won for the New York Giants. Both players were absolutely right. I, for one, had grown somewhat indifferent to Ryan's antics. Sure, it may have spoken volumes when he first arrived in New York, but it's a hell of a lot easier to successfully pull off the "there's a new sheriff in town" routine after three days on the job than it is three years. After watching this season slowly leak down the sink, Jets vs Everybody diatribes seemed like a thinly-veiled cover for the team's lack of talent. Much like a medicine loses a little bit of its effectiveness every time you take it, motivational techniques have a shelf life. Go back to the same well too often, and people start seeing through it. People like Brandon Jacobs. And McKenzie's quote serves as the strongest reinforcement of the "big brother, little brother" argument there is. If the Jets have a more quotable team, who cares? The Jets have a better record than do the Giants; who is going to remember that six months from now? Three and one were the only numbers that mattered. Three Super Bowls for the Giants and one for the Jets. Until something drastic happened, those numbers would continue to be the ultimate argument-ender in favor of the big brother.

This upcoming game counted as something drastic, though. Sure, the Giants and Jets had seen each other many a time before this particular week, but none of the previous matchups in recent memory had carried with it this kind of significance. For all intents and purposes, the contest was an elimination game. Because of the way everything played out around these two teams, the loser of this pivotal battle would likely find themselves excluded from the playoff race.

Long story short, the Giants won. Handily. The turning point came when the Jets were leading the game 7-3 around halftime and had the Giants facing a third and ten all the way back at their own one-yard line, an absolutely hopeless situation for the offense. But not in this case. Giants' quarterback Eli Manning took the snap, paused for a second, and then fired to wide receiver Victor Cruz, who was running an out route near the right sideline. Cruz caught the ball at the first down marker, slipped through the feeble arm tackles of two Jet defenders, then proceeded to run roughly ninety more yards down the sideline and into the end zone for a touchdown. After that, the game was really never the same. Of course, it didn't help matters that the ground and pound, roll up your sleeves, we-do-things-the-old-fashioned-way Jets ran eighty-four offensive plays and had Mark Sanchez pass on fifty-nine of them. Yes, somebody on the face of planet Earth thought that it would be a fantastic idea for Cardiac Mark Sanchez, in a game that pretty much determined whether the Jets would go to the playoffs or go to their couches, to throw a football fifty-nine times. I and most other Jet fans were thinking more along the lines of nine pass attempts than fifty-nine, especially given Sanchez's recent performance. Amazing. In one game, the Jets managed to kill all confidence in Mark Sanchez, offensive coordinator Brian Schottenheimer's career in New York, Rex Ryan's popularity in New York, Rex Ryan's boisterous predictions, GM Mike Tannenbaum's career, their own playoff hopes, their capacity to take over the city of New York from the Giants, and just about every single bit of progress that had been made over the last two years. And because it was Christmas Eve, I went with my parents to mass immediately after all of these things vanished. So in a nice, quiet church where everybody was thinking happy thoughts and the pastor was reading a cheerful sermon, I was silently fuming about why the Jets hadn't fired Brian Schottenheimer yet. Well, that and debating whether it was immoral to ask God for a decent quarterback.

Even during Christmas mass, these are the things that I was thinking about.

So that brings us to Week 17, the final week of the regular season. All playoff hope was somehow not lost for the Jets, but they would need tons of help to make it happen. Firstly, they'd need to beat the Miami Dolphins on the road, which was no easy task. Then, they'd need losses from no less than three different teams. Considering what we know about their history, the chances of that happening weren't fantastic. I'd completely given up on the season at that point, at least from a wins/losses perspective. The old coping mechanism for realizing your team sucks—lowering expectations along the way—kicked in almost immediately after the Giants game. Now, if the Jets simply played a decent game, I would be satisfied. Didn't care if they won or lost, just a decent, hard-fought game would be enough for me. 2010 Andrew would have considered this blasphemy, but I'd grown up since then. If we made the playoffs, great. If not, then there's more to life. Yes, the ultimate disappointment-proof plan was hatched . . . . and it took about three hours for the Jets to foil it. It's not the outcome of the game that did it for me—spoiler alert, the Jets lost and did not make the playoffs—but it was the sudden realization that one of my favorite athletes cared so little for his teammates or his fans that he casually disregarded both of them while the season collapsed around him. And, most of all, the disappointment stemmed from the discovery of the mile-wide chasm between the fans and this one particular player. The athlete in question? Wide receiver Santonio Holmes, only the hero of the Jets' entire 2010 campaign.

Deep into the fourth quarter, Holmes (who had been held without a catch so far) and offensive tackle Wayne Hunter exchanged some heated words in the huddle. Apparently, certain players weren't happy with Santonio's defeatist attitude and body language throughout the game, and they told him about it. Holmes responded by engaging in a shoving match with Hunter, the closest player to him that had been telling him to knock it the hell off. Several teammates stepped in between the two players to separate them while everyone else (me included) tried to pretend that the star wide receiver wasn't bitching out his entire team in front of CBS' cameras. Eventually, everything was broken up and Holmes was ~~given a timeout in the corner to think about what he did~~ sent to the bench for a play or two, presumably to cool off.

The problem, though, is that he never returned from the bench. After the game, Rex Ryan said that he didn't know why Holmes was benched, which is troubling because he's the head coach and "hey, my biggest offensive weapon isn't on the field when we need him the most" is usually a thing that coaches should notice. Nobody on the Jet coaching staff owned up to his benching and Holmes didn't say that he benched himself, so we may never know. But it doesn't really matter. All I remember is the sight of Holmes, the guy with the captain's "C" on his chest, sitting on the bench and looking totally disinterested in the game. Afterwards, multiple players called Santonio out for what can only be described as a lack of effort. Running back LaDainian Tomlinson said afterwards, "It's tough to follow a captain that behaves in that manner." I, too, can see how a team captain blowing his lid at a teammate and then quietly sulking on the bench during the most important two minutes of the year can be a drain on team chemistry.

Then came the Facebook update on Santonio Holmes' page, not even two hours later from Holmes. It simply read, "Time to make offseason plans!"

Yep, time to make offseason plans indeed. You know, I always expected there to be a certain disconnect between the owners (who were the driving force behind the lockout) and the fans. They bought the team, they're running it like the business that it is, and there's a tendency to forget about people like me when that happens. It's not likable, but it's at least semi-understandable. But I would have *never* expected this from a player like Santonio, not in a million years. The same guy who caught three game-winning passes and ran around Giants Stadium with his arms outstretched like a Jet couldn't even conceal his unbridled happiness that the season was over, his fans be damned. I don't think I'd ever felt so pathetic as a Jet fan. Sure, I'd been through the losses and the tough breaks. Those didn't even faze me anymore. This, though, absolutely crushed me, to the point where I thought about just giving up the Jets. It's one thing to put faith in something that let you down, but it's another to put faith in something that lets you down *and doesn't care*. And when all the stories started leaking out about him skipping team meetings, his incessant moaning, the times where he would walk into a film session late and lean his head up against the wall to fall asleep, not to mention how he apparently seemed pumped that the Jets' season was over, I couldn't ever totally forgive him as a fan. Even though I never suited up for a game, I stuck with my crappy team for almost the entirety of my life so far. Yes, I got that playing with the maddeningly inconsistent Sanchez wasn't fun. I understand that most of the team was not likable. But Santonio was still under contract, and his overall behavior alienated him from both his teammates and a ton of Jet fans. Many former supporters, teammates, and media personalities even dredged up the dreaded Q-word. It's the only curse word in sports, and to apply it to someone is to condemn them for life. This word is reserved for the rarest of cases, so much so that I hesitate to even use it. But it must be said, for the sake of posterity. Santonio Holmes, through his words and actions, earned himself the unenviable label of *quitter.*

Quitting is a mark of shame. Every quote you've ever heard from Vince Lombardi, Knute Rockne, or any inspirational sports figure essentially boils down to the fact that *quitting sucks.* If you ever want to start a confrontation with anybody in sports, just call them a quitter. (As Bill Simmons and Doc Rivers will tell you.) In athletes' eyes, it's better to be accused of cannibalism than it is to be accused of quitting. Sports is all about a one hundred percent, balls-to-the-wall, leave-everything-on-the-field mentality. It respects people who work a little too hard and care a little too much. Even though football's concussion era has toned that down to a startling yet appropriate degree, the basic attitude is still the same. To look around at a difficult situation and say, "Screw this, I'm outta here" is the antithesis of everything that sports are supposed to be about. That's exactly what Santonio Holmes did, and it's why I can't ever totally forgive him.

To put the cherry on top of the anthrax sundae that was the 2011 season, guess who played in the Super Bowl? Yeah, that's right, Super Bowl 46 was played between the New England Patriots and the New York Giants. My two least favorite teams met in the Super Bowl twice within six years. For all of the people who are reading this book and thinking, "Stop whining, Goldstein, my team's been through worse", I dare you to point to another instance where this has happened. The two least favorite teams of a specific franchise playing each other in the championship of their sport twice in six years? It has never happened before (as far as I can tell, anyways), and it probably won't happen again. I actually debated not watching the Super Bowl before realizing that it would be blasphemy to skip out on the one sporting event that's practically a national holiday. So I watched. And as I sat there at the end of the night, watching the confetti fall and the wrong team bring a Lombardi trophy back to New York, I realized that it was fitting in so many ways that such an unhappy season should end with an equally unhappy Super Bowl.

Thus, order was restored. The Giants reclaimed their hold on the city of New York for good. Most importantly, though, the same old Jets were losing again.

REVIS ISLAND

Part of the agony of being a Jets fan over the last ten years was the lack of consistency. I'm not talking about wins and losses; there are plenty of teams out there who can't post winning records every year. I'm talking about the individual players. I can count on my fingers the number of Jets players from 2002 to 2013 that I never worried about.

Here's what I mean by that. See, I think that a big part of building a great team depends on *knowing* what you're going to get from certain players. You need guys that you can point to and say, with confidence, "If I throw it to him on a one-on-one fade route in the corner of the end zone, I don't have to worry about whether he'll catch it." Or, "I don't have to worry about whether this guy can make an open field tackle, I know he can do it." In the ever-changing controlled chaos that is the twenty-two players on a football field, certainty is everything. The less certainty that exists and the more players that you have to worry about, the harder it is to make an effective game plan because that plan is contingent upon knowing exactly what the coach's players can and cannot do.

And when it came to the New York Jets, you were never quite able to be certain. The final five years of my childhood as a Jets fan have been epitomized by Mark Sanchez, a guy that made Jet fans' hearts skip a beat on every throw. Then, there was wide receiver Braylon Edwards and his severe case of the dropsies. (Wait a second, he's open . . . . that's a perfect throw behind the defense . . . . hold on, this is gonna be a touch—DAMNIT BRAYLON!). The performance of the Jets' entire offensive line seems to be an utter crapshoot. And my mom, who knows almost nothing about football, still lets out a beleaguered "Oh no!" whenever she sees Nick Folk line up for a field goal. I have to wonder what I'm going to get from just about every single one of these guys, just like I've had to wonder about dozens of Jets over the course of my fandom.

But Revis? I've never, not once, had to wonder what I was going to get from Revis.

The Jets took Darrelle Revis out of Pittsburgh University (Curtis Martin's alma mater!) with the 14th pick of the 2007 draft. Revis was known as a fundamentally sound corner who could cover anybody and everybody in college. He played man coverage, zone coverage, returned punts, and seemed to come up with the big play no matter where he was on the field. He wasn't afraid to step up into the box and tackle bigger running backs. He had the requisite toughness to jam just about every receiver at the line of scrimmage. And to prove that his college record wasn't a fluke, he performed so well at his college pro day that Arizona defensive backs' coach Teryl Austin said, "nobody walked away disappointed." Don't forget that Austin is talking about NFL scouts and professional coaches. Their entire job description when it comes to draftable players, if I'm going to be cynical about it (and I always am), is to find things to be disappointed about. That's just about the highest praise an NFL coach can bless a workout with. Really, he was everything that the Jets were looking for in a corner.

Revis' first two years on the Jets were quietly brilliant. He was only beaten for a touchdown four times in his first two years, which is astounding when you consider that opposing quarterbacks almost always throw at rookie cornerbacks as much as possible. Since important statistics for defensive backs aren't kept as diligently as they should be, we have no concrete way of measuring Revis' effect on a game. However, football analysts and astute fans began to see that, by the end of Revis' second year in the league, opposing quarterbacks stopped throwing the ball his way. They'd take a quick glance over at him and then immediately begin searching the other side of the field. When a defensive player is able to gain that kind of respect from opposing QBs *in only his second year*, you know that he has accomplished something significant.

The only problem with Revis' first two years was that, as usual, the Jets really sucked. His first year was the miserable 2007 season where the Jets went 4-12 and his second year was overshadowed by the 1-4 end to the season, not to mention Eric Mangini's firing. In 2008, the Jet defense ranked 29th in the league in both total pass defense and passing yards per game allowed. So while it was true that opposing QBs were looking away from Revis, they were looking directly towards the other cornerback, the unproven Dwight Lowery. When the Jets brought in veteran corner Ty Law to alleviate the problem, opposing offensive coordinators would put their shiftiest receivers on the aging Law, whose lack of agility meant that he couldn't cover nimbler guys like the Pats' Wes Welker at all. Had Revis played on a contender for his first two years, he would have generated lots of much-deserved, "Hey, that Revis guy is pretty good!" chatter. Alas, he was not playing on a contender and thus very few people appreciated how good he was.

Then, enter Rex Ryan. If you've watched more than a few Jet games or paid attention to Jet-related chatter over his tenure, you know that the "Rex Ryan LOVES to bring pressure!" tidbit has become a crutch for every single analyst and play-by-play guy in the business. However, most people don't realize the extent to which Ryan utilizes the blitz. It seems like the guy was put on this Earth to make life miserable for quarterbacks. He's bringing six guys on a fairly regular basis, having safeties pass rush and dropping linebackers back to where the strong safety should be and doing all sorts of crazy stunts, overload blitzes, and delayed rushes. The quarterback doesn't know when they're coming, who's coming, how many are coming, and where they're coming from. All they know is that it's coming. I honestly haven't the slightest clue how a new member of the Jet defense even starts absorbing everything that he has to know, and I certainly can't even venture a guess as to how anybody prepares for it.

So, what does all of that have to do with Revis? Well, you see, there's a little bit of a problem when you bring as much pressure as Rex likes to bring. Let me outline this problem for you. Blitzing is all about bringing at least one more pass rusher than the offense has blockers. So let's say the offense has six blockers (five on the O-Line plus the tight end), four wide receivers (two on each side of the QB), and the running back, who is lined up behind the QB. If we were to reduce this to its simplest terms (and believe me, things are almost *never* anywhere near as straightforward as my description will make it sound), that means Rex would send seven guys after the QB. That means there will be four receivers against four guys in coverage, unless the running back runs a route, in which case it's five against four in favor of the offense. (Now, obviously a coach would never have seven guys pass rush at once with any kind of regularity for precisely these reasons, but this example was just for the sake of argument.)

See the problem here? Blitzing as frequently as Rex does means that receivers are in one on one matchups with their defenders. If the coverage guy gets beaten downfield by his receiver, there's nobody behind him to cover up that mistake. And if the quarterback evades the blitz and sees his best receiver in one on one coverage (the other team's best guy almost always garners double coverage), then he's going to take advantage of that matchup by throwing the ball to him. It's just logical that if you're devoting more guys than you usually do to rushing the QB, then you're devoting fewer guys to covering the receivers.

In this case, the unenviable job of solo covering the league's best receivers on almost fifty percent of all passing plays, with absolutely no help whatsoever, fell to Darrelle Revis. He would now be playing for a boisterous coach and a team that people wanted to talk about, and his role was no longer ambiguous. In single coverage, no mistake can be pawned off on someone else not doing his job, mostly because there is nobody else, only Revis. He wasn't just a cog in the defensive machine anymore; he was the fulcrum around which the entire defense pivoted. The success or failure of Rex's scheme depended largely upon him. It was Revis versus the league's best in a one on one battle of wits, athleticism, and technical skill every week. And almost every single week, Revis won.

It started in Week one of the 2009 season, where he blanketed Texans' star wideout Andre Johnson all over the field and held him to four receptions for thirty-five yards in the Jets' season-opening win. The next week, he faced off against Patriots' receiver Randy Moss, who had hauled in fourteen catches the week before, and shut him down. Moss caught four passes for twenty-four yards and was generally rendered a non-factor.

And this is how it was for the whole season. The Colts' Reggie Wayne went up against him and had three catches for thirty-three yards to show for it. Carolina's Steve Smith tried his luck and caught one pass for five yards. Atlanta's Roddy White could only muster four catches for thirty-three yards. And Chad Johnson (excuse me, Chad *Ochocinco*) made the mistake of trash-talking Revis before both of the Bengals' games with the Jets (one to end the season, one in the first round of the playoffs). He caught two passes for twenty-eight yards over the course of both games. In the Jets' divisional round victory over the Chargers that year, San Diego QB Philip Rivers threw exactly three passes (out of forty) to receivers that were being covered by Darrelle Revis. By that point, there was a mutual understanding among the league's quarterbacks that Revis was the one guy that you shouldn't even test.

Revis isn't a physical specimen. He's barely six feet tall and weighs approximately two hundred pounds; measurables that aren't much different from any other cornerback. He isn't necessarily the fastest guy on the field, nor is he explosive enough to be feared as a punt returner (although he did return a few in college).

All Revis does is show up and shut receivers down. If you were to make a list of the things a cornerback needs to do in order to be successful, Revis would probably hit the most items on that list of any cornerback in history. He's strong enough to jam the best receivers in the league at the line of scrimmage, he can come up into the box to make tackles on running backs (some of which have at least thirty pounds on him), and he can outleap his man for jump balls (he had a 38-inch vertical at Pittsburgh University's Pro Day). When a receiver is covered by Revis, it's a fairly uncommon occurrence for him to *see* the football, much less catch it. The guy seems to instinctually know just the right angle to take on every single pass so that his body obscures the ball from the receiver's sight. There were times (and this happened somewhat frequently) where the guy Revis was covering, for just a split second, had no idea that the ball was thrown to him until he saw it bouncing across the turf.

Rex Ryan was and is prone to bouts of hyperbole, but even his harshest critics took him seriously when, after the 2009 season, he said, "This, in my opinion, was the best year a corner has ever had, the most impact a corner has ever had in the National Football League."

Hall of Fame corner Deion Sanders was also impressed with Revis' performance, so much so that he declared that Revis would be "the best corner in the game for years."

These two quotes cut to the real reason why Darrelle Revis decided to stage a holdout the next offseason. Revis was trapped in year four of a six-year rookie deal that would pay him approximately one million dollars, making him one of the most sparsely paid defensive backs *on his own team*. Can you imagine that? A player that stepped onto the field for every single defensive down and was one of the ten best players in the league would be paid less to be the focal point of the Jet defense than Mike

Goodson was paid to be the Jets' third-string running back. Rumor had it that there had been an unfulfilled handshake promise between Revis and Jets' management to rework his contract as soon as the season ended. When training camp came and the parties were far apart on the money, Revis decided to hold out. He showed up for some practices in June, sat out a handful of plays with a (cough, cough) hamstring injury, and then didn't return for training camp in July and August. It wasn't likable and it certainly didn't endear him to anybody, but it was explainable.

So, the Jets waited for Revis to name his price. Ten million per year? Fifteen million per year? Twenty? Revis responded not with a dollar figure, but simply by saying, "Higher than Asomugha."

Nnamdi Asomugha was a starting cornerback on the Raiders that many considered to be the best corner in the game before Revis took that title. When asked by a reporter if he'd accept a contract that was worth a dollar more than the one given to Asomugha, he responded, "It could be fifty cents more. Give me fifty cents more [than Asomugha], and we'll be OK."

This quote, along with the ones from Ryan and Sanders, taught me more about the way professional athletes think than anything else ever has. The monetary benefits that would come with a new contract were nice, but that wasn't the biggest reason for the holdout. It wasn't about the money, it was about the validation that came with the money. Revis had put himself through considerable amounts of pain, spent God knows how many hours in the weight room or the film room, and helped to drag a team that some said had no business making the playoffs to the verge of the Super Bowl. He was the best in the league. According to drive-time radio hosts? According to his fans? No, that compliment came from both his coach and the greatest corner to ever play the game. In a league full of hypercompetitive people who want to win at everything, whether it's football, business, or anything else, money is a measure of where a player stands on the NFL totem pole. I'm convinced that's the real reason why you rarely see athletes willingly take pay cuts when they don't have to. It's not because they're going to miss the extra few million dollars, it's because they feel like they're being knocked down a rung on the ladder. Revis might be called the best in the game, but I guess that it felt hollow to him if management didn't feel the need to (quite literally) put their money where their mouths were. What he really wanted was to be named the best at his position in the league, and that couldn't happen unless he got paid like the best player at his position.

However, most fans aren't wired anything like the way pro athletes are wired. There were outraged cries of "Selfish!" and "Just shut up and play!" coming out of both the Jets' fanbase and the media on a daily basis. At the time, I was firmly entrenched among the ranks of these irate fans who felt betrayed by one of their guys. In fact, it wasn't until just before I started writing this book, almost three years later, that I began to wonder why he *really* held out. I wasn't interested in getting behind his motives or trying to understand who he really was in the Summer of 2010. After all, he was the best player on a potentially Super Bowl winning team. The fans *needed* to see him out on the field, and we didn't care what it took to get him there. With the season impending, my desperation turned into anger. I was angry at Jets' management for not putting up the money, angry at Revis for wanting the money in the first place, angry at Rex for inflating Revis' stock, angry at the HBO show Hard Knocks, a documentary about life at an NFL training camp, for helping to blow the Revis negotiations into a bigger distraction than it already was; basically, I was just angry at anybody that had even the slightest connection to Revis holding out. Did all of these people actually do anything? Of course not. But, like in so many other instances, I was able to pretend that they did.

Eventually, Revis got his money. He didn't get the long-term deal that he asked for, but he did get an extension of two years that was worth a total of 32.5 million dollars. That equated to 16.25 million dollars, just a smidge higher than Asomugha's 16.14 million. The Jets realized that Revis wasn't going to budge on the dollar figures, and I'm convinced that it would have absolutely killed Revis to willfully miss games because of his contract. So, the two sides settled on a compromise that left both of them a little bit dissatisfied, which is exactly what almost everybody involved with the situation thought would happen all along.

Because of the circumstances surrounding the Jets in that particular offseason (Rex Ryan's Guarantee, Hard Knocks, etc), Revis became an NFL icon. He started doing nationally televised commercials. His jersey was among the most purchased from the Jets' team store. And among the commotion surrounding Revis' fantastic season and ensuing holdout came his now-famous nickname: Revis Island.

The new moniker was apt because the receiver that had the misfortune of facing off against Revis might as well not even be on the field. It really was like they were on an island and the space all around them was a zone in which no quarterback dared to throw the football. It took herculean strength or otherworldly agility just to get the slightest bit of separation from the guy. Every single game, the receivers played the part of Rocky and Revis played the part of Clubber Lang. No matter how hard they tried, they couldn't keep Revis off of them. When Revis locked a receiver down, it felt like there was nobody else on the field except for Revis and his man. You were all alone for the day and would count yourself lucky to catch four passes or gain thirty yards. Hell, you'd be lucky if the quarterback saw fit to even look your way. That was the power of Revis Island. The ability to choose a receiver on the other team and completely take him out of the game, to make it seem like he doesn't even exist, was an advantage that no other team besides the Jets had. One receiver, every single game, was sent to Revis Island; a particular area of the field that was so difficult to penetrate that quarterbacks eventually stopped trying.

Revis was immediately re-adopted as a fan favorite in New York, if for no other reason than the fact that it was such a treat to watch somebody who was so unbelievably good at his job on a week to week basis. Whether for better or for worse, fans will forgive a lot in exchange for on-field performance and winning. Jet fans *needed* Revis back because, like I said at the beginning of this chapter, he was the one player that you never had to worry about. Nobody ever had to wonder, even for a second, if Revis was going to be able to take care of the guy he was assigned to on a given day. I was watching a transcendent player go about his business and make it look so damn easy on a weekly basis, which is something that I had *never* seen before on the Jets. Yes, I loved Curtis Martin when I first became a Jet fan and he's still my favorite Jet ever, but he seemed too mortal to really be considered an otherworldly talent. Curt showed up, tried like every game would be his last, picked up his quiet 120 yards on 20 carries, helped the Jets win, and called it a day. Nothing about him or any Jet player before Revis made me think things along the lines of, "I'm watching one of the greatest players in the game's history" or "I'll remember watching this guy until the day I die." When fans know that they are witnessing a player that simply rises above the rest—and we know fairly quickly—we cheer like crazy for him. We cherish every single opportunity that we have to see him play and try to take in every single detail of it. We buy his jersey, his signature sneaker, his poster, his book (if he wrote one), his awful rap album (if he ever released one), his game-used socks, the coffee cup he drank out of that morning, just whatever we could. For instance, one day, my Grandpa gave me a game-worn Revis jersey that he won at a raffle and it was probably one of the greatest days of my life. (Thanks, Grandpa!) The next day, I was telling everybody at school who would listen about how I got a Revis game-worn. Everybody I talked to that possessed the appropriate football knowledge to appreciate what that meant reacted more or less the same way. *Whoa! You got an authentic Revis game-worn? That's awesome!* I guarantee you that no other game-worn Jets jersey (besides, of course, Namath's) would have gotten that reaction. He was becoming larger than life.

Revis started the 2010 season a bit shakily after a Week 2 matchup against New England, when Randy Moss beat him coming off the line of scrimmage and got behind him downfield, then cavalierly snatched a Brady pass out of the air with one hand for a long touchdown. It was the first time that I had seen Revis defeated in over-the-top coverage since his rookie year. After the game, word started to trickle in that Revis had a knee injury and would miss two to three weeks. I immediately began to hold my breath. Knee injuries are bad for anyone, but *especially* for somebody who has to turn and run with the league's best receivers step for step. Who knew if Revis was really going to be the same after he came back? What if 2009 was the only transcendent Revis season that Jets fans would ever get to appreciate? As Jets' nation began to have a collective heart attack, some naysayers predicted an end to Revis' dominance.

Revis' first game back was against the Minnesota Vikings on Monday Night Football, where he surrendered eighty-one yards and a touchdown to Moss, who had been traded to the Vikes the week before. The next week, he gave up seventy-four yards receiving to the Broncos' Brandon Lloyd. I remember all the experts saying the same thing. *He looks like he's grimacing whenever he has to run for a long time. He doesn't seem as explosive as he used to be. Guys are getting separation from him now. I don't know if he can sustain himself for the rest of the season.* For the first time, Jet fans were starting to worry about Revis.

And suddenly, it all went away. After holding his own against Green Bay, Revis squared off against Calvin Johnson of the Detroit Lions, a guy who many considered to be the best receiver in the league, and seemingly refused to let him intake Oxygen, much less catch a football. Every time Johnson tried to shove Revis aside and get inside positioning on him, he would jab him squarely in the chest and take him right off his route. Johnson would try to run downfield routes to test Revis' knee, but Revis ran with him as if he were tethered to his man with a rope. The cameras would focus in on the matchup all throughout the game and it looked inconceivable that Revis could win. I mean, Calvin Johnson is 6'5 and Revis is 5'11. It seemed like if the ball was thrown anywhere in Johnson's general direction, he would just be able to reach over Revis and grab it. But the master tactician had learned to deal with taller wide receivers. Every time the ball would be thrown to Johnson, Revis' fingers somehow emerged right in between Johnson's hands to deflect it away. Detroit QB Matt Stafford would glance over at Johnson and then immediately glance elsewhere. Yeah, Revis Island was back.

In the coming weeks, Andre Johnson (four catches for thirty-four yards), Chad Ochocinco (four catches for thirty-one yards), and Brandon Marshall (two catches for sixteen yards) would be forced to languish in anonymity on Revis Island. This trend continued during the Jets' improbable playoff run in 2010, when Revis was matched up against Colts' wideout Reggie Wayne, who had caught 111 passes (his career best) for 1,355 yards (nearly a career best). And that's before you even get to the fact that Peyton Manning, one of the greatest quarterbacks to ever play the game, was throwing him all those passes.

His stats against Revis? One target and one catch for one yard.

Wayne just seemed like he had no hope of getting a clean release off the line against Revis. It's like both teams (and the fans of both teams) forgot that the two of them were even on the field. They might as well have held their crucial one-on-one battle in the parking lot, because the game was 10v10 instead of 11v11. I'd be surprised if Wayne even laid eyes on a football for the majority of that game. That was the power of Revis.

Unfortunately, that would also be the lone saving grace amid the spontaneous combustion of the 2011 Jets. He became the one thing that Jets fans could cling to, the one advantage that we knew *for sure* we still had going for us, the one guy that we never had to worry about. Amid the depression and frustration of watching a Super Bowl window snap shut for who knows how long, Revis delivered what was possibly his most brilliant season yet. And it didn't matter. The Jets were once again a sideshow, a disappointment, the little brother to the Giants. Yes, Revis got his spot on the NFL's Top 100 list and the New York sports talk radio shows. But those words rang hollow, for both the fans and probably for Revis. For all his Pro Bowl caliber play and Hall of Fame hype, Revis was playing for a losing team in the most toxic of environments. And that was *before* things truly got worse.

During Week 3 of the ensuing 2012 season, the Jets were squaring off against the Miami Dolphins. It happened on a routine screen play, no different than the kind you'd see at least once or twice in almost every single game. Except this one was anything but routine. As the Miami running back caught the pass and turned upfield, Revis started running towards him to make the tackle. The next thing I knew, there was a pile-up around the ballcarrier and I temporarily lost sight of Revis. After a few seconds, everybody began to detach themselves from the pile and walk back to their respective huddles, leaving Revis lying helplessly on the ground. He gnashed his teeth in an obvious expression of anguish as he clutched his knee.

Oh, shit. The words came out of my mouth almost instinctively. (Luckily, my parents were not watching the game with me.) Nothing inspires those two words (or the sentiment behind them, for that matter) from fans more than seeing a player on your team in obvious pain, especially when he's holding his leg. Teams and players carry emotional weight with the people that support them, so injuries are doubly painful. Obviously, from a selfish perspective, injuries hamper a team's ability to win. But from a less self-centered point of view, injuries are the bane of a sports fan's existence because someone that you support, somebody who you've grown to respect, has suffered bodily harm. So we react the same way that you'd react if one of your friends had to get stitches or if your kid fell off his bike and broke some teeth. We're checking phones every half hour for updates, consoling each other, convincing ourselves that it didn't look that bad, whatever it takes to maintain hope. There is nothing, absolutely *nothing*, more stressful than to watch a favorite player get hurt on Sunday, and then have to wait until roughly noon on Monday to see how he's doing. And that whole time, you pretend to concentrate on whatever you're supposed to be doing while wondering if the guy is ever going to be the same again. In many cases, he isn't. So, in a multitude of ways, it's worse to win and watch a favorite player get hurt than it is to lose. And if that favorite player happens to be a future Hall of Famer that is both the centerpiece of the team and has gained the kind of respect from both fans and peers like very few ever have? Well, then you're *screwed*.

Revis stayed down on the field for about a minute or two as the Jet training staff and his teammates huddled around him. Eventually, Revis began hobbling around, favoring the leg that he hurt. He draped his arms around the trainers that came out to check on him and began limping off the field. Or maybe he ended up walking off the field by himself. And did he hurt his right leg or his left leg? I really don't know. I've tried to block out everything that transpired in those minutes. It's not something I like to remember, for obvious reasons.

For a little while, it looked like my fears were unfounded. Postgame reports said that Revis was talking with teammates like he always did after games. He was even walking around somewhat normally. The replays showed Revis falling to the ground untouched, so maybe he just tweaked something in his knee. Yeah, maybe he just pulled a hamstring again.

I remember that it was at break the next day when I got the news. After sitting down with some of my friends to eat lunch, I decided to pull out my phone and check Twitter for the injury report. After all, Revis' MRI was scheduled for mid-morning that day, so the results would probably be in. As soon as my Twitter feed loaded up, I immediately saw the two words that I had been afraid to see.

Torn ACL.

For any readers who are unfamiliar with sports injuries, torn ACLs are probably the most common season-ending injury in the game. When the knee is hyperextended, the anterior cruciate ligament (the ACL) is a threat to rupture. Because of the severe restriction on mobility that a torn ACL places on an athlete (not to mention the potential for damage to other parts of the leg), it almost always sidelines its victims for at least half a year. Most often, it's a full year. If the rehab goes perfectly, the guy returns in a year and goes back to playing exactly like he did before the injury. But more often than not, he'll return with some apprehension. Maybe he won't be able to cut as well as he used to. Maybe he won't be able to run as quickly. He'll probably never be the same.

All that was going through my mind as a tweet popped up a few minutes later confirming that Revis was, indeed, out for the season. For the rest of the week, every time I met a fellow Jet fan, we would just sadly shake our heads. They knew the same thing I knew; that without Revis, the Jets were finished. Matt knew it too, and he took some amount of pleasure in taunting me over it. (By the way, this seems like a pretty good time to mention that you should never taunt somebody over injuries on their favorite team. Not only is it a fantastic way to piss people off, but it's never a good idea to give karma a reason to work against you.) I can honestly say that it was probably one of the ten or twenty worst days of my life. He was the meal ticket. Amid the decaying ruins of the Ryan Jets, he was the one advantage that still remained. Most importantly, he was probably the only player that still resonated with fans. And then, suddenly, he wasn't there anymore.

These last six thousand or so words were by no means a eulogy for Darrelle Revis. He might come back stronger than ever, shutting down receivers and talking trash like he always has. But the strong possibility: no, the strong *probability* that he won't be the same player made me feel the need to include this chapter. As soon as trade talks and rumors that the Jets may no longer be able to afford him began to swirl, I realized that I might not get to see him in a Jets uniform ever again. That's the thing about transcendent athletes, they don't stay that way for long. Most fans don't appreciate that the first time they have one on their team. It usually takes something like an injury or a sudden retirement or even a slow and natural atrophy of athletic ability to make people realize what they were watching. That's what it takes for a lot of people, and that's what it took for me. It wasn't until he was injured that I took the time to search "Darrelle Revis" on Youtube, cue up some of his highlight tapes, and internalize all of the little things that I just described to you. That's when I really noticed, for the first time, how amazing at the game of football Darrelle Revis was. That's the first time when I tried to think like a receiver and figure out how anybody could possibly escape from Revis Island, ultimately concluding that it wasn't entirely possible. And I tried to think about whether I would ever, *ever*, see another cornerback as good as Darrelle Revis.

The answer to that question is probably "yes." After all, everybody's always looking for the successor. Athletes keep getting bigger, faster, stronger, and more durable. I'll probably see another guy who plays like Revis someday. But will I regard him like I regarded Darrelle Revis in his prime? No. Every sports fan remembers the first athlete that really captured their imagination and redefined what was possible in the world of sports. People's connection to that player will be stronger than their connection to any other, especially if that connection was formed in childhood, where sports carry a disproportionate amount of weight anyways. Revis was that guy for me.

Will I see better players than Revis? Probably. Will there be athletes down the road who can do what Revis did? Maybe. Will there ever be another Darrelle Revis? For me, no.

THE BIG APPLE CIRCUS

The transformation was nearly complete. New York had been taken from a contender to a nobody in the span of a year. The dynamic of the Jets had changed from close-knit and scrappy to dysfunctional and poisonous. When Rex came to New York, everybody wanted to play for the Jets. Now, nobody did. Suddenly, we were the doormat, the laughingstock, and the butt of everyone's joke. (Quite literally, as you'll find out later in this chapter.) We were back at the bottom, and it all happened in the blink of an eye.

Meanwhile, my fanhood had begun a transformation of its own. I realized that by this point (my Junior year in high school, to be exact), sports and the Jets had already reached the peak of their significance in my life. Every sports fan has one or two particular teams that meant far more than they should, and for me those two teams were the 2009 and 2010 Jets. After going through those seasons, sports started to be put in perspective. I no longer had the time to sulk about losses for days on end. Gone were the days where I could afford to let the Jets dominate my life. In a way, it was freeing. Suddenly, I no longer felt like we *had* to win. It would be nice, but we didn't *have* to. And that was a good thing, because somehow, the Jets managed to take a situation that was already dismal and plunge it even further into the garbage can.

Immediately after the season, third-string quarterback Greg McElroy went on a radio station in his home state of Alabama and called his Jets' teammates "extremely selfish individuals." He also stated that there were certain players in the Jets' locker room that "didn't care if the team won or lost as long as they got theirs and had a good game individually." He neglected to mention the names of the teammates he was referring to, but I'm sure that he wasn't talking about Santonio Holmes at all.

So of course, the tabloids and the national media felt the need to blow this up into a big thing. Plastered across the front page of ESPN's NFL section was Greg McElroy's quote, along with teammates' reactions to Greg McElroy's quote. And, of course, four columnists had to offer their take on what he said. Which, in turn, prompted the NFL's substantial Twitter emporium to start offering their opinions on it too.

My reaction, as well as the reaction of every Jet fan who watched any significant part of their season, was, "Really? There were selfish players on the Jets last year? You sure about that?" (Sarcasm doesn't work as well in print as it does in speech, I have found.) In other news, the sky is blue, the Pope is Catholic, and Rex Ryan is a little bit emotional. This wasn't exactly eleven o'clock news; I had pretty much resigned myself to the fact that some of my favorite players were selfish assholes when a fistfight nearly broke out in the huddle during the Miami game. You know, when the Jets were trying to make the playoffs and totally had tons of time to waste on trivial bullshit like, "Why is he getting thrown the ball more than I am? Is it because you don't like me?"

And that brings us to Santonio Holmes, who did a masterful job of slapping horse blinders on the Jets' management. (Warning: the irrational fan in me is about to make an appearance. Please don't mistake my rant for actual first-hand knowledge of Holmes' psyche.) If the Jets management did not cut him before February 13th, he would collect on a 7.5 million dollar roster bonus. So, he immediately set to the task of assuming the veil of contrition. He held a post-mortem meeting with Mark Sanchez to resolve their differences, a meeting not unlike the ones that he seemed utterly disinterested in attending leading up to the Miami game. He attended Sanchez's "Jets West" camp (after casually skipping it the year before) to gain better chemistry with his quarterback and to improve his route-running, two things which he also showed disdain for in the weeks leading up to the Miami game. This new good-guy Santonio seemed to be the antithesis of the Santonio of 2011 who, according to a team source, slouched against a wall and complained, "Why do I have to do this?" when Sanchez tried to organize the receivers after practice for a film session. Let's see, Santonio, why do you have to do this? To heighten the chance that you'll make the playoffs, it's your job, for pride and self-respect, it's your job, fans pay to see you, because being a Jet means something, because you want to be as competent as possible for your teammates, and did I mention the fact that IT'S YOUR DAMN JOB? You know, just to name a few.

Of course, when Santonio got his money, the buddy-buddy "look at what a good guy he is" stories about him disappeared. In fact, he ended up calling out the media in a July press conference. I'm just going to run his original quote, which was offered without the slightest hint of irony, and then move on. There's nothing that I could possibly say to condemn Holmes more than he condemned himself with the following two sentences:

> *If you guys want to be, and this is for the New York media, if you guys want to be a part of our team and want to feel so important, be there to support us, not try to break us down. Because (there's) not on day that we all step in that locker room and we try to break each other down, that we talk bad about the way that person played because it affects the team the way one person plays if they don't play to perfection.*

And then there was the issue of what to do with the guy Santonio spent most of the season feuding with. Mark Sanchez clearly regressed from a technical standpoint during his third year, which is traditionally a young QB's breakout year. I was at the point where I'd accepted reality; it was time to move on from Mark. He was an awful QB. The guy worked hard, said all the right things, and could never be faulted for lack of effort, but he just didn't have it. The correct course of action would have been to start him for one more year, let his contract expire, and start over. Or, as Grantland.com's Bill Barnwell so lovingly put it, "cut Sanchez after the season and have a ceremony so that the door can literally hit him in the ass on the way out."

But then, Jets' GM Mike Tannenbaum committed the number one most egregious offense in the unofficial "How Not to Screw Up a Team" handbook that I just made up in my head ten seconds ago. He began to make moves that fall into the "We need to do something drastic to get the fans talking about us" category. This used to happen all the time when there was a large disconnect between what people inside the organization knew and what the fans knew. You could *easily* get away with what the Jets were about to do if they did it during the seventies because fans didn't have that many sources of information. Now? We have Sunday Ticket, Twitter, All-22 film, and Adam Schefter. Fans are smarter these days and can understand why teams trade thirty-year old running backs that just had big years or stockpile as many draft picks as possible. It's this same level of intelligence that allows fans to see through everything that I'm going to describe in the next paragraph or two.

Peyton Manning, a surefire Hall of Famer and the guy who had beaten the Jets in the 2009 AFC Championship game, parted ways with the Colts after sitting out the entire 2011 season due to injury. Rumors immediately started circulating that the Jets were contacting Manning and expressing interest in him. Whether or not these rumors were true, they must have immediately ceased when Manning noticed a few things. Namely, that the Jets didn't have the first dollar available in their salary cap to pay him with, he'd be stepping into a toxic locker room atmosphere, he'd have to directly compete with his brother for attention (because they'd be playing in the same city), he would be standing behind an unstable offensive line, and he would have virtually no viable receivers to throw to. So, he did what any thirty-five year old QB who wanted a half-decent team and the chance to win a Super Bowl would do in his situation. He avoided the Jets like the plague and eventually signed with Denver.

So not only did the Jets miss out on Manning, but they now had to deal with the rumors that they had lost confidence in Sanchez. So, to reaffirm their phantom belief in the struggling QB, they gave him one of those out-of-the-blue votes of confidence that usually precede a pink slip. Well, attached to that vote of confidence was a three-year contract extension with over twenty million dollars of guaranteed money, but still. You know those moments as a fan where your favorite team's management just makes a move that's so terrible that there's no other appropriate reaction besides, "What the hell?" This was most definitely one of those times. After signing that deal, Mark Sanchez made more per year in base salary than the following quarterbacks; Aaron Rodgers, Cam Newton, Robert Griffin III, Andrew Luck, Russell Wilson, Colin Kaepernick, and Alex Smith. Go ahead; let that sink in for a little while. Mike Tannenbaum looked at *Mark Freaking Sanchez* and thought that he was worth more, per year, than Aaron Rodgers was. (Note to everybody who doesn't watch football: Sanchez was not half as competent as Rodgers is/was.) That move didn't just kill what remained of the salary cap, it beat the salary cap upside the head with a baseball bat and buried it alive like Joe Pesci at the end of *Casino*.

And this is all before we got to the Jets' signing of Broncos' quarterback and cult icon Tim Tebow, who I considered including in this book's description to boost the number of page views on amazon.com. I tried like Hell to talk myself into it, like all fans try to do with their teams' signings. *Maybe they brought him in to motivate Mark Sanchez. Maybe Tony Sparano, our new offensive coordinator, has a special use for him that we just don't know about yet. The Jets are going nowhere anyways, so why not give it a try? Hey, if nothing else, at least he's a good guy to have in the locker room.*

So, to review, I convinced myself that Mark Sanchez, already under an unfathomable amount of pressure from his fans, coaches, and teammates, needed more pressure in the form of a highly polarizing backup QB in order to succeed. I was able to persuade myself that the one guy who held the magical key that would unlock Tebow's hidden value was Tony Sparano, one of the most inept Jet employees of my lifetime and a guy who somehow found ways to get *less* impressive results than did the fired Brian Schottenheimer. And I somehow managed that the attention and intense scrutiny that went with signing Tebow (not to mention his limited worth on offense) was worth it because he was a great guy to have in the locker room. Whenever I'd make these arguments, my friends just nodded their heads at me and smirked at each other. *OK, buddy. Whatever you say.* As soon as I started getting the same reaction that I got when trying to defend Sanchez, I should have known right then and there that Tebow and the Jets were exactly what everybody said they were; a horrifyingly awful match in almost every way imaginable.

Well, maybe I shouldn't say that. The Tebow signing worked perfectly in one very important sense. See, nobody was talking about the Jets anymore. All of the possible "Rex Ryan said something controversial!" storylines were worn out. The unbearable "Does Mark Sanchez have the talent to be elite?" conversation was short-lived. (Not short enough, if you ask me or any other sensible Jet fan who had seen Mark Sanchez play a full game.) Even the whole "Ground and Pound" mantra and "the Jets are winning the old-fashioned way!" thing had grown more and more untrue by the game over the course of 2011.

Fans had grown tired of the same old Jets, and both the owner and the GM were quickly losing the capacity to put fans in seats, given the absurd price of tickets. So, they probably started looking at what type of fans *did* attend games and quickly discovered that most of the real fans were driven away. In this day and age, who was going to waste gas and time for a vastly overpriced and mediocre product when you could just stay home and watch the game instead? So, that left corporate tickets, well-to-do fans, people with connections, people with season tickets in the family, and generally people for whom money was no object. A lot of them were casual fans, people who couldn't even rally the enthusiasm for a proper J-E-T-S! chant. (I witnessed firsthand evidence of this a few months later.) That meant a greater proportion of people who didn't totally care how the Jets did, people who weren't necessarily spending all of Sunday glued to their couches, people who could easily be fooled by splashy names and cheap stunts. This schism between the real fans and the bandwagon fans (anybody who started loving the Jets immediately after they started winning) or the "I went to the stadium just to say that I went" fans allowed the Jets to make money through jersey sales, increase ticket purchases, and earn enough publicity for multiple lifetimes.

So now, everybody was talking about the Jets again. That is, everybody who didn't know a thing about football. Every single day, I had to hear the same thing over and over. *So, how about Tebow? What is Tebow going to do? Are you excited about Tebow? You don't look as excited as you should be. Tebow? Tebow! TEBOW!* (I'm going to sound like a curmudgeon or, even worse, a complete jerk for the next paragraph, so bear with me.)

I didn't like these people. They represented everything that the Jets' brass started serving when they stopped catering to the actual fans. Every time I heard someone say, "I'm rooting for the Jets because of Tebow!" I wanted to smash my head against the wall. They didn't pass the test yet. They didn't suffer through any agonizing losses. They hadn't watch the Jets horribly butcher their draft picks. They probably couldn't even name three other players. It seemed less like they were football fans and more like thirteen-year old girls at a Justin Bieber concert. I knew that these people would scramble for the lifeboats as soon as the ship started to sink, as soon as they realized that the team they had been fooled into supporting absolutely sucked. I hated that they were gullible enough to be fooled by management's publicity stunt, I hated that I was initially fooled by management's publicity stunt, and I came to regard everybody who so much as spent more than thirty seconds discussing Tim Tebow as a pretender who was unfit to support the New York Jets.

(So, yeah, this wasn't exactly the happiest time to be a Jet fan. With that, I'm going to climb down off my high horse, ditch the jerk persona, and turn back into my usual, affable self.)

And of course, if any of the fans took a ten-second break from the rampant Tebow speculation, the crush of media that surrounded him at all times would rush to fill the dead air with all due haste. ESPN went so far as to put a "Tebow Cam" on him at Jet practices and devote over half of their flagship show, *Sportscenter*, to live footage or debate over a guy that would serve as the punt protector and backup quarterback. Keep in mind that this happened *during the Olympics*. Yeah, screw the greatest sporting event on the face of the Earth, let's see Tebow watch Mark Sanchez throw! It was a good thing, too, because if that Tebow Cam never existed, the mundanities of the poor guy's life would never have become public knowledge. *Did you see Tebow blow his nose yesterday? Do you think he has a cold? Hey, look! There's Tebow listening to music as he warms up! Wait a second, is that Tebow talking with Rex Ryan? Wow, this is the greatest television ever!* Now actually seems like a great time to mention that even after his one playoff win in Denver, he was almost universally deemed as unfit to be a starting quarterback by various NFL scouts. And now he had a camera named after him.

With the incredibly dumb "Tebow vs Sanchez" controversy swirling, anonymous players in the Jet locker room taking shots at Tebow in the media, and a historically puke-inducing preseason in the rearview mirror (it took the Jets until their third game to score a touchdown), the lovable misfits took the field for their first game against the Buffalo Bills. Opening day against the Bills, the same way it was ten years before when I watched my first game. Looking back on it, that first game against the Bills was a simpler time, a time when I could just watch the Jets' game and enjoy it. No cynicism, no worrying about the outcome, nothing. If there's one thing that I want parents with young kids who read this book to walk away with, it's to really savor your kid's first game. Even if they don't understand it, make sure to point things out to them, get them excited, and take tons of pictures. You know, parent stuff. Why?

Because when kids are five and six, they don't understand bad contracts and sensationalist media coverage and anonymous quotes in newspapers. For them, the game is just that, a game. They'll get disproportionately happy if their team wins, bummed out if they lose, and forget about it either way in an hour or two. They're the ones that have it right. They love their team, root for them, want to watch the game with other fans, and ultimately treat sports like what it should be, the best diversion from life in the world.

As that Bills game approached and I looked back on an excessively unhappy offseason, I realized that I needed to be more like that too. Watching the games was becoming a burden for me and I found myself, for the first time in a long time, not looking forward to Jets games as much as I used to. It was almost like a chore I needed to get through. My Dad's question of "If they make you so sad/angry/insane, then why do you keep rooting for them?" started to carry more and more weight in my mind. I saw, for the first time, how being a fan could interfere with the enjoyment of the game. I needed to stop caring as much. And I did.

If you read my first book, *The Football Volumes*, which is on sale for the low, low price of $14.95 on amazon.com (seriously, buy it now. You know you want to.), then you know how much I love the RedZone channel. For those of you who don't know what that is, it's basically a TV channel that operates from 1:00 P.M. to approximately 7:30 P.M. every football Sunday that jumps from game to game based on where the most interesting things are happening. Since I was writing the first book at the time and needed it to watch the out-of-town games, I was somehow able to convince my parents to buy it.

The Jets blew out the Bills 48-28 that day, and I think I might have flipped to that game four or five times over the course of three hours. The rest of the time I spent riveted to the RedZone channel. See, I'd spent so much time fixated on the Jets, that I seemingly forgot that there were no less than thirty-one other teams in the league. As I whipped around from game to game, none of which I had a rooting interest in, I was instantly reminded why football was so much fun. For the first time since that Pittsburgh game, I noticed how a subtle shake of the receiver's hips turned the cornerback the wrong way for a split second, just enough time for the quarterback to step up, square his feet and throw him a perfect spiral. I started to take my eye *off* the ball, and instead place it on the offensive line or the linebackers or the running back that had just swung out into the flat. I was able to do all of these things because, for a change, I was watching the game for fun. No worrying about the results. No prospect of heartbreak if the Jets didn't deliver. Just football, pure and simple.

After three weeks of football therapy (and one devastating Darrelle Revis injury), the 2-1 Jets were slated to play the 2-1 San Francisco 49ers at home. Like we always do once per year, Dad, Grandpa, Jamer, and I piled into the Mercury Mountaineer and made the trek to the Meadowlands. As soon as I walked into the stadium (after a delicious tailgate meal of burgers, chili, brats, and other stuff that's probably clogging my arteries as we speak), I was instantly struck by how few people were wearing Jets' jerseys. My section had about a dozen Niners fans in it, which would have been totally unheard of just a year earlier. As I looked out over the rest of the stadium, the solid sea of green that I had seen the first time I walked into the stadium now contained uncountable flecks of red and gold in it. The awful team (they were *much* worse than their 2-1 record would suggest, as you'll soon see), the ticket price hikes, the RedZone, the personal seat licenses, and a variety of dumb front office movies had worked their magic. As kickoff approached, I would have estimated that at least twenty-five percent of the fans that I saw were either wearing no football apparel or wearing Niners Jerseys. And that's not counting the people up in the boxes, who almost certainly had little to no rooting interest. Before the game started, retired wide receiver Wesley Walker, a Jet for over a decade, was brought out before the game to lead the crowd in the traditional J-E-T-S chant. When I heard that chant in person during my first trip to Giants stadium, it was so loud that I couldn't hear myself think. But on that day, I could have turned to Jamer and had a perfectly audible conversation over it.

And then, the Niners proceeded to kick the Jets' ass up and down the field for four quarters. Up front, the Jets were just lifeless. Every single play on both sides of the ball featured at least one Niners' lineman ramming his counterpart forward or even knocking him down to the ground. The Jets couldn't get a thing going offensively; eventually, it came down to either Sanchez throwing an incompletion or Shonn

Greene barreling into a brick wall for a yard and a half. Perhaps the only memorable moment from the entire experience was the fan behind me that consistently yelled "PUNT!!!" at the top of his lungs every time the Jets would get the ball back. Given how inept the Jets' offense was that day, it wouldn't have been a bad idea. The score was only a modest 10-0 in favor of the Niners at halftime, but the majority of the Jets played poorly enough for the score to be 31-0 at the half. It was only a matter of time before the Niners broke the game open.

The Jets trailed 17-0 at the outset of the fourth quarter and had the ball near midfield when Sanchez threw a decent spiral to Santonio Holmes on a shallow out route. Holmes caught the ball as he fell to the ground in front of two Niners defenders. Then, for seemingly no reason whatsoever, Holmes released the ball from his left hand. It wasn't an unintentional snafu where the ball slipped through his hands; he actually tossed the thing directly into the chest of the cornerback in front of him. The football was flicked backhanded as if he were trying to throw a frisbee or something. It actually took the Niners' cornerback a second or two to pick it up after it hit the ground, presumably because he couldn't believe what an enormous, perfectly-wrapped gift he had just been handed. When he did pick the ball up, nobody was within five yards of the open path straight down the sideline and into the end zone, a path that he was more than happy to take. Ensuing replays showed that Holmes went to the ground untouched and remained that way when he inexplicably flipped the ball away. As it turned out, he had suffered a bone displacement in the foot (also known as a Lisfranc injury) as he ran his route and, believing that the play was over, threw the ball away in order to hold said foot. Unfortunately for Holmes, the play was not over. So not only had the Jets surrendered a touchdown in one of the most embarrassing ways imaginable (in about nine weeks, Mark Sanchez would find a way to top this by a factor of roughly a million), but the only guy on the offense that inspired any fear whatsoever in opposing defenses was now gone for the season. Fantastic.

At that point, we collectively decided to cut our losses and make our way out of the stadium, still surrounded by sarcastic cheers, heads shaking sadly back and forth, "WE WANT MCELROY!" chants (referring to third-string QB Greg McElroy), and plenty of beleaguered frowns among those who chose to remain in their seats to the bitter end. Of course, most fans didn't and chose to proceed out of the stadium also. Ordinarily (or at least judging by the last time I had went to a Jets game and seen them lose), people would be cursing and calling for people's heads after something like this happened. You'd get people spitting, yelling "THE JETS #(%*@ SUCK!!!" at the top of their lungs, maybe throwing a thing or two on the ground in disgust, and generally doing all of the things that I used to do when the Jets lost a game. Was it mature and responsible? Nope. But did it leave any doubt in onlookers' minds whether or not that person cared about the Jets? Hell, no. So, it was tacitly condoned.

After the Niners game? Nothing. Just people calmly walking to their cars and leaving. I don't know who these regular people with apathetic expressions were or what they wanted, but I wanted to know what the hell they had done with the old Jet crowd. Then, after a second, it hit me that I was becoming just like them. Maybe I'd matured and realized that sports didn't matter so much. Maybe the team was just so bad that I couldn't allow myself to even think about the prospect of hope entering the equation, thus preventing any possible disappointment. Maybe, just maybe, the Jets didn't mean as much to me as they used to. And if that was the case, then was I really becoming one of those bandwagon fans that I'd always hated? I really didn't have any of the answers, and I wasn't in the mood to find them after the Jets were beaten 34-0 by San Francisco. All I knew was between this game and my growing interest in the other thirty-one teams, I was becoming less of a fan than I used to be, and I wasn't sure whether or not it was a good thing.

So on the season went, the Jets achieving mediocrity and shooting themselves in the foot all the way. As predicted, the Tebow controversy reared its ugly head at nearly every crucial turn. In typical Jet fashion, offensive coordinator Tony Sparano flicked a burning cigarette onto the tank of gasoline by bringing in Tebow for about three ineffective plays every game, only to banish him to clipboard duty for the remainder of the contest. This produced the difficult-to-pull-off double whammy of getting people talking about Tebow and (rightfully) criticizing the Jets for their use of him, while still totally destroying his confidence and level of respect for the coaching staff, thus rendering him even more useless should he ever be needed. So that was turning out exactly as badly as everyone but me thought it would. Revis and Holmes were injured for the year. The "Sanchez is about to make the leap!" angle was long dead and bore no hope of resuscitation. "Ground and pound" was still a joke, a mantra that proved just as lifeless as the ferocious units it used to describe. Teams ran the ball for five yards on the Jets' front seven nearly as often as Shonn Greene or backup RB Bilal Powell dove into the opposing defense for two. The halcyon days were over, the Jets of just two years prior a distant memory.

And there was more frustration ahead on their schedule. A heartbreaking overtime loss in New England that was fueled by a big dropped pass from rookie wide receiver Steven Hill. Two games against top-flight teams (Houston and Seattle) that completely and totally outclassed the Jets. A huge 30-9 divisional loss to the Dolphins that virtually ensured the continuity of an almost decade-long AFC East title drought. Easy wins against Indianapolis and St. Louis to bring the Jets' record to 4-6 and set up a showdown with New England to potentially save the season. Dueling forces of crushing hopelessness and desperate hope. A team that was perplexing, awful, promising, and never boring. Yeah, the Same Old Jets were back.

The Jets' season reached the tipping point on Thanksgiving night in Giants Stadium against the New England Patriots in a matchup that was utterly representative of the natural order of business between the Jets and the Pats. New England, ruthless and efficient as always, went into Indianapolis to face a quarterback named Andrew Luck five days before they played the Jets. Luck was a rookie, the number one pick in the previous year's NFL draft and hailed as the best quarterback prospect to come along in twenty years. But by the time the game ended, there wasn't enough left of Andrew Luck or the Colts to scrape off of the Gillette Stadium turf. Brady and the Patriots beat them by a score of 59-24, a final tally which is normally reserved for games between top college teams and the hapless patsies they schedule in week one as warm-up games. Luck was intercepted three times by the Pats' secondary and had two of them returned for touchdowns. He was also hit a total of six times. Just another Sunday for the rejuvenated Patriot Machine.

Meanwhile, the Jets were on the brink. They *needed* to beat New England in order to have any chance at a divisional title or even a Wild Card playoff berth. The season had been disappointing and the team had played poorly, but not disappointingly enough to exterminate the last glimmer of optimism from its fans, nor poorly enough to eliminate themselves from playoff contention. I entered the game hoping for a change of fortune, that *somebody* on this team would step up and take things over, yet I knew that it probably wasn't going to happen. But regardless, my parents and I made sure to get home from Thanksgiving dinner on time to see if the Jets had one last miracle left in them.

I sat down on the couch just as Al Michaels and Cris Collinsworth were welcoming the viewing audience to MetLife stadium, ~~an inescapable quagmire of disappointment~~ the home of the New York Jets. Suddenly, my hard-to-describe sixth sense triggered. Remember when I wrote in the Pats' chapter about how I *knew* that the Jets were going to win after the Dennis Byrd moment? Well, the same thing happened to me before the kickoff. I *knew* that the Jets were going to lose this game. And I would be right. But *how* they would lose it is something that I never, ever could have imagined.

The first quarter was played to a scoreless draw as the B-roll shots of the New York City skyline led into the commercials. Both teams had played reasonably well up to that point, but neither one of them had really seized the advantage. But that would soon change. Towards the end of the quarter, the Patriots embarked on a long drive that brought them close to the Jet end zone. Three yards away, to be exact. Those three yards would be masterfully negotiated by the bane of the Jets' existence, Brady to slot receiver Wes Welker, on the first play after the commercial break. 7-0 Pats. On New York's next drive, the ball was marched deep into the Pats' end before a Shonn Greene fumble gave possession back to New England on their own seventeen yard line. I had a feeling that this wasn't going to end well.

I had to wait all of about thirty seconds for my fears to be realized. Brady took the snap from under center and threw a strike to running back Shane Vereen on the left sideline. For some odd reason, none of the Jets had thought to cover him. Which, of course, meant that between him and the end zone stood nothing but a whole lot of green. I think a Jet defender got close enough to dive and get the tip of his finger on Vereen's jersey when he was almost in for the touchdown, but it didn't matter. After a quarter of scoreless football, the score had become 14-0 Pats in just over five minutes.

I decided that the ensuing commercial would be a good time for me to take a bathroom break and maybe heat up some Thanksgiving turkey leftovers so I could drown my sadness in sweet, sweet gravy. When I exited the restroom, however, I was genuinely concerned that I had been in there for an hour, but I checked the clock and it was only four minutes or so. My concerns, of course, were based on the fact that the first thing I saw on my TV screen as I turned the corner into my family room was a New England Patriot player holding the ball over his head in the end zone. Well, that and the score at the bottom of the screen now read "NE: 21, NYJ: 0." I did some quick guesstimating in my head and deduced that the commercial break was two and a half minutes long, which meant that the Pats must have somehow gotten the ball back from the Jets and scored a touchdown in approximately one minute. But how the hell did they do it?

NBC then showed the slow-motion replay. Mark Sanchez took the snap from under center and turned around to his fullback, as if to hand the ball off. However, the guy who was presumably supposed to take the ball ran past Sanchez and into the line, mistakenly assuming that his responsibility on that play was to block, not to run with the football. The running back that was lined up behind said fullback started running horizontally and away from Sanchez towards the left sideline, as if he expected to catch a pass. (Given the way that Sanchez was playing at that point in his career, it was a fairly unrealistic expectation.) So, at the top of his dropback, Sanchez still had the ball on a designed running play with nobody to hand it off to. He proceeded to do the only thing he could do at that point, which was run the ball himself. Sanchez started barrelling full-bore into the pile in front of him, searching for gaps, just like a running back would. As he neared the line, he began to brace himself against a collision with the defense. Instead, the intrepid quarterback accidentally collided with his own blocker, who was thrown back into him by the Patriots' defensive tackle. The force of the collision jarred the football loose from Sanchez's arms and onto the grass. Patriots' safety Steve Gregory picked up the ball and ran it back in for a touchdown.

Actually, that paragraph was a little bit complicated, so let me tell you what happened a little more bluntly. Mark Sanchez fumbled the football after colliding with his own offensive lineman's ass. That's right. In a do-or-die game, the franchise quarterback committed a turnover after being attacked by an ass. For those of you who aren't football fans, I swear that I'm telling the truth. I really am. There's, like, footage and eyewitnesses and everything. A football player fumbled the football upon smacking into his own teammate's backside. This happened.

Almost immediately after I saw what had transpired, I started uncontrollably . . . . laughing. I mean, if you can't laugh at stuff like this, then what the hell can you laugh at? Yeah, my team was pathetic, but this set a new standard, both for the Jets and every single team that would play football at every level for all of eternity. A guy ran into someone's butt and fumbled. Nothing was ever going to top that. It was as if the football gods were saying, "Alright, let's see how much of this ridiculousness Andrew can bear before he stops taking this so damn seriously." Ultimately, I couldn't even fathom getting the least bit sad over the Ass Attack. It's the kind of thing where you just have to shake your head and smile. Hey, my team sucked. They weren't good enough to get where people wanted them to go. It happens to everybody eventually. (The "not good enough" part, I mean. Not the Ass Attack. That was fairly unique to the Jets.) Two or three years ago, I probably would have screamed at the TV and sworn never to watch the Jets again. However, the Assault (see what I did there? Pretty clever, am I right?) made me realize that I can't keep acting like losing a football game was the same as suffering a real-life tragedy, because it isn't. That was something I knew for the longest time, but never really acted on until Mark Sanchez ran full-bore into the rear of the guy who was blocking for him. It made me appreciate the randomness of football, of sports, of life. Sometimes, stuff happens. Wacky, zany, weird, and totally out of left field stuff. And there's nothing you can really do about it besides acknowledge that it happened, laugh at it for awhile, and move forward. And if it took the Ass Attack to teach me that, then so be it.

Quick tangent on the aftermath of the Rump Bump. (You have not lived until you've experienced the feeling of sheer and utter ridiculousness that comes with typing the words "Butt" and "Fumble" into an online thesaurus to try and come up with a new term for everything that occurred in the last three paragraphs.) The thing caused an Internet riot. In fact, I think that Twitter came very close to undergoing spontaneous combustion. It ran away with the number one spot on Sportscenter's Not Top Ten (a countdown of the ten most facepalm-worthy moments in sports from the past week) by the widest margin that anything has ever won by. The score might have been 85-15 in favor of the Ass Attack being worse than whatever pedestrian blooper occupied the top slot before it happened. Being the person who committed whatever lame error that stumbled into the number one spot the week before was like being the last number one golfer in the world before Tiger Woods took over. The play kept its Worst of the Worst slot for forty consecutive weeks before ESPN decided to mercifully retire it, even commemorating the play with a SportsScience segment about the physics of what happened in those six seconds. Along the way, it spawned Twitter hashtags, YouTube videos, thousands upon thousands of columns/blog posts, dozens of jokes, and a lifetime's worth of misery for poor Mark Sanchez.

So, as you can probably guess, the rest of the game did not go swimmingly for Gang Green. In fact, I hadn't quite stopped laughing in the aftermath of the Ass Attack when Joe McKnight received the ensuing kickoff for the Jets. He began to make his way up the field and weave his way through blocks when, if you can believe this, he collided with his own teammate's backside and fumbled the ball . . . . .

OK, I kind of made that up. You know, just to see if I could fool the non-football fans into believing that it happened again. (Admit it, you wanted to believe me for at least a second or two.) But I added the "kind of" qualifier because I *didn't* make up the part that involved McKnight fumbling the football. He successfully avoided all asses, but he unfortunately couldn't avoid the helmet of Patriot coverage man Devin McCourty, which solidly connected with the football as McKnight fell to the ground. Up in the air the pigskin flew, turning end over end about two and a half times before Patriots' wide receiver/special teams ace Julian Edelman snatched it out of the air and ran it back the other way for a touchdown. Yes, the score went from 0-0 to 28-0 in roughly six minutes. The score also went from 7-0 to 28-0 in just over one minute. By halftime, the score was 35-0 and offered little to no hope of getting significantly better. I at least thought that the Jets would stand a fairly good chance of covering the ten-point spread, but it now looked like it would be an uphill battle to lose by twenty.

That's when I did something that I'd rarely done before and swore that I would never do again in my life. I turned the game off before it was finished. See, I used to think that turning the game off early was akin to abandoning your team. You made the choice to root for your guys, and you don't get to bail on them early. I felt like it was your obligation to stay and watch the whole thing. So, during all of those Jet losses, which happened over the course of all those miserable Jet seasons, I forced myself to stay and watch for the entirety of the game. Which, of course, would just make me more miserable and unhappy than I already was and ensured that I would go to bed thinking about what had happened. It had become, like so many other aspects of rooting for a team that consistently disappoints, an exercise in self-loathing. If you weren't willing to put yourself through it, then you had lost the right to call yourself a real fan, or something like that.

But that night? I just changed the channel. And later on, I went upstairs and wrote about the game for my first book without fighting back any feelings of disappointment whatsoever. Here's a little bit of what I wrote.

There was almost no depression at any point of the Jets' season or that New England game. Is this what I'm turning into? Am I even a real fan anymore if my team loses this way and I find myself only marginally caring? I've had my one team that meant too much (the 2010 Jets), and ever since then I've never felt like a Jets' loss has ruined my day or even a single minute in that day. This is something that non-sports fans will never understand. A non-sports fan would read this and say, "great, you're finally becoming normal." But "fan" is short for "fanatic", and I don't feel like I'm as fanatical as I used to be. Some people say that their teams have driven them insane, but the Jets have driven me sane. I find myself no longer living and dying by the box scores and the draft picks like I once did. I don't know whether to be angry at the Jets or thank them. I watched that game and felt nothing whatsoever. No remorse, no anger, no sadness, nothing. I watched until the score went to 35-0, and then changed the channel to The Godfather marathon. And I spent the rest of the night watching Michael Corleone and not thinking about the Jets or that game in the least. After that 45-3 loss to the Pats on Monday Night Football in 2010, I couldn't sleep. I stayed up all night just thinking about what had happened. I don't think I got one hour of shut-eye that night. This loss never even crossed my mind until I started writing this. Maybe it's for the best.

And you know what? I still feel that way. It took too many unnecessary tears shed, pillows punched, overreactions (both good and bad), teams that meant too much to me, and minutes spent on football, but I finally arrived at a better place. And then, about six months later, I started asking questions about the process. Which moments mattered? Why do we react so strongly to sports? What is the fan experience like, and why do some people not understand it? Why have very few people even attempted to find answers to these questions? And, most importantly, why haven't I tried to yet?

Heck, you could probably write a book about it.

EPILOGUE

That pretty much brings us up to now. It took a second book, thousands of words, and way too many 11 P.M. to 3 A.M. writing marathons, but I think that just about covers it. Well, almost covers it. You see, almost every good story about past events, whether it be told in the form of written/typed word, verbally, or through film, usually has some kind of retrospective conclusion. You know, just something to put a nice bow on the proceedings and to provide some final insights into the characters before the credits roll. A good narrative should keep you repeatedly asking the question that the teller of the narrative wants you to ask, which is often "What happens _____?" What happens next? What happens to this character? What would have happened if he didn't do that? What happens to this place? Not only does the storyteller have to find the most effective ways to both answer those questions and incite the listener to keep asking them, but he/she also has to pick just the right time to stop answering them. It's a little bit easier for me to choose when to stop this story since I had a definitive timeline (My first Jet game at age five to the present), but it's still tough to choose *how* to stop.

The question of how to wrap things up is especially difficult for this particular story because this was never, at any point, a narrative that was supposed to make you ask, "What happens?" You may have asked that question incidentally, and I'm certainly not going to discourage your interest in that side of the story. However, in my opinion, that's not the interesting part. In fact, you can just type "New York Jets" into Google, go to their page on nfl.com, and knock yourself out reading about what happened. That story has already been told, and while it might have needed some re-telling in order to frame everything else that I was trying to get across, it was definitely the lesser story in this book.

The Jets' story was just the backdrop upon which I could tell my story, which borrows pieces from the tales of other faceless, nameless fans (at least to me, anyways), and creates something original. That's the beautiful thing about being a fan; that you are guaranteed both a shared experience with other people and a unique experience for yourself because everybody reacts to that shared experience in different ways. *That's* what

I wanted to capture by writing this book. For the fans, I wanted to create something that would make them reflect on and think about their own story. For the non-fans, I wanted to capture what it's like to be a fan, so you can finally understand why we exist, what we're really like, and how we operate. More than anything else, I wanted you, the reader, to *think*.

In fact, as you flipped through the pages of this book, I wanted you to engage in a dialogue with *yourself* more than you engaged with me. Not an out-loud dialogue, mind you, because that would just be weird if you were reading this in a public place and talking to yourself as you read it. No, just an internal dialogue that you might have while you're reading it or (hopefully) some length of time after you've put the book away. I didn't want to lead you into asking me the questions that I wanted you to ask. No, I wanted you to come up with your *own* questions to ask *yourself*. I hope that you read about how I reacted to some things and asked yourself, "What would I have done if that happened?" My purpose was to help you gain a different perspective on your favorite team. That's all. I know that these last couple of paragraphs might have made me sound like a wordy blowhard, but I can't help that.

There is no right or wrong way to interpret this book because, much like the games I write about, it's going to inspire different reactions from different people. (This sentence was specifically included to prevent an English teacher in 2075 from making his/her students do explications of passages out of old, tattered copies of *Growing Up Green*.) And much like there is no correct way to interpret the book, there really is no correct way to end it. I mean, I suppose that in the superficial sense, it will end in a few pages when I try to put as much of an ending on this story as I can. But that only answers the "What happens?" type questions that you direct at me. The story isn't really over until all of the questions stop being asked and all of the answers stop being given. So in that sense, *you* control when this story ends. If it inspires thought, discussion, action, a deeper appreciation, really *anything* on your end, then my story as a fan will continue as a part of your own.

If there is one larger truth that I was hoping to get at through this book, it's that everybody has a story. I've chosen to (hopefully) work in the fields of sports commentary and sports journalism because I love the stories that are behind the box scores and the win-loss records. I thought that a good way to begin my career in these fields would be to get in touch with my own sports journey before I start asking for the stories of others. I also figured that as long as I was going to take the time to assemble my story, I might as well share it with others, with the simultaneous goals of entertaining the reader through my own experiences and inspiring them to think about what went into their own, both as a sports fan and as a human being. These two stories are not mutually exclusive; in fact, I just spent a whole book trying to show the degree to which sports mingles with life. I guess what I'm really trying to say here is that revisiting your own story and listening to the stories of others, whether from sports or otherwise, will teach you new things about both yourself and the world around you. A story is something that everybody has and nobody can ever take away from you, so embrace it, add on to it as frequently as possible, and extract everything that you can from it.

And now that I'm re-reading those last two paragraphs, I realize that I *really* sound like a wordy blowhard. So that probably means it's time to wrap this thing up.

Before I do, though, I want to bring my story up to the date of this book's completion. After the Pats game, the Jets descended into an atmosphere of hopelessness that I had never really seen before, but I didn't really mind. It was almost better for the team to just be hopeless and leave no doubt about it than to do their usual routine of offering the illusion of hope, only to yank it away. They got two ugly wins after the Pats game to put them within a game or two of the playoffs with three weeks left to play, but absolutely nobody was fooled. Sanchez was a lame duck quarterback, the Tebow experiment had predictably blown up in the Jets' face, the salary cap was being strangled by bad contracts given out over the previous few years, and practically everybody on the team was a threat to leave. It was under those conditions that the Jets lost their last three games by a combined score of 69-26 to three other teams that would finish under .500.

The first thing that happened after the season ended was the unceremonious dumping of GM Mike Tannenbaum. He was replaced by Seattle Seahawks' GM John Idzik, but not before a few more pink slips were distributed. New offensive coordinator Tony Sparano and quarterbacks coach Matt Cavanaugh were both fired. Defensive coordinator Mike Pettine's contract was allowed to expire.

Then, the floodgates opened in earnest. Dustin Keller, Shonn Greene, Bart Scott, Brandon Moore, Eric Smith, and Sione Pouha all left the team. Just like that, almost a third of the players who had been the starters on that January night in New England were gone. A month later, Darrelle Revis was traded to Tampa Bay for draft picks, and the Jets had finally erased the last vestiges of success.

The architect, a GM that had assembled a team that looked like it would contend for championships throughout the next decade. Revis Island, the franchise's most iconic player since Namath and a surefire Hall of Famer. The mentor that was supposed to be the Burgess Meredith to our next savior. The old-school offensive coordinator that was supposed to turn the Jets back into the bullies of the NFL. The defensive mastermind who helped build the fearsome Jet defense from nothing. The core of players that would define Jet football now and forever. All of them, gone in one offseason.

Mark and Rex. They're all that's left, and both of them are hanging on to their jobs by a thread. After two straight losing seasons, they've been given a covert and unofficial ultimatum of one year. If they can't achieve at least some success in 2013 with a severely outmatched squad, they're gone. When a coach drafts a rookie QB, his fate often becomes tied to the fate of that signal-caller. So if Mark goes, then Rex is almost sure to follow. The Jets tried to find their Brady and Belichick. At various points, it looked like they succeeded. But now, we know that they have failed. They are relics of the Tannenbaum era and, considering that Idzik just spent an entire offseason systematically dispatching every single significant Tannenbaum hire, it can be assumed that the QB and the coach will exit soon and the purging will be complete.

The future of the team now rests squarely upon the shoulders of the 2013 draft class. With the first of their two selections in the draft's opening round, the Jets took a promising young corner from Alabama named Dee Milliner to fill the gaping hole in the defense that Revis left. The Jets' other first-round selection went towards defensive tackle Sheldon Richardson, who will be tasked with restoring a once-ferocious run defense. And perhaps none of their draft picks were more important than the one they made in the second round; quarterback Geno Smith. His job? Be the successor to Joe Namath that the Jets have waited forty-five years for, do everything that Jet fans expected (but never got) from Sanchez, and lead the Jets to a Super Bowl victory. Come on, we don't ask for much.

But maybe it doesn't matter all that much anymore. Maybe the Jets are just one piece of the puzzle. See, during the process of writing my first book, I was forced to look beyond the Jets. I had to know every single team just as well as I knew my own. I always did that anyway, but now I was forced to do it on a deeper level. Every week, I watched Joe Thomas effortlessly keep the defensive end at bay. I would watch J.J. Watt ferociously rip two offensive linemen to shreds on his way to the quarterback. Adrian Peterson's otherworldly juke move, Andrew Luck's surgically precise footwork, Jacoby Jones' blazing acceleration, these are all things that I learned to appreciate more after watching their games. And as I began to step more and more outside of the Jets' bubble into the whole world of football, I realized that for all these years, I was missing out on a pretty good game.

Somewhere along the line in my Jets' fanhood, I started loving football. Sure, I'm still a Jet fan and I probably always will be. Yes, I'd rather be strung up to the Meadowlands goalposts than miss a Jet game. But it's no longer just about the Jets; it's about the game itself. Every single week feels like a new gift just asking to be opened, as opposed to another exercise in futility. Instead of sitting around and waiting for the Jets to either win or lose, I've started watching all of the other games too, even some of them in other sports. You know, I always thought that sports were only fun if you were rooting for a team or a player. Entertainment and enjoyment be damned, you *had* to pick a side. Now? I just root for a great game and a few things that I've never seen before, just like everybody else. The eras of people like LeBron James, Albert Pujols, J.J. Watt, and—yes—even Tom Brady are too awe-inspiring and far, far too fleeting to waste on rooting against them at every turn. The same applies to great teams, great stories, and memorable moments from all around sports. I found that if you waste the opportunity to appreciate the great ones, you'll end up looking back on it in a few years and saying, "Wow, I really missed out." When I get older, I don't want to tell people that I forgot everything about Tom Brady and the Pats, just because I didn't like them. I want to say that I took in sports because I loved them, not simply because I chose the Jets when I was five years old. And now, I can truly say that. In the words of the great sage Ferris Bueller, "Life moves pretty fast. If you don't stop and look around once in a while, you could miss it." And since sports tend to be a fairly good reflection of life, well, I figured that I should probably stop and look around in that world as well.

The best part about my childhood as a Jets fan, though? I'm still a fan. After all of the gut-wrenching losses, the euphoric highs, the epiphany that I need to stop taking sports so seriously, the last paragraph that's filled with flowery language about how I've learned to love life more, writing this book, and all of the little moments in between, I still can't help but be a Jet for life. I mean, this is my team. You don't get a mulligan on your favorite team and even if you did, I wouldn't want one. Like I said earlier, I want to be there on the day that the Jets finally break the glass ceiling and win it all. I want to go to the victory parade and give random people wearing Jet jerseys big bear-hugs. I want the story to have its Hollywood sports movie ending. And even if that day never comes, the laughs and the lessons and the unquantifiable number of memories that the Jets have given me are more than enough to have made the whole thing worthwhile.

(But seriously, that day is going to come soon. Any year now. No, really, I feel like they could maybe even do it this season. What, you don't think so? Come on, you enjoyed reading this book, right? The least you could do is humor me by nodding your head . . . . . .)

(Thank you for humoring me, reader. This has been a fun chat. Maybe we can do it again sometime.)

AUTHOR'S COMMENT

Some people who know me and/or know about my first book, The Football Volumes, have asked a lot about what's in my future with regards to writing. Let me take this opportunity to try and preemptively answer a few questions that you, the reader, might want to know the answer to. As a throw-in, I'll even answer a couple queries that you almost certainly never wanted to know the answer to.

OK, serious questions first . . .

This is your second book in two years; are you just going to keep writing one every year?
Nope, this will be my last one for at least six years.

Wait, why specifically six years?
I'm setting aside four years for my undergraduate degree and two years for grad school. I anticipate being too busy in college to have enough time available for writing another book. In fact, time and opportunity were both very much of the essence when deciding to write this one. This is my last year living in the comfort of my home and with a relatively stress-free schedule, so I figured that I might as well write another book if the motivation and concepts were both still there.

So you'll start another one after you get out of college?
Probably not even then. I plan to write more books at some undetermined time in my life, and I will (hopefully) be writing and/or talking about sports for a living. However, I'll probably be too preoccupied with other stuff to write a book for a long time after college.

What made you decide to write a second book so soon after the first one?
First of all, I knew that there would probably be no better time in my life to write a book than in the upcoming year (my senior year of high

school). For the rest of my professional life in sportswriting/sportscasting (if I have one), I'm going to have word counts, bosses, deadlines, assigned topics, and things that generally don't lend themselves to being creative. On top of all that, I'll have to worry about my career, starting a family, my financial well-being, death, taxes, my air conditioning unit breaking, and all of the other things that go along with being over eighteen. I had one last window to write whatever I wanted with, generally speaking, no real-world responsibilities. That's a chance I couldn't pass up.

However, I also wrote this book because I felt like I was in the right frame of mind to do it. My childhood was almost finished and sports had started to assume its proper place in life. I still loved sports and the Jets enough to write with emotion, yet I was old enough to be appropriately introspective about how I changed as a result of being so tightly attached to this one particular team. It's not as if I decided that I had to write a book just because this was my last chance; in fact, I really wasn't planning on writing another one. The concept had to be right, and I happened to stumble into a workable one.

You came up with your last book idea while you were bored in free period at school. Do you have a more inspiring backstory for this concept?

It was 2:30 in the morning at Sports Broadcasting Camps: Boston. (Shout-out to everybody in SBC Nation!) I couldn't fall asleep and was going on my third hour of staring at the ceiling. Suddenly, I got the idea to write this book, took out my laptop, and did pre-writing until about 4:30, after which I fell asleep with my laptop balanced precariously on my legs. The movie rights for the story behind the creation of this book are still available, believe it or not.

O.K., now for the answers to questions that absolutely *nobody* was asking. Still, if you want to know a few facts about me that will give you the chance to make small talk if we ever meet, here they are.

Favorite Ice Cream: Chocolate with fudge on top, perhaps with gummi bears too if I'm feeling adventurous.

Favorite Music/Musicians: Tie between Bruce Springsteen & the E Street Band and Frank Sinatra. I love listening to both of them and they're so completely different that I can't choose between them. Generally, my iPod is full of classic rock and stuff released before the mid 80s. Billy Joel, Aerosmith, Ray Charles, and The Beatles are all well represented on my regular rotation of music. Like I said earlier in the book, I was born at least twenty years past my time.

Hobbies: Playing the piano, tracking storms (especially snowstorms), video games, playing tennis semi-competently, playing basketball incompetently, watching sports very competently, and writing (hopefully competently), to name a few.

Pets: One dog, a twelve pound Shih Tzu/Poodle mix named Roscoe. Quick Roscoe story: One day when I was home alone, she took Dad's socks and ran around the house with them because she (rightfully) thinks that she owns the place. I took them away from her and put them into Dad's sock drawer. Ten minutes later, I hear a noise coming from my parent's bedroom. I'm terrified because I thought that somebody had broken into the house or something. I walk in only to find Roscoe standing on her hind legs with her front paws inside each of the drawer handles, shimmying the thing open. She then grabbed the socks and walked out of the room, thoroughly pleased with herself. Heck, I wasn't even mad, I thought it was amazing.

Random quirky things about me: I talk to myself all the time, I try to get up before 5:30 A.M. every school day, I'm just about useless until I've had at least half a bottle of water in the morning, I try to drink at least four bottles of water per day, I'll listen to Eye of the Tiger before significant events (big tests, emceeing my school's talent show, etc) and either run around or punch something for the entire duration of the song, and I never learned to snap my fingers or whistle.

ACKNOWLEDGEMENTS

This book would not have been possible without support from a multitude of people—more than I can possibly hope to remember, anyways. So if I neglect to mention you in the acknowledgements, my apologies in advance. And if I accidentally thank you in the same manner as I did in my first book, well, sorry about that too. With those two things said, here we go:

Thank you to every teacher that has ever had me in their class. Special thanks go to Mr. Lucker and Mr. Levandowski for writing my college recommendations and turning them in promptly. The college process is a stressful enough when you're not writing a book at the same time, and you guys made it that much less of a pain for me. Hats off to you guys for that.

Another big shout-out needs to go to every single person in SBC Nation. I'm a nine-year veteran of Sports Broadcasting Camps and enjoyed the hell out of every single one of those years. I can't list every single impactful camper, counselor, and speaker by name because I'd be here until the Jets win a Super Bowl if I did, but all of you know who you are and know precisely what you did for me. Thanks a ton for giving me the best week of my year for the past decade.

I would be remiss if I didn't mention what a joy AuthorHouse publishing is to work with. They've been very cooperative throughout the entire process and worked with me even when I wasn't the easiest to work with. It's very difficult to find an overall satisfying experience when publishing a book, and I can't thank AuthorHouse enough for providing that experience.

Thanks to all of my friends for making my life more hilarious, more interesting, and more enjoyable over the past decade-plus. Special thanks go to Liam, Matt, Ray, and the rest of my football-watching buddies for influencing this book. Just like the last book, you guys were more of a help than you know. Also, Ray, I'm gonna beat you in fantasy football one of these years. Seriously, it's going to happen. One of these years, I swear.

Thank you to Bill Simmons, Rich Eisen, Chris Berman, Andrew Siciliano, and every other sportswriter/sportscaster that inspired me to both write this book and pursue my current career path. As you guys were doing your jobs, I was looking at a computer monitor or TV and becoming more certain that I wanted to do exactly what you do for the rest of my life. Without all of you, this book is either of marginal quality or not written at all. So thanks for that.

Thank you to my family for collectively being my number one fans throughout both the book-writing process and my life. I don't know what I'd do without you guys.

Of course, special recognition has to be given to a couple of specific people within the family. My grandma and grandpa introduced me to football, steered me toward the Jets, watched dozens of games with me, and did a million other things that made my childhood better.

Then, there are my mom and dad, who are acknowledged in this book for, you know, having put up with me over the course of the last eighteen years, especially when the Jets are playing. It couldn't have been easy, but you guys successfully raised a child and sent him off to college. Take the rest of the day off and read this book—goodness knows you deserve it.

Many thanks go to Roscoe, my dog, for being the greatest stress reliever anybody in the world has ever had.

And finally, thanks to the New York Jets for quite literally making this book possible. I'll always be proud to be a Jet fan.

Made in the USA
Lexington, KY
09 December 2014